C000145591

Rocío G. Davis, Jaur
Ana Beatriz Delgac

Ethnic Life Writing and Histories

Contributions to Asian American Literary Studies

edited by

Rocío G. Davis
(University of Navarre)

and

Sämi Ludwig
(Université de Haute-Alsace Mulhouse)

Volume 4

LIT

Rocío G. Davis, Jaume Aurell,
Ana Beatriz Delgado (Eds.)

Ethnic Life Writing and Histories

Genres, Performance, and Culture

LIT

Cover Design: Mariangel Gonzalez

Bibliographic information published by the Deutsche Nationalbibliothek
The Deutsche Nationalbibliothek lists this publication in the Deutsche
Nationalbibliografie; detailed bibliographic data are available in the Internet at
http://dnb.d-nb.de.

ISBN 978-3-8258-0257-8

A catalogue record for this book is available from the British Library

© LIT VERLAG Dr. W. Hopf Berlin 2007
Chausseestr. 128 – 129
D-10115 Berlin

Auslieferung:
LIT Verlag Fresnostr. 2, D-48159 Münster
Tel. +49 (0) 2 51/620 32 - 22, Fax +49 (0) 2 51/922 60 99, e-Mail: lit@lit-verlag.de

Distributed in the UK by: Global Book Marketing, 99B Wallis Rd, London, E9 5LN
Phone: +44 (0) 20 8533 5800 – Fax: +44 (0) 1600 775 663
http://www.centralbooks.co.uk/acatalog/search.html

Distributed in North America by:

Transaction Publishers
New Brunswick (U.S.A.) and London (U.K.)

Transaction Publishers
Rutgers University
35 Berrue Circle
Piscataway, NJ 08854

Phone: +1 (732) 445 - 2280
Fax: + 1 (732) 445 - 3138
for orders (U. S. only):
toll free (888) 999 - 6778
e-mail:
orders@transactionspub.com

Acknowledgements

The editors of this volume would like to thank the Fundación Universitaria de Navarra, for funding for a research project that helped organize the 5th MESEA Conference in Pamplona in May 2006. We also thank the College of Arts and Letters of the University of Navarra, the Ministerio de Educación y Ciencia (Acciones Complementarias 2005; Ref. HUM2005-25390-E), and the Gobierno de Navarra for support for the conference and the publication of this volume.

Table of Contents

Ethnic Life Writing and Historical Mediation: Approaches and Interventions

Rocío G. Davis, Jaume Aurell, and Ana Beatriz Delgado

Critical discussions on the intersection between life writing and history inspired the dialogue that led to this collection. In the context of the fraught ethnic politics in our increasingly globalized world, negotiating with historical memory has become both a cultural obsession and a powerful political weapon. Though we now generally agree about the use of memory (and the writing thereof) as a legitimate source of historical truth, we need to continue to examine the *ways* in which these historical mediations occur. Importantly, as Jacqueline Dowd Hall suggests, we need to explore "the phenomena that travel under the sign of 'memory and history.' First, personal memories (the chains of association that seem to come unbidden to the mind, rely on concrete images, and split and telescope time); second, social memories (the shared, informal, contested stories that simultaneously describe and act on our social world); third, history (the accounts we reconstruct from the documentary traces of an absent past); and, finally, political imagination (the hope for a different future that inspires and is inspired by the study of the past)" (442-443). These different phenomena function simultaneously in the ethnic life writing exercises examined in this volume, giving the texts a Janus-faced perspective, and complicating our notions of how previously discrete methodologies function in changing situations.

This volume presents some of the results of the Fifth Conference of the Society for Multi-ethnic Studies: Europe and the Americas (MESEA), held at the University of Navarra in May 2006, entitled "Ethnic Life Writing and Histories." The essays collected here are highly interdisciplinary and focus on how processes of literary creativity and historical inscription blend to produce texts that require nuanced readings on many levels. This strategy is multiply enhancing as a discursive tool because the autobiographical perspective presented in the texts may be analyzed not merely as a way to negotiate historical contexts in order to inform the reader, but as a tool that illuminates the creative activity of writers or filmmakers. Half the essays focus on Asian American texts, inviting crucial connections and insights on the ways ethnic concerns are reflected methodologically. Publishing a comparative analysis in a series on Asian American literary studies favors the strategic intersections between the work of writers of diverse ethnic groups or national affiliations who consciously negotiate issues of ethnic self-representation and history.

From a theoretical perspective, the work of Karl Weintraub, Philippe Lejeune, Hayden White, Paul John Eakin, Jerome Bruner, and Jeremy Popkin, among others, have expanded our views on the ways in which life writing enriches our readings of public experiences, on the one hand, and how these creative performances become historically valid documents, on the other. Weintraub posits that autobiography achieved its prominence when we acquired a historical understanding of our existence; the life writing text then became an important cultural artifact, part of "that great intellectual revolution marked by the emergence of the particular modern form of historical mindedness we call historism or historicism" (821). From a more literary point of view, Eakin, in *Touching the World*, describes autobiography as more than "an imaginative coming-to-terms with history" because "it functions itself as the instrument of this negotiation" (144, 139). These reflections authorize the use of autobiographical writing as interpretative frames for historical information, validating the methodology of life writing for historical discourse.

Conscious of the complexity of the interaction between the subjective and objective in the telling of stories, historians and literary critics have increasingly granted authority to singular voices, considering them "unconventional" yet reliable perspectives. Autobiography has gained important scientific and academic ground as a valid source for negotiating with the past—viewing a public story through stories of the self. The increasing fascination of the critics with life writing is based on the possibilities of the triple dimension of the word "auto-bio-graphy": *autos*, the portrait of the author's self that emerges from the text; *bios*, the narrative of the life that it contains; and *graphe*, the writing of the text itself (Olney 236-267). The history of a particular context, the story of a singular life, and the act of narration of that story are integrated in one text. For this reason, historians, even those who have written their autobiographies, often reveal their reluctance and suspicion regarding a genre that appears to privilege the subjective. Jeremy Popkin, for example, in the introduction to his *History, Historians, and Autobiography*, presents an illuminating caveat to the ways in which we read historians' life writing: "My training as a historian makes me acutely aware of the risks one would run by accepting as gospel truth everything these autobiographers have written about themselves, but evaluating their completeness and factual accuracy has not been my main concern" (9). Understanding this position, we nonetheless argue that life writing can be not only a potentially productive source for a nuanced reconstruction the past, but also an invaluable document for discerning processes of identity. We do not conceive autobiographies as a "dangerous double agent," moving between literature and history, fact and fiction, subject and object (Marcus 7) but rather as a privileged way to access personal and collective forms of subjectivity in changing contexts.

Autobiographers themselves often describe their ambivalence regarding the use of their texts in historical contexts. Robert Rosenstone subtitles his family memoir: *"The (Mostly) True Story of My Jewish Family."* He conceives this memoir as a mosaic of memories that re-created certain experiences, transforming *lived* experience into *narrated* experience. Telling the story shifted the experiences' epistemological status, complicating notions of "reality" or "fiction," or "literature" and "history." Rosenstone argues that through this process of transformation of the past into written memories via words (or images, or sounds), "we attempt to simulate a lost word, but the life we bestow upon the dead is not one they would recognize as their own" (xi). A professional historian himself, Rosenstone illustrated how, after decades of the hegemony of the great narratives and the long-term historical structures, historians are becoming more and more convinced of the privileged function of the singular "stories" in the making of "history." The reality of the past does not lie in a collection of data but in an accumulation of stories. These stories are always told by those who have experienced them. It is now considered naïve to maintain a blind trust in official records, because these too are subject to limited or partial perspectives. Personal and collective memory creates a space where fact, truth, fiction, invention, forgetting, and myth are so entangled as to constitute a renewed form of access to the past. This theoretical assertion also provides a deep experiential reflection, because, as Rosenstone concludes, "ultimately, it is not the facts that make us what we are, but the stories we have been told and the stories we believe" (xv).

Taking our lead from Rosenstone's affirmation, the editors of this book posit that ethnic identity is not only shaped by the "stories we have been told and the stories we believe," but also, and more importantly, by the stories we tell. The act of telling and writing one's story affirms as it performs identity. This idea links the articles in this collection: the intersection between the discourse, practice, and social function of life writing, history, and ethnic identity. Our approach is based on a transversal methodology that links genre studies and historiography, using the strategies of each in order to arrive at new conclusions about the writing of the history of globalization, immigration, racial and ethnic negotiation, privileging non-official histories in the process.

The first two essays in the volume, reflections on the writing of autobiography, describe the processes that direct self-inscription in specific contexts. Shirley Geok-lin Lim positions her autobiography, *Among the White Moon Faces*, in dialogue with academic writing, embodied memory, and the historical and social material that contextualizes all Asian American writing, thus illuminating the making of a private and historical self out of individual memories. Seeking for the story of her life a form that would accommodate "the interiority of poetry and a different external scaffolding: drama and narrative drive," Lim explains how she deploys images of her embodied self to locate herself in a family story and also in the shifting political practices in Malaysia and the United States. Carmen Pearson's essay, the introduction to her family memoir about her grandmother, the first Carmen, describes her sense of responsibility as the heir of her grandmother's diary and her struggles to uncover a history of multiple dislocations, seeking the balance between private stories and public contexts. As she says of her family: "We are not the people who have written history; instead, we have always remained in that silent fringe of the middle class, living our lives largely within the domestic, somewhat isolated from extended family, from politics and from a culture we were born into." Transcribing, interpreting, and also trying to publish Carmen's diary, Pearson also negotiates the politics that govern ethnic self-representation. Both these essays, reflections on the self located in history and politics by persons who have engaged the genre of autobiography, invite us to consider how the act of life writing may be directed of controlled and how the texts function discursively in society.

Jerome Bruner's reflections on the nature of autobiographical writing as historical mediation are useful for this discussion. Noting the development of the ideas that have validated autobiography as history, he explains a series of discourses involved in the autobiographical act: first, he posits autobiography as "a discourse of witness: accounts of happenings in which one participated if only as an observer. These accounts are most often marked by the past tense, by verbs of direct experience such as *see* and *hear*, and by declarative speech acts. Witness creates existential immediacy for both the writer and the reader" (Bruner 45). When the "witness," as is often the case in ethnic life writing, is not necessarily the writer but a relative or a member of the community, the genre's conventions allow the reader to receive the information as coming from a witness. In a sense, the writer bears witness to the witness. The autobiographer's position as receiver and preserver of personal or community stories authorizes her voice, granting a similar immediacy to the narrative.

Historical mediation, thus, requires two previous phases: first, a recognition of the power of personal narratives inserted in the public forum to engage historical and cultural issues, in order to challenge dominant mainstream versions which have often hidden, misrepresented, or invalidated these stories. It also suggests how, to an important extent, individual identity is constituted in relation to family and national history. Second, historical mediation requires a commitment to preserve these stories from disappearing and provide the ethnic communities with potentially empowering narratives. In a sense, these motivations function simultaneously on the personal and collective level. So, though the autobiographical act is primarily a personal one, autobiographical writing exists for public interpretive uses, "as part of a general and perpetual conversation about life possibilities... In any case, the 'publicness' of autobiography constitutes something like an opportunity for an ever-renewable 'conversation' about conceivable lives" (Bruner 41).

The essays by Terry DeHay and Lavina Shankar analyze texts produced in similar circumstances. DeHay's reading of Mahmoud Darwish's autobiography, *Memory for Forgetfulness*, situated in a single day during the Israeli siege of Beirut in August 1982, elucidates how violence compels the articulation of memory. Positing that all of Darwish's work can be read "as an intervention in the narrative of his people and demonstrates the creation of a national narrative as an on-going process," DeHay validates reading this personal account in the context of a national story, partly as a form of recovering and preserving memory and partly providing Palestinians with a necessary narrative of selfhood. Shankar analyzes Meena Alexander's 2003 revision of her 1993 memoir, *Fault Lines*, a task the Manhattan author felt was imperative after having lived through the 9/11 bombings in New York. Again, a violent event becomes the trigger for memory. Alexander finds herself revisiting what she had previously written, in order to work through its validity, its completeness, and its function in her present life. Impor-tantly, she revisits the notion of nationhood and belonging, which were crucial points in her first memoir but which she felt compelled to re-address in the new context of a city shattered by violence. Both these pieces, which foreground historical events as catalysts for the articula-tion of memory, bring private recollection into the public—even "national"—sphere.

Bruner also stresses the role of autobiography as a "discourse of interpretation," *diegesis* in the classical sense, which organizes the elements of the story and "places them in evaluational frames (instances of 'struggle,' of 'devotion,' or whatever). Diegesis has a way of being more subjunctive than mimesis: it considers paths not taken; it is crouched retrospectively and counterfactually; it is more apt to ride on epistemic verbs like *know* and *believe* rather than see and hear; and it is usually crouched in the present or timeless tense" (Bruner 45). The interpretative element Burner refers to is illustrated in several of the essays in this collection, notably a series of articles that examine the ways in which autobiographers negotiate generic possibilities.

Three essays explain the advantages to the use of graphic art, photography or film to represent or interrogate specific events in twentieth-century history. Pin-chia Feng's essay on the text and film versions of Abraham Verghese's *My Own Country*, discusses the politics of representation in complex situations, describing the ways ethnic subjectivities are enacted vis-à-vis questionable group identities and how these may be represented in writing and film. By focusing on the ways communities are formed—ethnic as well as, in this case, the community that grows out of the experience of AIDS in a small town— she unveils the interaction that determines ways of representing belonging. Min Song's comparative study of Miné Okubo's *Citizen 13660* and Marjane Satrapi's *Persepolis*, focuses on the advantages of the graphic novel as a form of life writing that illuminates "the trope of looking back during times of transition in state power." Discussing childhoods experienced in internment camps and during the Muslim Revolution in Iran, he posits that both graphic artists use their multilayered form of representation to call attention to the "discursive poverty" surrounding the historical experiences they represent. Finally, Eleanor Ty's analysis of Denise Chong's *The Girl in the Picture*, the biographical account of Phan Ti Kim Phuc, the South Vietnamese girl in the emblematic 1972 picture of the napalm bomb, negotiates "the tightly woven intersection of biography, politics, and history, the fluidity of global subjects in an age of transnational crossings at the same time as it raises questions about competing discursive forms of image and text in contemporary society." As she analyzes these issues, Ty also explores the ways Chong's texts transcends biography to become a form of immigrant personal and collective history for a generation of Vietnamese people caught in perpetual warfare.

This interpretational process leads to Bruner's third point, "stance," referring to the "autobiographer's posture toward the world, toward self, toward fate and the possible, and also toward interpretation itself" (45). For ethnic autobiographers, these crucial points define the ways in which the author conceives of the text as entering the critical dialogues established in ethnic historiographical writing. Bruner notes that the task of the autobiographer consists in uniting the discourses of witness, interpretation, and stance to create a story that has both verisimilitude and negotiability (46). By negotiability, he refers to "whatever makes it possible for an autobiography to enter into 'the conversation of lives'. In other words: "Are we prepared to accept this life as part of the community of lives that makes up our world?" (Bruner 47). Quoting Hayden White, Bruner affirms the final result of autobiography's historical quality: "one cannot reflect upon the self (radically or otherwise) without an accompanying reflection on the nature of the world in which one exists. And one's reflections on both one's self and one's world cannot be one's own alone: you and your version of the world must be public, recognizable enough to be negotiable in the 'conversation of lives'" (43).

Bruner's analysis ends with a vital proposal: the conversation of lives that is, ultimately, the aim of these life writing exercises. In this context, questions that historian Carolyn Steedman asks about the making and writing of the modern self resound: "Who uses these stories? *How* are they used, and to what ends?" ("Enforced Narratives" 28). One way in which these texts renegotiate our perspective on the past is by obliging us to revisit our notions of memory. Specifically, two tropes— "countermemory" and "postmemory"—may be usefully deployed in this context. The trope of "countermemory"—interrogating "the gaps that always exist between what is told and the telling of it" (Holquist xxviii)—functions in multilayered ways here, to resist the prejudices, erasures, limited perspectives, or inventions typical of official versions of the past. The narrators of these autobiographies function almost as builders who, according to Sidonie Smith and Julia Watson, take up "bits and pieces of the identities and narrative forms available and, by disjoining and joining them in excessive ways, create a history of the subject at a precise point in time and space" ("Introduction" 14). Smith and Watson note that this kind of narrator can evaluate as well as interpret the past, creating a "countermemory" that "reframe[s] the present by bringing it into a new alignment of meaning with the past" ("Introduction" 14). Indeed, Edward Said notes the collective nature of a knowledge production oriented toward "presenting alternative narratives" that "forestall the disappearance of the past" and constitute a kind of "countermemory" with its own counterdiscourse that will not allow conscience to look away or fall asleep" (31).

Ultimately, these authors seek to represent a truth that lies beyond documentary evidence, although they might need the documentary evidence to verify particular experiences. The kind of memory work involved in these autobiographical exercises illustrates what Marianne Hirsch calls "postmemory," "distinguished from memory by genera-tional distance and from history by deep personal connection" (22). Significantly, her term also signals the nature of this kind of memory, which is constitutive of the process of ethnic life writing: postmemory becomes "a powerful and very particular form of memory precisely because its connection to its object or source is mediated not through recollection but through an imaginative investment and creation" (Hirsch 22). Indeed, this form of invention of memory is characteristic in cultures where issues of heritage operate in the present to develop ethnic communities. We can also discern the process by which various groups use these forms of memory to adapt personal and national origins to changing political and transnational paradigms.

Two essays on Chicano autobiography illustrate these points. A. Gabriel Meléndez's survey of Chicana auto/biographical strategies— from La Malinche and Sor Juana Inés de la Cruz to Denise Chávez— marks the continuity, presence, and agency of an autobiographical impulse for Chicanas, who, in diverse ways, negotiate the vexed issue of gender, psychological, class, and racial borders. Philip Bracher's essay on Oscar Zeta Acosta's *Autobiography of a Brown Buffalo*, traces the form of self-representation that one of the most emblematic figures of the Civil Rights era. Bracher suggests that this autobiography is deceptively simple: by a sophisticated use of narrative perspective, Acosta undermines the reader's assumptions and revists possibilities for Chicano identity formation.

But, more specifically, how do these autobiographical texts mediate history? The first manner of historical mediation might simply be the recovery and safeguarding of particular stories from historical erasure. Manuela Constantino and Susanna Egan posit that the autobiographical text functions like "a museum in which the past can be preserved and explained to present generations" (108). The curator of the museum, so to speak, is the author herself, who selects the forms in which memory is resurrected, presented, and preserved. Importantly, the writer contextualizes these stories, which blur the boundaries between historical accounts and personal memories. In the act of writing, the writers brings these hidden or disenfranchised stories back to life, firstly as access to a valid identity for themselves and then as a usable past for a community. Indeed, "auto/biographers 'here and now' stake their claim on collective identity 'then and there'. As they do so, they transform the relevance of their new belonging precisely because of the cargo that they carry" (Constantino and Egan 110). For this reason, the history re-presented in autobiographies is always a re-enactment of the past, performance rather than spectatorship. The element of performativity in these texts gives accounts of the past specific personality, nuancing negotiations with the present.

The second form of historical mediation involves a more direct dialogue with public histories. By inserting personal stories into official discourse, they contribute to the process and progress of historical revisioning. Because of the valuable emancipatory work done by life writing texts, autobiographies have become authoritative as historical narratives of ethnic communities, multiplying sources of knowledge and memory, altering perspectives on the past and present, opening up possibilities for the future. Importantly, these personal texts prevent historical erasure as they help attain a sense of group identity, which may serve as a basis for political mobilization. As Angelika Köhler posits in her essay, family memoirs by Victor Villaseñor and Sheila and Sandra Ortiz Taylor evoke "an awareness of their cultural roots that can function as a referential framework for their own processes of self-positioning within the contexts of their family histories in particular, but also within those of American cultural history in general." By examining issues of border identity, class divisions, and possibilities for self-representation, Köhler proposes a reading of these texts as important documents that engage the history of an ethnic community.

In Asian American studies, a related paradigm involves autobiographical (as well as fictional) texts about the Japanese internment in the United States and relocation in Canada, an event that finally received recognition and redress from both Governments. Though we cannot contend that the autobiographical writing on the internment was indispensable in achieving this end, we do argue that the texts invalidated many official accounts of the time, disproving the Government's position. Moreover, these texts interpellate history in a more epistemological sense. Ajay Heble, discussing the forms of writing Canadian history, asks telling questions in this context: "who has the institutional power to determine who speaks (and who doesn't speak) and to determine whose histories count as knowledge and whose get disqualified as unpleasant and inharmonious noise. What's the relation, these texts compel us to ask, between those who teach, produce, or authorize history and those who live it?" (27). Patricia Chu's analysis of Japanese American narratives of "return" invites us to rethink the ways in which these public histories have been narrated. Her comparative reading of

Lydia Minatoya's *The Strangeness of Beauty* and the published letters of Mary K. Tomita, a *nisei* stranded in Japan throughout and after the war, raises provocative questions about Japanese American historical positions and the duties of citizens who disagree with their governments in wartime. Her essay discusses Japanese American identity and political agency, highlighting a politically questioning sensibility in this crucial period in Japanese and Japanese American history.

Finally, these texts mediate history by proposing a textual and cultural model for present and future communities. Using Leigh Gilmore's ideas on autobiography, we argue that "autobiographical performances draw on and produce an assembly of theories of the self and self-representation; of personal identity and one's relation to a family, a region, a nation; and of citizenship and a politics of representativeness (and exclusion). How to situate the self within these theories is the task of autobiography, and entails the larger organizational question of the ways selves and milieus ought to be understood in relation to each other" (135). As noted earlier, we must call attention to the ways in which "the cultural work performed in the name of autobiography profoundly concerns representations of citizenship and the nation" because "autobiography's investment in the representative person allies it to the project of lending substance to the national fantasy of belonging" (Gilmore 135). Ihab Hassan's and Edward Said's memoirs are thoughtfully read by Ioana Luca in this context. The titles of their autobiographies—*Out of Egypt* and *Out of Place*, respectively—already signal the national dislocation that these literary critics experience personally and which, in sophisticated ways, will mark, as their autobiographies attest, their intellectual endeavors. In particular, Luca notes how their specific fields of research—postmodernism and theories of orientalism—are closely connected not only with these scholars' personal histories but also with the ways they engage their past.

These ideas critically complicate notion of life writing's historical mediation *in* and *for* the present. Though most of the material in autobiographies is set in the past, we acknowledge the autobiographer's task of selection, ordering, emphasis, and formal choices. We have to discern, in our analysis of the texts, how particular events are selected because of particular meanings they have for the writing present, more perhaps than for the remembered past. Pirjo Ahokas's reading of the challenges to the neoliberal paradigm of postethnicity in recent texts by Alice Walker and Maxine Hong Kingston reminds us of the discursive possibilities of life writing. By demonstrating how *The Way Forward Is with a Broken Heart* and *The Fifth Book of Peace* perform an ongoing process of identification and disidentification with culturally pervasive public discourses, she shows how they generate forms that promote revisions of imposed systems of ethnic identification.

As we highlight the ways in which life writing mediates history, we could ultimately ask ourselves whether because these autobiographies so effectively engage history and oblige us to rethink our forms of access to history, are the boundaries between autobiography and history still valid? Caroline Steedman's preoccupation with this issue provides a usable answer. She asks: "What function does the historical past serve me in *Landscape for a Good Woman*? I am very eager to tell readers, close to the beginning of the book, that what they are about to read is not history. At the end, I want those readers to say that what I have produced is history" (*Past Tenses* 45). The essays in this volume, in diverse ways, support notions of the fusion of forms, discourses, and conversations. Ethnic writers who engage autobiography are increasingly conscious of the discursive possibilities of the form, inspiring them to participate more actively in the dialogues on history and culture that mark our changing world.

Works Cited

Bruner, Jerome. "The Autobiographical Process." *The Culture of Autobiography*. Ed. Robert Folkenflik. Stanford: Stanford University Press, 1993. 38-56.

Constantino, Manuela and Susanna Egan. "Reverse Migrations and Imagined Communities." *Prose Studies* 26.1-2 (April-August 2003): 96-111.

Eakin, Paul John. *Touching the World: Reference in Autobiography*. Princeton, NJ: Princeton University Press, 1992.

Gilmore, Leigh. "Limit-Cases: Trauma, Self-Representation, and the Jurisdictions of Identity." *Biography* 24.1 (2001): 128-139.

Gossman, Lionel. "History as (Auto)Biography: A Revolution in Historiography. *Autobiography, Historiography, Rhetoric*. Eds. Mary Donaldson-Evans, Lucienne Frappier-Mazur, and Gerald Prince. Amsterdam & Atlanta: Rodopi, 1994. 103-129.

Hall, Jacqueline Dowd. "'You Must Remember This': Autobiography as Social Critique." *The Journal of American History* 85.2 (September 1998): 439-465.

Heble, Ajay. "Sounds of Change: Dissonance, History, and Cultural Listening." *Essays on Canadian Writing* 71 (Fall 2000): 26-36.

Hirsch, Marianne. *Family Frames: Photography, Narrative, and Postmemory.* Cambridge: Harvard University Press, 1997.

Holquist, Michael. "Introduction." *The Dialogic Imagination: Four Essays* by Mikhail Bakhtin. Ed. Michael Holquist. Trans. Caryl Emerson and Michael Holquist. Austin: University of Texas Press, 1996. xv-xxxiii.

Lejeune, Philippe. *On Autobiography.* Ed. Paul John Eakin. Trans. Katherine Leary. Minneapolis: University of Minnesota Press, 1989. 185-215.

Marcus, Laura. *Auto/Biographical Discourses: Theory, Criticism, Practice.* Manchester: Manchester University Press, 1994.

Olney, James, "Some Versions of Memory/Some Versions of *Bios*: The Ontology of Autobiography." *Autobiography: Essays Theoretical and Critical.* Ed. James Olney. Princeton, NJ: Princeton University Press, 1980. 236-267.

Popkin, Jeremy D. *History, Historians, and Autobiography.* Chicago: University of Chicago Press, 2005.

Rosenstone, Robert A. *The Man Who Swam into History: The (Mostly) True Story of My Jewish Family.* Austin: University of Texas Press, 2005.

Said, Edward W. "The Public Role of Writers and Intellectuals." *The Public Intellectual.* Ed. Helen Small. Oxford: Blackwell Publishing Company, 2002. 19-39.

Smith, Sidonie, and Julia Watson, eds. "Introduction." *Getting a Life: Everyday Uses of Autobiography.* Minneapolis: University of Minnesota Press, 1996. 1-24.

Steedman, Carolyn. "Enforced Narratives: Stories of Another Self." *Feminism and Autobiography: Texts, Theories, Methods.* Eds. Tess Cosslett, Celia Lury, and Penny Summerfield. London & New York: Routledge, 2000. 25-39.

Steedman, Carolyn. *Past Tenses: Essays on Writing, Autobiography and History.* London: Rivers Oram Press, 1992.

Weintraub, Karl J. "Autobiography and Historical Consciousness." *Critical Inquiry* 1.4 (June 1975): 821-848.

White, Hayden. *Tropics of Discourse: Essays in Cultural Criticism.* Baltimore: The Johns Hopkins University Press, 1978.

Jaume Aurell is Associate Professor of History at the University of Navarra, Spain. He has published articles in *Rethinking History, Biography, Viator,* and the *Journal of Medieval History,* among others.

Rocío G. Davis is Associate Professor of American Literature at the University of Navarra. Her most recent publication is *Begin Here: Reading Asian North American Autobiographies of Childhood* (2007).

Ana Beatriz Delgado is a Teaching Assistant at the University of Navarra, and has recently completed her doctoral dissertation on Canadian literary biographies.

Academic and Other Memoirs: Memory, Poetry, and the Body

Shirley Geok-lin Lim

A subject that has played on the periphery of critical discourse for a number of years and has recently come to the fore is the question of ethics and truth-telling in the genres of memoir and autobiography. I am senior enough to recall those heady days when scholars and readers welcomed works of genre-bending as if acts of miraculous levitation, when Maxine Hong Kingston's *The Woman Warrior* set the bar for how much further a book may be read as memoir while composed also of texts of fiction, from the stories of the No Name Woman, to the retelling of the exploits of the legendary Fa Mu Lan heroine. Kingston enunciated for many of us the impossibility of constructing definitively the boundary between fact and story, truth and imagination. As she said of *The Woman Warrior*, "we cannot find the seams where a myth leaves off and a life and imagination begin" ("Personal Statement" 24). In short, Kingston reminds us, who might need such reminding, that we spend much of our lives in our heads, and that life writing is as much about writing, those artifacts of imagination, as it is about the lives such works inscribe.

Today, however, any uncritical, unproblematized celebration of postmodern transgressive plays sounds a little hollow; pushed a little harder, the fuzzy line between factual life event and imaginative inscription begins to look less like postmodern aesthetics and suspiciously more like old-fashioned lying, or to put it euphemistically, invention. Genre blurring is in danger of becoming less brave experiment circulating in a literary domain and more strategic commodified discourse driven by marketing considerations. The recent James Frey controversy, as illustrated in the seemingly trivial matter of whether it is important that the author had been in jail for less than a day (as testified to by witnesses and records) or incarcerated for three weeks (as is claimed in the memoir) and why such accurate facticity or lack of it may be significant for his memoir, has made mainstream many of the theoretical battles of positions that scholars have been debating in the last three decades. I wish to approach this debate from the angle of my own experience in writing my memoir, *Among the White Moon Faces.*

I am frequently asked what it was like writing a memoir. Now, I ask you, what kind of question is that? I have yet to be asked what it is like to write a poem or a short story, and I have written many more poems and short stories than memoirs.

Still, the question is canny in catching the assumption that something more visceral is or should be happening when someone sits down to write her memories of events. We expect an embodied relationship between memory and the person remembering; what Steven Robins in his essay, "Silence in my father's house," calls the relationship between "memory and narratives of the body." The story, we believe, is already imprinted indelibly, prior to its voicing, in the neurons of the teller, waiting for the appropriate moment to be made visible or, in the case of the memoir, literal, to another. Unlike fiction, we expect with life writing genres not invention and novelty but real life and actual events re-narrated; the past, under threat of extinction, re-membered. Baldly stated, writing a memoir implies re-living or re-experiencing a provable past.

Philippe Lejeune tells us as much in his concept of the "autobiographical pact." Beginning from the position of the reader, Lejeune defines autobiography as "retrospective prose narrative written by a real person concerning his own experience, where the focus is his individual life, in particular the story of his personality" (4). Apart from the use of the masculine pronoun, Lejeune's definition appears admirably to fit my memoir, *Among the White Moon Faces*; for here I am, a real person, who has written a retrospective narrative on experiences that focus on the story of my personhood, if not personality.

Lejeune, however, distinguishes the memoir from the autobiography. Memoirs do not fully meet his requirements for autobiography, as they are neither solely about an individual life nor particularly about the narrator's personality. Some Asian American critics, moreover, have been only too eager to agree with Lejeune in his framing of the autobiography as a historical discourse covering "a period of two centuries (since 1770)" and dealing "only with European [or Eurocentric] literature." The Chinese American author and editor Frank Chin, in an influential essay, attacked autobiographies by Asian American authors such as Maxine Hong Kingston as works of Christian propaganda; the genre, being so inextricably associated with European, that is, Christian literature, thus of propagating false histories of Chinese misogyny and historical villainy in order to sell images of Chinese assimilation to a gullible white American readership. Chin's criticism constructs the fraught issue of deformations of ethnic and race identity as processes integral to what he calls the European Christian genre.

Extending and modifying Lejeune's paradigm, one may note that in approaching life-writing in the American grain, we need to take into account that the writing of American lives—indeed, arguably, of every life—is almost always already more than that of an individual personality, for it is almost always already riven by and conscious—if not critically addressing issues—of racialization, gendering, class and regional formations, and many other forms of social identity processes. That is, an individual's "personality," to repeat Lejeune's use of this common abstraction, is almost always already constructed in American life writing as part of larger troubling social, economic, and political structures and forces. We see this enlargement in Frederick Douglass's autobiography, in W. E. B. Dubois's *Souls of Black Folk*, Edith Eaton/Sui Sin Far's "Leaves from the Mental Portfolio of an Eurasian," in Kingston's *The Woman Warrior* and *China Men*, and so forth. If we accept Lejeune's definition of the autobiography, authors who self-identity as a member of a collectivity—national, racialized or in any way marginal (ethnic, minority, female, disabled, etc.)—cannot write the iconic autobiography that reduces the narrative to only individual personality, that is, self-writing. Rather, what we call life writing perforce takes on the shapes of genres related to but distinct from autobiography: history, documentary, journal, essay, even poetry. The "I" in i-dentity misleads us into reading within a tunnel vision of self isolated from other selves; whereas we may instead conceive of that "I" as embedded, apprehended, and acknowledged in relationship with community, as in the wedded wording of "iden-comity": an I-self hinged upon its unstable hyphenation with Others. André Vågan, in his projected study of South African narratives, cites Richard Werbner's astute observation that "[a] historical approach to memory takes it as problematic that intractable traces of the past are felt on people's bodies, known in the landscape, landmarks and souvenirs, and perceived as the tough moral fabric of their social relations—sometimes the stifling, utterly unwelcome fabric of social relations."

In February 2005, I was invited to speak at a memorial symposium held at Columbia University to celebrate the life of Caroline Heilbrun, who had killed herself at the age of 77, as she had years earlier promised she would do. The symposium selected eight university women who had written what the organizers termed "feminist academic memoirs." While I resisted having my memoir reduced to this sub-genre of the pedant, I admitted it was perhaps inevitable that *Among the White Moon Faces* should have been so categorized, written as it was in response to an assignment, pushed aggressively by the well-known academic feminist, Florence Howe, and published by a quasi-academic press, the Feminist Press, housed in the City University of New York.

Still, I argued then, my memoir's motivation was in contradistinction to the intellectual deconstructive currents of postcolonial theories. A strong authorial motive, as I can vividly recall, was to seize in prose those uncertain moments, yet certainly surviving as embodied traces, that up to 1994, when I began writing the memoir, had continued to emerge, involuntarily, and in spasmodic fashion, through the years. I had understood for a long time that specific memories, a term that cannot fully connote the independent disrupting violence of these mental acts, defined a subject—me—that was as different as a thumbprint from anyone else. In retelling my life, a major thread from early childhood to motherhood was the ways in which my body, the object of, subjected to and subjecting others to physical acts, of violation, violence, itself enraged and brutal, was the conduit to imagination. The formation of an interior consciousness of self, of interiority itself—the secretive, private, individualized, rankling sensibility from which came my poems—had everything to do with the familial, public violence that shaped the content of those involuntary mental images I call memory. In that talk, I argued that such formative violence and corresponding interiority characterized the shaping of my imagination; so that my memoir is not about an academic personality but rather about the growth of a poet's mind. Here is one such moment as replayed in the memoir:

> I remember one splendid Sunday morning when we four children,
> Beng, Chien, Jen, and myself, clung to each other's shoulders, and

Beng hung on to Father's, who swam out to the horizon, unafraid that the four of us might drop out of each other's grip into the salty waves. Father was a strong swimmer. As a boy he had jumped off the bridge into the Malacca River in weekend play, and his love of the sea blinded him to the danger he was leading us through. The water rushed like a living current over us; we were suspended above the drowning element by the power of my father's body.

Were we seven, six, five, three? All four of us did not add up to my father's years, although he was still a young man. Remembering his body, I need to count to materialize it out of the myth of muscle and salt water. A man of twenty-eight, lean, muscular, bearing on his shoulders the exposed naked slippery bodies of four children, each destined to grow larger than he, whose little fish bodies he could so easily have shrugged off, dropped over the horizon's edge, to return unencumbered, a free male. Instead I feel his calves kick, his arms arc and flash in a flight through welcome space. His teeth gleam white, a father shark, as he turns his handsome head, laughing at our squeals, taking pride in our fearless faith.

Because my father loved his children, I have kept faith with him, through the years of living with his pursuit of women, his gambling, and his rages. The bond I sewed tight between my father and me was illicit. In a Chinese family, perhaps in every family, daughters must be wary of their love for their fathers. We are constrained as daughters; the ties that strain us to our fathers are tense with those constraints. A vast because fearfully crossable boundary must separate girl-child from male parent. I wonder if all daughters suffer a revulsion about their fathers' bodies, instinctively reacting to save themselves from unacknowledged dangers.

As a child I adored my father's body. When I slept with my parents, before even more children arrived to remove me to a newly purchased iron-frame bunk bed, it was my father's body I reached out to touch when I roused in the night. He was warm and solid; it made me happy to touch his flesh lightly with my fingers, then drift back into sleep. So, in that serpent-like familial swim, with a brother gripping me around my neck, clinging to another brother as he clung to another who clung to my father's confident body, all of us children extruded from my father like grown sperm, links in an unbreakable, undrownable chain, the meaning of my father's life made manifest to him....

My father beat me on many occasions. Every time he slapped me, raised the cane and cut me on my legs, my shoulders, my back so that the raised welts were also deeply grooved and bloodied, I hated him. My eyes would blank and hurt and in my ears I heard the chant, "I hate you, I hate you."

That silent chant gave me an enormous sense of secret power. I never begged him to stop beating him, never cried, although my throat burned with stifled feeling and my head spun from the violence of his slaps. The rattan's whipping cuts were like knife-tongues of fire that licked the flesh and stayed and stayed. I hated him as much for humiliating me as for the pain. I felt public shame, for he beat me in front of anyone, my brothers, the neighbors, visitors, and relatives. I never asked what drove him to these maddened episodes. I knew it wasn't me. He beat me viciously once for dropping a spoon and breaking it; on another occasion when he thought a hawker had cheated me.

The only time I felt private shame when he beat me was the first time. A five-year-old stay-at-home, I was fascinated by my older brothers' sophistication, the news they brought home each day from school. They said different words, played different games, and owned large shiny books with photographs and drawings and stories in them. I felt my chest tighten with the desire to possess what was in their mouths and heads. My brothers shared a secret joke that galvanized them with mirth. I stood outside the circle of two and spied. They whispered, pretending not to see me. They formed circles with the thumb and first finger of their left hands and stabbed the round air with the fingers of their right hands, a secret sign that hailed them as partners and insiders. It was an understanding that they shared, and they slyly glanced at me to see if I had caught it form them, then yelled, "Go away!"

I ran outside into the evening air with their secret. I was elated, for I understood the sign. I knew how to form that circle and how to penetrate it. I ran to my father who was just closing up the shop. He was moving yet another wood plank into its grooved position, completing the wooden wall that shut the shop each night and transformed it into a home. There was no one else for me to play with. I tugged at his arm and showed him the secret I had just mastered.

But his face reddened. His eyes took on that crazed glower, only this time, for the first time, it was directed at me. I was horrified, but it was too late. He put the plank against the wall, went inside, dragging me with him, and caned me. I do not remember how many times the feather duster descended. Perhaps, because it was the first time, the switch came down for three cuts; perhaps it was more. After that evening I knew I could not depend on my father's love.

Later, as I approached ten and eleven, I understood the meaning of the sign, and the memory of his rage shamed me. The shame is unspeakable. I am covered with confusion. Did I, five years old, know that power of the sign? What secret was I breaking open as I tugged at his arm, smiling? Why am I still ashamed? Am I shamed by his uncontrolled use of power over my small female body, his displaced, repressed fears? Or by my child's desire for him, the man whom I had approached as my playmate, my partner, with whom I wanted to share the secret of the circle?

When my father beat me for the first time, the horror that filled me as I sobbed through that evening was not simple horror at pain, the sting of the rattan switch on my buttocks. It was also the horror at the acknowledgment of the break, that he had forcibly set me aside from himself, asserting a presence so alien that it could turn the lithe pliable rod on my flesh and cut me. My father became a fearful stranger to me then; as he gripped my arm, cursing in the growing darkness, and brought the rattan down on me, he appeared simultaneously to melt away, to lose his familiar contours, and to harden, to loom as a featureless man to whom my screams and tears signified nothing. My lifelong sense of the evening as the hour of abandonment, when one looks into the world and is overcome by one's aloneness, begins with that beating.

And the shame. For I understood clearly that it was what I had done that had changed this man from father to monster. Something in my desire for him, that tug on his arm, the sharing of a sign, had toppled something in him. His rage was inexplicable otherwise…. The buoyancy of the five-year-old looking up into her father's eyes as she showed him the sign she had just learned from her brothers never returned. I can mark that moment as the consciousness of another self, a sullen within, hating the father who beat me.

Hate does not explain love, but it sharpens love, in as much as it gives us the power to see the fragilities of the object of our hate. From the moment my father beat me, I became aware of his weakness rather than of his power. While I feared the pain of his canings, I never came to fear him; instead I came to acknowledge the depth of my responses and the interiority of my feelings. His blows drove me inwards into misery that cannot be spoken. I felt the power of my unhappiness, and therefore the power of my personhood. I learned to love my father again because I pitied him, and I pitied him because he gave me the power to hate him. (*Among the White Moon Faces* 31-34)

Thus, to the question, what kind of life is to be discovered in a poet's memoir: seduced by the epistemology of postmodernism, we may be tempted to accept a version of such life writing as writing, just another text that defers correspondence or identity in a series of webs of difference. Vågan's reading, however, framed through Pierre Bourdieu's concept of habitus, argues, "In the heart of memory lies the dialectic relationship between narrative and experience. This implies that memories from the past are discourses of identity. The memory/identify nexus is both phenomenological—when we know implicitly who we are and what circumstances that made us so, and an explicit construction; when we narrate certain stories of our selves to make certain impressions (Goffmann 1975). But even if our memories ought to support our view of identity, it can also threaten to undermine it, whether the past is something we wish to distance ourselves from, or it is filled with gaps such as amnesia." Shifting from both Lejeune's reader's and the postmodernist philosopher's positions, to the location of a writer of memoir, I affirm that there is something in a memoir that is more than the identity of the text; and that is the identity of the private and social body that is doing the writing; the embodied correspondence between writerly subject and narrative.

What is embodied memory? Arthur Glenburg argues that it is a form of cognitive structure that "arise[s] from bodily interactions with the world," "evolved in service of perception and action in a three-dimensional environment... to facilitate interaction with the environment" and results in "embodied representations, which are in fact mental models" (1). As memoirist, I tell the story that my body has lived through. Inscribing the memories that fire in my cerebellum, I intuitively understand that the past is seldom gone. To paraphrase William Faulkner's famous dictum, the past is never past; it returns as an individual's psychological experiences—in trauma, flashbacks, guilt, pleasure, associations, recognitions, wisdom, aches, neuralgia, dreams, nightmares; in a society's records of birth and death certificates, census questionnaires, photographs, letters, legal and archival documents, wills, legacies; and in family and communal bodies as hereditary diseases and in the form of related bodies and so forth.

Cognitive psychologists such M. L. Anderson, G. Lakoff and Johnson, and F. J. Varela have argued for an "emerging viewpoint of embodied cognition [that] holds that cognitive processes are deeply rooted in the body's interactions with the world" (Blutner). The move "to grant the body a central role in shaping the mind" (Wilson) may well be incorporated into how we think not just about our selves, that is, our identities, but also about how we think about writing these identities into our lives. In counter distinction to the widespread position that life writing is only or chiefly about writing—or, using related terms, only about discourse or textuality—I would claim that life writing or identity writing, to use an alternative phrase, is also about bodies, about memories that are embodied.

Remembering what it was like to remember for the first time, I return to a particular set of scenes that played themselves out when I was about three years old. The scenes were always recalled in double sequence, as a single drama, rather like a reversed before and after triumphal picture of the 90-pound weakling transformed into that buffed up body, Mr. Atlas. And like that double portrait, this memory sequence repeated a narrative of a personality, a subject identity, a life, so much so that from an early age, for as long as I had known I wanted to be a writer, I knew I would write down this story. This is the memory as I finally wrote it down in spring of 1994, almost half a century after the dual events occurred.

> Before there is memory of speech, there is memory of the senses. Cold water from a giant tap running down an open drain that is greenish slime under my naked feet. My mother's hands are soaping my straight brown body. I am three. My trunk is neither skinny nor chubby. It runs in a smooth curve to disappear in a small clet between my two legs. I am laughing as her large palms slip over my soapy skin which offers her no resistance, which slips out of her hands even as tries to grasp me. I do not see her face, only her square body seated on a short stool and a flowered *samfoo* that is soaked in patches.
>
> The same open area, the same large green-brass tap above my head, only this time I am crying. My anus hurts me. My mother is whittling a sliver of soap. I watch the white piece of Lifebuoy grow

> sharper and sharper, like a splinter, a thorn, a needle. She makes
> me squat down, bare-assed, pushes my body forward, and inserts
> the sliver up my anus. The soft is soft, it squishes, but it goes up
> and hurts. This is my mother's cure for constipation. I cry but I do
> not resist her. I do not slide away but tense and take in the thorn. I
> have learned to obey my mother. (*Among the White Moon Faces* 10)

Using the language now available to me as a Western-trained academic, I can describe these events narrated as traumatic, tracing the child's loss of original pleasure in her body through the pain of penetration as a figure for her socialization into a kind of femininity ruled by the mother; a mother, moreover, whose lesson for the girl-child is a prefiguration of a future in which women are subordinated to bodily regulatory systems premised on the universality of women's pain: penetration, mutilation, containment, breakage, birthing. This gloss, however, is unnecessary if the inscription of the body in pain is manifest in the re-telling, a manifest purchased in the Imaginary, substantiated in the Word, and marking that moment when the Symbolic and the Real become fused in the autobiographical pact, when story and history, self and other, word and body, are co-generated in the genre's text.

To elaborate, according to several psychotherapists, early traumatic experiences can become locked into patterns of chronic muscle tension. These tension states preserve such embodied memories which are thus able to be retrieved and resymbolized in future psychological processes (see, for example, Wilson and Keane's *Assessing Psychological Trauma and PTSD*). No wonder then that that dual scene replayed itself over and over again ever since I could remember remembering. Today, psychologists understand this involuntary repeated replayings as "flashbacks"; what I categorize as an embodied memory asserting its presence like a physical ghost, the sensory sharpness of lived experience like bright jagged lightning illuminating the night of the past and showing not empty landscape but a world full of corporeal actors and things, full of colors and violent actions in the darkness. Waiting to cross a street in heavy traffic, chatting with an acquaintance, reading a book, eating a meal, the scene of my mother's penetration of my three-year-old body would flash involuntarily into view; and again I would tell myself, here is what you must write. That is, even before the actual writing, I held that memory as an identity for writing, the promise of writing. It was this memory of the body, singular, idiosyncratic, yet also resonant of common childhood powerlessness and of female suffering that, to my mind, shaped my particular interior life, the identity of that self to which my memoir finally turned.

One of the reasons why many things appear to us as past is that we escape them. The past is often less pleasant than the present, and even when it appears more pleasant, the contrast between pleasurable past and painful present itself may lead to further pain. The repressive mechanism that encourages forgetting is so common and intense precisely because it possesses strong survival value. What happens then when a memoirist returns to and writes of traumatic memory? That time for me came in when I began writing the memoir for Florence Howe and the Feminist Press. Recovering at home after a radical hysterectomy, composing on an ancient Apple computer, immediately after writing the passage above, I felt a watery blister had been pricked and the fluid of that life event leaked out. The notion arrived in the form of this actual sensation; I saw and felt the blister deflating, and this particular flashback has never recurred since.

A woman in the audience that had elicited this writing account from me said that she found the loss of the flashback sad. With the devastating destruction of memories brought on by Alzheimer's and other degenerative diseases, the disappearance of a traumatic memory may not be a celebratory but a tragic moment. All memories, she claimed, painful or otherwise, are significant and should be preserved. Her rueful observation seems to be rather common; Lisa Knopp, in a recent collection of essays, also notes: "what seems like the purest, most self-contained type of creativity—turning the events, images, and ideas of one's life into a written story—is a destroyer. Writing about one's memories, trimming, padding, moving them around, reshaping them until they fit a readable or 'tellable' form, changes those memories in great or small ways. What the writer remembers after her act of creation is not her memory of the event that is the subject of her essay or story, but the written account of her memory" (cited in *Chronicle of Higher Education*, B4). Of course, both my interlocutor and Knopp miss the irony that memory is more effectively preserved in the condition of writing than as embodied story, in the condition of a text that will continue to exist long after the person who had narrated it is gone. These critical interventions, however, do suggest a primary problem about the writing of a memoir. In the transference of a privately coded story to a public document, something is lost. The secrecy of private memory, its residence in the skull case of an individual, the profoundly binding identification of story with hidden self, that is, the psychological integrity of memory, is irrevocably changed in composition—in the long industrial processes of printing, publishing, marketing, distribution, and reception.

When I first began drafting this talk, I thought of the writing of my memoir in the contrasting metaphors of organic and constructed processes. A memoir, I wrote, preserves memory; but, like canning, the process of preservation materially changes the original. The analogy lies not simply in the difference between fresh and canned fruit but between fruit borne fresh and green on a living tree—the tree of an individual consciousness—and the fruit plucked, preserved, and sold on the shelves of mega-bookstores. Somewhere in the final memoir, edited, reviewed, placed between covers, is the experience of the three-year-old child, carried over almost fifty years. In my first draft of this paper, defiantly I added, *to tell the truth, I was glad to lay down that burden. The fruit was hard and bitter. For over forty years it would not ripen. I plucked it. I did not sweeten it. If language is a preservative, it has other purposes than for a marketplace. The salts and spices that had preserved corpses as well as fruit and meat possess strong social and religious values in many civilizations. We no longer mummify humans, understanding death as that final condition from which there can be no further vital transformation. But language, the word, is breath, not death. If memory speaks in the memoir, then memory lives outside of the individual skull case, and it lives in language. That is the difference between memory and memoir, the difference between what is embodied and therefore must die with the body and what is externalized in the technologies of culture and may live.*

But, on second thought, second draft, this binarized distinction between organic and constructed memory, rearticulated as the difference between mortal memory and perhaps immortal prose, appears inadequate. Rather than privileging one form of memory over the other material form in print, Daniel Levy and Natan Sznaider have argued that "it seems more fruitful to identify the different historical and sociological conditions of memory cultures" (91) and so have taken up

Jan Assmann's distinction between "two memory types": "communicative memory, based on group-specific carriers" and "cultural memories that can exist independent of its carriers" (91). "What is at stake," according to Assmann, as cited by Levy and Sznaider, "is the transformation of communicative, i.e. lived and in witnesses embodied memory, into cultural, i.e. institutionally shaped and sustained memory" (91).

Memory has become a highly contested term. We seem to be getting to a point when we no longer recognize its legitimacy, as if in a postmodern era, a collective Alzheimer's has set in civilizationally. In place of memory, we now are cautioned about false memory, informed that all memory is socially constructed, that the boundaries between memory and fictivity are blurred, that personal memory is only part of collective memory, that memory is radically provisional and subjective and hence open to differentiation, ambiguity, obscurity, manipulation, erasure, and worse. Glenberg, for example, theorizes that memory is rooted in perception filtered through the subject's determination of "its usefulness to us," a usefulness "directly determined by our bodies, that is, what is useful to one person is not necessarily useful to another." Yet all these theories emphasizing the social constructedness and provisionality of memory do not conclude that memory is never to be trusted. Rather, they underline the complex relationship between body and memory and between embodied memory and the language in which that memory is both stored and storied.

The troubled and unstable relationship between language and embodied memory suggests also certain dynamics and modes of operations in the processes by which embodied memory—internalized and associative—comes into language, is reconstructed or imagined, vocalized, narrated, reproduced, transformed into life and identity writing. A dialectical process is at work by which embodied memory is transformed into writing, or by which language is affected and changed or charged by embodied memory. John Sutton, discussing the porous nature of memory, cites Marius Kwint on the "sensuous and physiological dimensions of embodied memory": "human memory has undergone a mutual evolution with the objects that inform it... the relationship between them is dialectical. Not only does the material environment influence the structure and contents of the mind, but the environment must also have been shaped along the lines of what persists in the mind's eye." Sutton goes on to argue, "It's just because representations in the brain are partial and action-oriented that external cognitive scaffolding and tools of many varieties supplement our relatively unstable internal memories."

One can usefully speculate that some of these "external cognitive scaffolding and tools," used to supplement "our relatively unstable internal memories," come under the rubric of rhetoric, and, practically, appear more and more frequently as readily available and purchasable items. Workshops on memoir writing proliferate, offered as two-week summer courses in prestigious institutions like the University of Iowa, as seminars in creative writing departments all over the United States (Vivian Gornick, for example, a well known East Coast feminist intellectual and writer for *The Village Voice*, teaches memoir writing at the University of Arizona in Tucson), and as community classes offered by organizations such as the YMCA and by private individuals. Entire textbooks now promise to teach undergraduates as young as seventeen advanced courses on life writing to be "shared with a public readership" (description of Winifred Bryan Horner's *Life Writing*). One such textbook, Susan Wittig Albert's *Writing From Life*, sub-titled "Telling Your Soul's Story," offers the reader "a guided writing program that will empower any woman to pick up a pen and chart the geography of her unique and fascinating life," promising an array of "exercises, meditations" and "the practical tools you need to get it all on paper" (back cover, *Writing from Life*). My knee-jerk skepticism in response to such broad claims that unproblematically associate a pedagogic schema with customizing a unique story, however, needs to be ironically contextualized in my own practices as a teacher of writing; for, as a writing teacher, facing twenty-five young eager clueless students, I also clutch at the closest scaffolding and tools, urging students to find their unique voices while stretching them on the same rack.

Teaching life writing compels me to consider the dialectical relation-ship between the external scaffolding provided by the practices taught in expository and narrative writing classes and the unstable memories internalized in brain and body circuitry. This complex dialectics is itself restlessly deconstructed by the company it keeps, by the specificity of its multiple contexts. At the University of Maryland campus, for example, a working group on life writing is said to do "intersectional work" with the Material Culture/Visual Culture, Structure and Agency in Education, and Intersectionality and Globalization working groups. An interdisciplinary conference on cross-cultural life writing and self-representation, we are told, has brought together "scholars working on life writing, self-representation and cross-cultural encounters in literature, history, anthropology and art history." A course description on 20th Century Life Writing notes that life writing covers forms as diverse as poetry, retrospective autobiography, memoir, personal essay, letter, journal/diary, and welcomes graduate students in literature, creative writing, history, women's studies, psychology, education, and other disciplines. Frequently, the reception to my memoir appears to arrive from as broad and interdisciplinary, even multidisciplinary, public readership as these many examples suggest. A graduate student writing her dissertation on women's island autobiographies, began her interview with me with this question: "A startling number of personal-history works—including your autobiography *Among the White Moon Faces: A Memoir of Asian-American Homelands*—by women immigrants, particularly from 'Third-World' countries, have been released in the latter half of the twentieth century, particularly in the 1990s. How do you account for the high number of these particular narratives?" The identities encompassed in her single question include American national, immigrant, women, third-world, twentieth century, and genre—autobiography, personal history, and narrative. Perhaps all memoirists encounter such academic readings. My answer on this occasion was to clarify a historical context for reading the multiple identities suggested by my memoir; such historical and social materials contextualize all Asian American writing, and, as I argued earlier, they illuminate the making of a public and historical self out of the individual's memories.

As author I have tried to stay away from writing about my writing: that is a subject I continue to believe more proper to readers than to the writer herself. D.H. Lawrence's caution: Trust the tale, not the teller, has haunted me since I first came across it at the age of sixteen. No author should be trusted on her work, for what more massive swamp for egotistical self-deceit can lie ahead than authorial self-evaluation? Yet many readers seem to insist on such writerly self-judgment and self-reflection. Even as I was completing the final draft of the memoir,

Florence Howe called me to say that she wondered why I had not written about my development and public recognition as a writer.

My first response, and still my response today, is that there can be little more boring than such representations. The innocent pride of first achievement; the enormous interior rooms of self-doubt and egotism, the many hours of composition; the soreness of rejections and highs of prizes and awards: these subjects are better treated as expository prose, and what I wanted for the story of my life was the interiority of poetry and a different external scaffolding: drama and narrative drive. Yet over and over again, I meet questions such as these, from scholars and academics.

Occasionally, an interview question allows me to clarify issues of identity that the life story appears to have left unfocused, to set the record straight as it were. To conclude, while my memoir is chiefly read as U.S. ethnic, it is in fact transnational, threading between at least two subjectivities, a Malaysian Chinese and an Asian American. Because Malaysia and the United States have very different political constitutions and governmental and ideological structures in which both the Malaysian Chinese and Asian American identities are marginal, and because the autobiographical subject becomes embedded temporally in these different socio-political economies and rights, the book contains in fact at least two memoirs, in which discourses of citizenship rights denied to Chinese Malaysians brush up against the loss of ethnic community vitality for the American resident alien: the passage from one dark complex habitus to another as complex and dark being perhaps the central dilemma narrated in this story of assimilation for one kind of Asian coming to America.

In many interviews, despite my protests, I am obviously talking about my life writing, just as in drafting this talk I am writing about the writing of my life writing. Such looping hyper-reflexivity, a meta-critical life writing discourse, is one of the ironic developments of a writing practice that is above all reflecting on the identity of a self. As a memoirist, however, I confess to a preference for the specific concretions of language constructed in dialectical relationship to embodied memory. As much, I hope, can be suggested through these kinds of stories about the cognitive role of the body in the formation of our mental maps of ethnic, gender, and cultural difference as can be understood through reflexive schema constructed after the fact of life writing.

Works Cited

Albert, Susan Wittig. *Writing From Life: Telling the Soul's Story*. New York: Putnam, 1996.

Anderson, M.L. "Embodied Cognition: A field guide." *Artificial Intelligence* 149 (2003): 91-130.

Blutner, Reinhard. Abstract of Masters Thesis: http://www.blutner.de/proj.html (Viewed on Aug 5, 2006).

Chin, Frank. "Come All Ye Asan American Writers of the Real and the Fake." *The Big Aiiieeeee!* Ed. Jefferey Paul Chan, et al. New York: Meridian, 1991. 1-92.

Douglass, Frederick. *A Narrative of Frederick Douglass, an American Slave*. (1845). New Haven: Yale University Press, 2001.

Du Bois, W.E.B. *Souls of Black Folk*. (1903). New York: Barnes & Noble, 2003.

Frey, James. *A Million Little Pieces*. New York: Anchor Books, 2003.

Glenburg, Arthur. "What Memory Is For." *Behavioral and Brain Sciences* 20 (1997): 1-55.

Horner, Winifred Bryan. *Life Writing*. New York: Prentice Hall, 1996.

Kingston, Maxine Hong. *China Men*. New York: Knopf, 1980.

—. "Personal Statement." *Approaches to Teaching Maxine Hong Kingston's The Woman Warrior*. Ed. Shirley Geok-lin Lim. New York: Modern Language Association Press, 1992. 23-25.

—. *The Woman Warrior: Memoir of a Girlhood Among Ghosts*. New York: Knopf, 1976.

Knopp, Lisa. *The Nature of Home: A Lexicon and Essays,* University of Nebraska Press, 2002, cited in *Chronicle of Higher Education*, Sept. 27, 2002: B4.

Lakoff, G. and M. Johnson. *Philosophy in the Flesh: The Embodied Mind and Its Challenge to Western Thought*. New York: Basic Books, 1999.

Lejeune, Philippe. *On Autobiography*. Ed. Paul John Eakin. Trans. Katherine Leary. Minneapolis: University of Minnesota Press, 1989.

Levy, Daniel, and Natan Sznaider. "Memory Unbound: The Holocaust and the Formation of Cosmopolitan Memory." *European Journal of Social Theory* 5.1 (2002): 87-106.

Lim, Shirley Geok-lin, ed. *Approaches to Teaching Maxine Hong Kingston's The Woman Warrior*. New York: Modern Language Association Press, 1992.

Lim, Shirley Geok-lin. *Among the White Moon Faces: An Asian American Memoir of Homelands*. New York: Feminist Press, 1996.

Robin, Steven. "Silence in my father's house: Memory, Nationalism, and Narratives of the Body." *Negotiating the Past: The Making of Memory*. Ed. S. Nuttall and C. Coetzee. Cape Town, South Africa: Oxford University Press, 1998. 120-140.

Sui Sin Far (Edith Eaton). "Leaves from the Mental Portfolio of an Eurasian." 1909. *Mrs. Spring Fragrance and Other Writings*. Ed. Amy Ling and Annette White-Parks. Urbana: University of Illinois Press, 1995. 125-132.

Sutton, John. ("Porous Memory and the Cognitive Life of Things": http://www.phil.mq.edu.au/staff/jsutton/CognitiveLifeOfThings.htm   as retrieved on Sep 17, 2006 08:48:38 GMT.

Vågan, André. "That's who we are! Narratives and embodied memories among 'coloureds' in Wentworth, Durban, South Africa." Hovedfagsstudent, Institute of Social Anthropology, University of Oslo. Autumn, 1999, unpublished paper.

Varela, F. J., E. Thompson, et al. *The Embodied Mind-Cognitive Science and Human Experience*. Cambridge: Massachusetts Institute of Technology, 1993.

Wilson, John P. and Terence M. Keane. *Assessing Psychological Trauma and PTSD*. New York: Guilford Press, 1997.

Wilson, Margaret. "Six Views of Embodied Cognition." *Psychonomic Bulletin and Review*, forthcoming: http://philosophy.wisc.edu/shapiro/PHIL951/951articles/wilson.htm (Viewed on Sep 13, 2006).

Shirley Geok-lin Lim, Professor of English at the University of California-Santa Barbara, has published *Reading the Literatures of Asian America*; *Approaches to Maxine Hong Kingston's* The Woman Warrior; *Transnational Asia Pacific*; *Power, Race and Gender in Academe*; and *Transnational Asian American Literature*, among others. Winner of the Commonwealth Poetry Prize, she has also published short stories, a memoir (*Among the White Moon Faces*, an American Book Award winner), and two novels, *Joss and Gold* and *Sister Swing*.

My Name is Carmen but this Story is Not Mine
An Introduction to "Searching for Carmen: A Mexican-American Odyssey"

Carmen Pearson

My name is Carmen but this story is not mine.

It was my grandmother who was the Carmen, born to a new century as Carmen Barragán Dorcas on 22 May 1900, in San Luis Potosí, a state nestled deep in Mexico's colonial heartland. She was the second child of four and the only daughter of María Dorcas Berro and Luis Barragán Garate.

María Dorcas Berro was a woman from the Basque country who met and married her brother's schoolmate, a Mexican-born Luis Barragán. The story of their meeting is that Luis was furthering his studies in engineering at the Sorbonne in Paris at the time of the courtship, having consumed what information he could at the university in San Luis Potosí and in other Mexican universities. No doubt enthused and encouraged by the expansive Porfirio years of the late nineteenth century, this young engineer sought the newest theories and technological advancements to help modernize his country.[1]

So María Dorcas Berro left the old country for the new, as most Europeans have, for something better. There is no written history of her family that I can find and nothing to truly verify if she ever saw her mother again or if her father and brother visited her in Mexico. I'd like to think they had, but these facts are lost. Of María Dorcas's life, there remain only two or three faded photographs and the foggy memories of her eldest grandchildren.

> "She sewed. All the time, she had a needle in her hand. She sewed and sewed…"
> "She loved her grandchildren very much."
> "She preferred speaking French over Spanish."
> "She was very religious…"

---

[1] President Porfirio Díaz led Mexico from 1876 through 1910 and, at different times, is either credited with leading his nation into modernity or faulted for leading Mexico's people into revolution.

"She returned to San Luis Potosí with her sons from New York after her husband's death there. She buried him back there in New York City. I'm not sure where… No one could earn a living in San Luis Potosí in those days and so they moved to La Ciudad de Mexico and then she lived alone in an apartment, earning money from teaching languages and catechism."

And that is all I have of her life—those few facts and my father's memory of María Dorcas Berro's only daughter, his mother, Carmen, running out to the hammock near the woodpile and crying and crying when the telegram was delivered, announcing her mother's death. How painful would it have been for Carmen Messinger Barragán to sit alone and mourn on a hammock near her stone farmhouse in Upstate New York, so far from Mexico? From my father's memory of this dark day, I assume María and her daughter, Carmen, although separated for many years and miles, were close and that she must have been a good mother.

Carmen, my grandmother, sewed and loved her grandchildren very much. She must have been like her mother. She too spoke in French and Spanish and English. Perhaps her mother had taught her this as well. Our Lady of Guadalupe always hung near Grandma's four-posted bed and we would stare up at this dark Madonna as we lay curled in her arms and were taught to read. I do not know if I could say that Grandma, Carmen, was very religious. Her Catholicism was very private. Sometimes she would pull open her drawers and we would stand on a stool and take peaks at her neatly folded piles of embroidered handkerchiefs and scarves. A musty smell of perfume penetrated those wooden drawers. Beneath the linens, she would lift her prayer beads and we would ask her questions about them. She'd begin to explain the saints and then smile and laugh and shake her head and tell us we were "ignoramuses," tucking her beads and other life back into their private fold.

She had married a gringo: tall, blond-haired, blue-eyed, with ancestors whose arrival to the hostile and cold shores of the northern coast of the Americas rivaled her own European ancestors' in Mexico and eventually ended up at a small farm in Upstate New York.

As is the case with many children, we lived within the domestic. I have since learned that this is not the case with all children, but in those days and within our family, life and history and drama were within our own walls and stories. It never occurred to us, American born, to ask Grandma how it felt to be foreign because we never thought she was. We never asked her about "acculturation" or "assimilation" or "discrimination" because we lived within our walls. We thought that the discord in that house over issues of the Virgin of Guadalupe and prayer beads and bills and money and our noise and my father's heated accusations to his father of Carmen's mistreatment were purely matters of domestic discord. We did not know that the dramas within those walls emanated to the world outside, nor would it have helped if we had. Alone and within those book-lined walls, we could hardly settle the dust. Had we ventured beyond the threshold, the strong winds of the outside would have made any calming or explanation impossible.

But now, those walls and the people who were my family are all long-since gone. A hug, a kiss, a smile, a candy from Grandpa's jar can no longer settle the dust—and so I wander outside the threshold of a domesticity that once held me and soothed the unanswered questions. I do not know if Carmen ever felt that she belonged. I do not know if she ever thought enough that way to even ask the question. Although she fled to the United States from Mexico with her family during The Revolution as a teenager and never really returned with the exception of a few short visits to her homeland, she never became a U.S. citizen, not even after she birthed my father in New York. What should I make of that fact? Did she always think, as many immigrants have, that she was always a foreigner and would eventually return home?

My father, still embittered over his father, explains that he never encouraged Carmen to take out U.S. citizenship because he held to his delusions of grandeur that they would, together, return to Mexico and buy an hacienda and live happily ever after. So, was Grandpa this story's villain, the capitalist who was looking for an edge—for a way to acquire a lifestyle in a foreign land that was no longer possible in his own? It would be easy to paint Grandpa as a villain and his villainy as the ugly American would make this a simple tale to tell, but the fact of the matter is much more complex than just that. Carmen adored her husband. She adored him even when everyone shook their heads. Carmen loved and mourned her husband and their hard lives together even after he died.

A feminist might try to explain this love by saying that Carmen Messinger Barragán, raised with all the patriarchal culture of the Catholic Church, was taught to adore the man and it was inevitable that she would play the martyred female. It is a story as old as Christianity itself and maybe that is the truth; but there are irritating facts that don't quite fit. In modern terms, we would say "Carmen had independent agency." She alone, despite all her family's misgivings, chose her husband. Although he was her brothers' close friend and even charmed her parents as he came and went, searching for mining claims and working with the family in various engineering projects both in the U.S. and Latin America after The Revolution, no one in the family wanted Carmen to marry him. Evidently, a safe marriage to a respectable Mexican man and second cousin was already arranged by the family. After the chaos and danger of The Revolution had settled, the brothers gradually returned to their country and wanted their sister to do the same. She refused. I cannot imagine the pressure Carmen felt, three brothers and how ever many cousins and her own parents, pleading with her not to marry the charismatic blue-eyed American... "Oh," Grandma would sometimes say, particularly in times when Grandpa had slumped down into one of his darker moods, "he was so tall and that blond hair... and his eyes, they were so blue..."

Was it all really that simple? Was Carmen swept off her feet by his good looks and charm? Was all that happened—that gave us life, U.S. citizenship rather than Mexican, a pure matter of infatuation?

Even our father will not begrudge his own father's good looks and charm. He remembers, almost in awe, "When he walked into a room, all eyes turned to him. He filled the room." Is that what Grandma fell in love with? A man who could fill all the empty spaces? Is that why she was able to put up with and even sympathize with his moods? She'd lost her father. She'd lost her country and a place in society that might have been her own had history been written differently. Did the blue-eyed, intellectual gringo fill some of that emptiness? Did she live vicariously through him?

Maybe in her dreaming moments she did, but not in her everyday life. The Depression made everyday living a hell with little room for dreaming. Without money, Carmen and her husband moved from the squalor of New York City and, with the assistance of a New Jersey spinster aunt's teaching pension, they bought an isolated farm in Up-state New York. There, without plumbing, without roads in the winter, no matter how hard times were, they would have food—or so this was the theory. The reality was that Carmen's husband was ill-suited for a hard life of physical labor, made of something softer than his Carmen. It was she, the girl from a soft and warm land who, taught to embroider, taught herself to wallpaper the stone walls with newspaper to keep the drafts from her only child. It was Carmen who ran to the henhouse late at night to keep the hens and their precious eggs from freezing. It was Carmen who swung the machete in the fields to clear the brush. It was Carmen who miraculously produced money from her sewing when the tax man came by to repossess the property. It was her husband who retreated from a world so much less than he had imagined and read poetry aloud as his wife toiled.

But, during those same hard years, my father recalls that between the milking and the hauling and the worrying over bills, Grandpa filled the house with intellectuals, drifters from New York City and around the world without a place to go. The debates echoed from the kitchen table and the clinking of the brandy glasses would continue on into the wee hours of the morning. These friends came and went and some stayed on for months, with no place else to go.

> "There were Russian Jews, Germans, and other intellectuals and artist-types from the city... They would sit up all might in the kitchen, arguing... Sometimes, I would get jealous because they would take my mother from me... My father and some of them once organized the first milk strike in New York State, demanding better prices for the independent farmers... They came and went and they all loved Carmen."

My father turns to my sister and I, remembering, thinking, "You girls are like her. She could be on her hands and knees all day, scrubbing, laboring—but then, she'd take a bath and dress for dinner and set the table and arrange some flowers and all that ugliness would fade in the candle-light..."

Is this what Grandpa gave his wife, in return for all he took? Moments where the drudgery and poverty faded and Carmen could let her mind wander from the constant gnawing fears of dispossession? I recall their trips to Canada in their later years. When her age caused us to worry over Grandma's drive to the local market—let alone locales beyond that—she would wave good-bye to us, propped up on a pillow and commandeered by Grandpa beside her in the old Buick, searching for the land of tomorrow. Grandpa's dreams had shifted in those last years and he believed the future lay north of the 49th parallel. Was it Grandpa's tenacity and insistent belief that somewhere he would find the Lost City of Gold or The Happy Valley the quality that Carmen loved so much about him—despite how far-fetched and crazy it all seemed at the time? Or, was her compliance, car wrecks on the Trans-Canada Highway, and discomforts in those last years just another way to placate a difficult old man? Our grandmother never explained, nor expressed a bitterness for life's turns, at least not aloud. When we were older and would ask, she would somehow say that the ups and downs were part of the history of the world and that was the only way to understand one's own story...

And here I am. It is 2006 and I sit in a little room in the barn, staring down at my grandmother's daily journals, wondering what I can create from the broken pieces. The words. And I wonder, why should anyone care to even read this story and what is it I am really looking for? A place in history where I can touch a moment with my fingertip and claim an understanding —a right? And for what? It is all in the past.

I sit and look out over the dirty late winter snow and feel the chill that blows in through the thin walls off the Canadian Rockies just to the west and I wonder. Once again, am I repeating a family history, far from the land where I was born, married, just as the women before me, to a foreigner? In each generation, the climate seems to be growing colder and the landscape more remote. María lived in Mexico. Carmen lived in New York. This Carmen lives in the foothills of Alberta in a land where winter can stretch from August to June. I rub my feet along the electric heater and think about belonging, about nationality, about a logical explanation for our movements and lives. Has it been the destiny of the women in our family to discover ourselves in distant lands or are we just chaff in the great winds of chance and capitalism—blown across the landscape with each boom and bust?

Did Carmen wonder where she belonged? Did María Dorcas? Need I? We are not immigrants in the traditional sense of the word. When Americans think of immigrants, we think of European families, piled up at Ellis Island; of pioneers traveling across the prairies, clutching their children to their sides on their bumpy Conestoga wagons; of war refugees; Cubans exiles; starving Haitians on flimsy boats; of Mexican workers dodging Border Patrol near the Río Grande during the dark hours of the night. We are none of those. As far as I can tell, we are all women, who, again, with independent agency, made personal choices resulting in our immigration. We are not the people who have written history; instead, we have always remained in that silent fringe of the middle class, living our lives largely within the domestic, some-what isolated from extended family, from politics and from a culture we were born into.

Do our stories even matter? Probably not as much as others'. Relative to others', our hardships are miniscule. We are a minority who, in the big scheme of things, are a statistical insignificance. We all married outside our nationalities. Are we the modern versions of *La Malinche*?[2] Can we be accused of selling out our own? Of crossing the line for personal gain? Of muddying the pure races? Or, are we the mothers of new nations not yet fully formed?

With all the moves in our lives, someone always carefully packed the daily journals that Carmen maintained throughout her adult life. "Someday," my mother repeated, "someone needs to do something with Grandma's journals…"

The last time my mother repeated that—gesturing to the old attic in her Colorado ranch house, I did not know at the time that I would never hear her voice again. She wasn't ill, spilling out her last words to me that day. She was healthy and vibrant and merely allowing her mind and conversation to idle after a big holiday meal. No one knew she would die the next day and I'm sure she didn't know the impact that those words would have on me. They were my mother's last and like the Carmen before me, I went off like a wounded animal, and cried and cried when my mother died. She was a good mother too.

---

[2] *La Malinche* (also known as Doña Marina and Malintzin) is viewed not only as the mother of mestizos—but also as the symbol of national betrayal (and sometimes, a whore). See Sandra Messinger Cypress's *La Malinche in Mexican Literature*.

And so now I sit, alone, with a little cardboard tomato box. Inside, each worn leather journal holds a year, beginning in 1945, ending in 1977. My father says there may be more. Grandma would have been forty-four when she began her journal in January of 1945. I too am forty-four. I muse: is there a significance in this coincidence? And then I wonder, why did Grandma keep these journals? There was the practical matter of keeping track of business and meetings—but was there something more?[3]

Daily journals are very different from memoirs or autobiographies. There is a lack of reflection, an immediacy, what a narratologist might refer to as the "episodic" rather than "diachronic self."[4] In actual fact, there is very little to work with unless the fictional imagination is employed to recreate a life and time.

I read some of the entries for January 1945. There is a column of numbers. Is this money? Survey calculations?

84
$8.2 - 2.9 - 1.0 - 1.0$

Tuesday January 2
Literary Guild 123-1049

And so it goes. January 5 calculates the hours of what seems to be a hired hand. She writes: "Elmer started Monday." This is followed by a

---

[3] In her book review of *Inscribing the Daily*, Elaine Neil Orr writes that studying women's diaries "illustrates the need to develop reading strategies that are appropriate to women's life writing practices…. the content and form of women's diaries continue to be of interest to women's studies scholars because these texts disclose how women construct knowledge, how they negotiate power in their particular cultural contexts, how they relate interpersonally, and in some case, how they come to healing through writing" (892). See also, Barbara Rylko-Bauer's "Bring the Past into the Present:," where the author examines "History-write-large" in "intimate family histories" (4) and Valerie Raoul's "Women's Diaries as Life-Savings" where the author argues that women's diaries can be empowering.

[4] See Battersby's article "Narrativity, Self and Self-Representation," which responds to Strawson's "Against Narrativity." See also Eakin's "What Are We Reading…?", Lisa Zunshine's "Theory of Mind," and George Butte's "I Know That I Know…"—all of discuss the creation of "self" relative to the narrative process.

listing of jobsites. Elmer's hours are carefully added. He'd earned $100 for what looks like a month of labor. During those years, Grandpa must have given up on finding his fortune in the mines of Santa Domingo and settled down to the grueling business of land surveying through the heavy brush in Upstate New York, with Carmen by his side.

There is nothing so far to even indicate a life, a woman, a Mexican exile. However, on Tuesday, January 9, the entries change and the skeleton of a life begins to appear. Carmen writes:

> Xmas list:
> George Clifford
> 1168 N Edgmont St
> Hollywood Calif
>
> Argonzonis
> Lourdres 54-Mexico D.F.

So far, I do not recognize these names, but on the page for January 10, the list continues. Now, it is her three brothers, scattered in those years:

> Adrian
> Frontera. 19 Bis – 0

During those war years, Mexico prospered and so did Carmen's brothers. Hence, her hard life in war-rationed New York became even more of a contrast and conundrum to her family south of the Border.

The lists go on for pages, more names from Mexico:

> Miguel Dorcas Beno
> Dueno 33 – Mex.

I eagerly wonder, could this be María Barragán Dorcas' brother? I read on…

> Joe Freeman
> 301 E 38th N.Y.C.

This man's name, I recognize. His book, *An American Testament*, published in 1938 by the Left Book Club sits on my shelf, identifying its author as editor of *The New Masses*. According to my father, Joe Freeman and his wife were his parents' very close friends during those years. I lift the book from the shelf and it falls open to a worn page. The author discusses the events leading up to his early years in New York: "[t]he outbreak of the Russo-Japanese War in 1904 aroused no enthusiasm among Jews…" (24). Freeman goes on to explain how "[c]oming to America at seven was like being born again" (26). However, this rebirth was not without its trials. As Freeman recounts his assimilation into American culture, he reflects that the greatest hardship was not learning the language, nor avoiding the street gangs, nor the poverty. It was the fear of loneliness. He concludes by writing: "The dream [and antidote for this fear] came: to have friends who you love and who love you" (30).

It is hard to imagine, reading the strong words about alienation and loneliness in this worn text and knowing that Carmen would have read each word many times that she did not wonder about nationality and belonging and the history of her own people as well. It is also easy to understand why she would have felt an affinity to these immigrants.

There are no more entries until Saturday April 7:

> Aunt Viola was sick, all day. I fixed things and cleaned a chicken in the afternoon. We went to survey at Kripplebush for Caulfield, we took Farrandito along. He wanted to see us survey.

"Farrandito," my father, would have been eight at the time. Aunt Viola was the aunt of Carmen's husband, Etienne Farrand, Sr. and I have been told that she adored and spoiled him and, in fact, raised him when he fell out with his own parents and left home at an early age. Aunt Viola is the retired teacher and spinster, the one who provided the down payment for Whitfield Farm and the one whose pension helped carry the family through the hard years and who also helped to raise my father, "Farrandito," while Carmen worked in the field.

> Sunday – April 15
> I sewed all day and made a blouse of blue and white stripes for the slacks. It turned out very pretty.

She lived too far to attend Church regularly. On Sundays, at least, she did not go to the field and work. Instead, Carmen sewed. Did the threads she drew on those long Sundays somehow pull her back to a world that was more her own? The entries continue, describing the rain, Auntie's bad health, that she has sewed pajamas for "the boy" — her son. The pages continue with entries about the rain, about neighbors coming to pick up loads of hay, about surveys and of her husband's being elected as the trustee of the Whitfield School, of more rain, of 4-H meetings... And then, on Thursday May 3, at the bottom of the entry, after sentences about the rain, the surveys, the man who delivered the cow and "got in the ditch," the first sentence in Spanish appears: "*Me enferme hoy en la noche.*" Why, I wonder does she write this [about feeling ill in the night] in Spanish? And for that matter, why, since this is a personal journal, isn't everything written in Spanish? On the next page, Saturday – May 5, she writes:

> Father McDonald came. He wants Farrandito to come to church. He might make his first communion.
> On Sunday, May 6, she continues: "We went to Church in Rosendale. I hope Farrandito can make his first Communion..."

The tension she must have felt over her only son's communion and her husband's lack of faith are all but hidden in these entries with the exception of the word "hope."

As I eagerly leaf through the pages of Carmen's journals, places and faces and stories appear to me, but I stop and close 1945. This is meant to be an academic project, not a self-indulgence. The questions that have been haunting me for months flood back.

Even if I do proceed with this project, how do I explain the first un-chronicled forty-five years of Carmen's life, her childhood before The Revolution? The terrifying train ride out? The years in Laredo, San Antonio, Florida, New York? Her marriage? The early years when one painful miscarriage flowed into the next? And, what do I do to imagine the days when her journal entries simply read, "Surveyed" or "It rained." And, how do I explain what I'm truly searching for in this narrative?

In "Memory and the Archive in Contemporary Life-Writing," Michael Sheringham offers encouraging words, suggesting that the story lives in the tension of what has been inscribed and what is lost to time.[5]

---

[5] Sheringham writes: "It may be naïve to see the document as material proof of the past state of affairs, independent of the constructions we put on it; but to forego this anxiety does not dispose of the documents' claim to some sort of authority [...] [and in this, there is a conjoining of presence and absence which invites us to reconstruct] [...] [knowing that] we can never reconstitute the temporal chain that separates us from the moment of its inscription" (51).

Other narratologists, such as Galen Strawson, suggest that perhaps I am creating "a self" as I construct this narrative, that what I'm truly searching for is a sense of identity found within the process of assembling the story itself.[6] However, when I read this, I immediately think: I'm not that interested in me. But, I wonder: what is it then?

Last year, I traveled to Mexico to visit relatives I have not seen in thirty years. The premise was to hear and collect their stories and recollections of Carmen. I found myself walking with distant cousins through the streets of San Miguel de Allende and San Luis Potosí.

"Could we find the house that was once theirs?"

"Was this the Church they attended?'

"Did they offer confession over there?"

And then, we emerge from the *Tunel Ogarrio*, a 2300 meter tunnel constructed between 1897 and 1901 that separates *Real de Catorce* from the rest of the world. Rubbing hips with the donkeys whose ancestors, along with traders and miners, speculators and laborers once filled this valley; we walk, hand-in-hand: "Grandfather Luis worked in the mines here. We have been told he was the mayor here."

We wander past the pelota wall, *La Plaza de Toros*, the crumbling aqueducts and stop to stare up at the slag piles from mines named *La Purísima, Milagro, Concepción, Dolores*, and *Santa Ana*. We stop on *El Puente de Purísima*. She says, "Grandfather probably helped to build this bridge."

We wander on and enter the cool luminescence of the Church of Guadalupe and watch the Pilgrims as they, in turn, offer their prayers to St. Francis of Assisi, just as they have for centuries. Eventually, we discover what must have been the city hall. The mayors' pictures adorn the walls. We search eagerly for a familiar name, but the portraits stop in the thirties.

There are a few American tourists around. They look at me, somehow knowing, despite the company I keep and my silence that I am not from this land. Stubbornly I turn from them. My cousins tighten their grip with mine and I wonder: do I actually feel as though the land and the streets are any more mine than they are a tourist's simply because my family once lived and worked here? What difference does the past

---

[6] See Galen Strawson's "Against Narrativity."

matter now? Do I really think that the land will speak to me in a way it wouldn't to tourists, to *los extranjeros*? I look over at Regina. She kneels beneath the Virgin of Guadalupe and weeps. I do not quite know why, but I stand in silence and in awe—over something that was lost. Alone, she and I walk amongst specters. We look into dark alleys, simultaneously imagining our ancestors walking along these same cobbled streets.

It was almost a year ago when I sat across the table, shocked at the Chicano publisher's vehement outpouring concerning my proposal over this project—and shocked at my own *naïveté*.

"It is the story of the enemy, why would anyone care?" he burst out.

I swallowed, knowing that he was no longer interested in any form of publication of my grandmother's diaries or of a narrative built up around them. Really, I'd known that since before he'd said a word. He'd looked at me as he arrived, in disbelief and, I think, in disgust. I'd stood up from the table and tried to shake his hand. He held his arms to his side and stared up at me. I towered almost two feet above his dark head and in that moment, I believe I could hear his thoughts:

"You are NOT a Carmen..." Or, at the very least, "you are NOT the Carmen I expected..."

This was nothing new. My name was given to me because it was the name of my Grandmother. But that Carmen was small and black curls surrounded her expressive dark eyes and face. Me? I am tall and was very blond when I was young and although my eyes are brown, they seem washed out, like earth plowed too many times, compared to those of my relatives. Even my brother and sister pestered me when I was young that I must have been adopted because I was so different from them. Their hair was black and thick and their complexions were a rich olive. Although I sometimes wondered myself that my parents hadn't made a poor choice in names, I always knew I was a Carmen.

We had lived in a time and in a place where a child's name received deep consideration. It was not a matter of which flower or movie star or constellation a parent might like. Instead, it was a matter of which relative would be honored. Wrong choices caused family feuds that lasted for years, sometimes for generations. Living in such a time and place, people would turn to me and smile, trying to explain to themselves and to me the strange and seemingly inappropriate choice of name, "Oh, your parents must be big fans of the opera..." And before I could explain that we'd never seen an opera in our lives, they would continue, "dark and lusty and independent..." They'd smile at me and I'd blush. "Well, not actually, it was my *abuelita*, I'd explain..." —trying to sound convincing with one of the only Spanish words I could pronounce with confidence. That done, the speakers would inevitably dismiss me as a genetic throwback and move on, sometimes adding, "Well, it is a pretty name."[7]

On this particular April day and to this particular man, I seemed an impostor, not worthy of the name. I wanted to tell him that I understood and felt both the honor and burden in having been named "Carmen" and it was for this specific reason that I had come to him. But he didn't give me a chance. The pounding interview continued.

When I finally accepted that I had very little in common with this man and what he represented and his cause and that, in complete ignorance, I had stepped into a minefield and had threatened his hard won position of power and that he would never publish a word I wrote, I decided that I should at least view the tremulous hour as a learning experience.

There has been long debate over the word "Chicano" versus "Mexican American" versus "Mexican-American" versus "Mexican." Certainly, I only ever heard my grandmother refer to herself as the latter and I never heard my father call himself anything but an "American," certainly not a "Mexican-American" or "Mexican American." The *Chicano/a* is a distinctive and hard-earned identity that includes those who live in Anzaldúa's *Borderlands* and those who labor as an invisible population in the U.S. and those, similar to other ethnic minorities, who were forbidden entry to public places, to schools, to neighborhoods. Vicki Ruiz offers one of the most succinct discussions of these different terms in her introduction to *From Out of the Shadows: Mexican Women in Twentieth Century America.* She writes:

---

[7] The name "Carmen" —her Saint's day is July 16—is derived from the *Virgen del Carmen*, the Virgin Mary of Mount Carmelo; from the Old Testament, her story involves the prophet Elias' retreat to a cave in Mount Carmelo near Haifa (Israel). She is the patron saint adopted by mariners and fishermen.

> Women of Mexican birth or descent refer to themselves by many
> names–Mexicana, Mexican American, and Chicana (to name just
> three). Self-identification speaks volumes about regional, genera-
> tional, and even political orientations. The term Mexicana typically
> refers to immigrant women, with Mexican American signifying
> U.S. birth. Chicana reflects a political consciousness borne of the
> Chicano Student Movement, often a generational marker for those
> of us coming of age during the 1960s and 1970s. Chicana/o has also
> been embraced by some of our elders and our children who share
> in the political ideals of the movement. (xiv)

Although it was the work of the *Chicano/as* scholars that brought me to
realize that someone might be even remotely interested in Carmen's old
diaries, I now appreciate that hers is not *their* story. However, even as
the interview with the Chicano publisher pounded on, I was not willing
to concede, as this publisher wished I might, that hers was not a story
worth telling. Finally, I had just about enough and something rose up
and poured through my polite schoolgirl veneer:

"So," I asked, "is history only to be written by victors?"

The publisher stopped and looked over at me, "Well, no…" he con-
ceded.

"Well, what then?" I asked. I understood that he felt it his respon-
sability to publish and publicize the hardships and the atrocities his
people had suffered and continue to suffer, but I could not understand
his anger about my family.

He began again. "They fled during The Revolution because they were
of Porfirio. They were the oppressors…"

I vaguely remembered that both my father and grandmother had said
how the whole family loathed government just as a matter of principal
and would have been happy to have been left alone to build their dams
and roads in peace.

"But, your family benefited from those years," the Chicano publisher
pointed out.

And again, the blood was on my hands. In the state-run education of
New York in the seventies, I had been taught, along with the Gettysburg
Address and the names of the battlefields of the American Revolution,
that it was our people who were responsible for destroying the Native
culture, for oppressing the Blacks and for damaging the environment.
Today, this fact was just one more sin to be added to the list and the

burden I was meant to carry. I could only seek consolation in the fact that we were really never important enough to be true oppressors and villains because, as far as I knew, we were usually too occupied with the business of surviving. But, even with this fact in mind, I knew we could still be accused by some of buying into an oppressive economic force and were therefore complicit with all these injustices.

I sat at the table, staring at my fork and then started. "We didn't benefit too much." I looked over at the Chicano publisher. "We lost everything but what we carried inside us."

Even here, he found fault. The fact that our family could find jobs state-side because of the education their privilege had allowed them was a dark mark against them. Sure I couldn't win this debate, I tried one last turn: "The only thing I know is that we were always brought up to be proud of our Mexican heritage. We never knew shame from that." Silenced for a moment, he considered what I said, and concluded: "that is because your family moved so far from the conflict. They buried themselves in some obscure farm and tried to recreate the *hacienda* some place else..."

It seemed odd to think of Whitfield Farm as an *hacienda*, but there was no winning and so I made one last comment and stopped. "Whatever they did wrong or right, they raised us to be both interested and proud in our heritage. If cultural discrimination and hegemony is the enemy, then maybe they avoided some of that."

The sting of that interview still chills and inhibits me and so it was with interest that I read the words of Genaro M. Padilla in *My History, Not Yours: The Formation of Mexican American Autobiography*. In his text's preface he explains his political difficulties as a Chicano in proceeding with his studies which included the writings of those he considers "*ricos*" or landowners.[8] As much as he too would like to exclude these

---

[8] Padilla writes: "This book represents my understanding of the ways in which Mexican American autobiography came into formation as a personal and communitarian response to the threat of erasure. Understanding did not come easily.... I more than once decided to abandon the project for political reasons. I would not spend my intellectual life arguing on behalf of people I probably wouldn't have liked in person. But the more I read their narratives, and the more social and political history, newspapers and letters I read, the more I came

individuals' stories from his own, he admits that he cannot. He writes: "Theirs are [also] autobiographical narratives of dispossession [and, I would like to add, "In some cases, theirs are also the narratives of maintenance and repossession...]" (x).

With Padilla's words, I feel somewhat buoyed that a narrative built around the words in Carmen's diaries might be worthwhile. In some ways, Padilla admits that such stories are not the ones he wishes he had—but, since they are all there is, he will accept them and proceed. But, I wonder... Is there a value in these words, beyond the scarcity of others? Could it be argued that the words and memories of the middle class struggle contribute a necessary and integral link to an explanation of cultural shifts, of human struggles, movement, and the very formation and evolution of nation states?

Once more, looking for comfort, for guidance, I turn back to the tomato box on the floor, to some thirty years of records—jotted down in a few brief words and stored for years in the loft of a barn. These are our family archives. Again, I ask myself: how do I recreate a meaningful history out of so little and if I do, isn't it presumptuous and even neo-colonial to imagine that in exploring and recreating those streets and hills that they might come to be any more mine than they were before—or, that there is really a place on this earth I can cast any claim to at all? I cling to Carmen's diaries as though the answer is somehow hidden in their pages and I persist and wonder if I will search again for specters in the back streets of the villages around Pamplona and if I will walk the beaches on the Bay of Biscay, trying to find some traces of María Dorcas Berro and of a footprint that might bear any resemblance to my own.

Most likely I am not the Carmen you expected and the Carmen I try to describe is probably not the Carmen you hoped to find here, but, maybe like Padilla, you will come to appreciate that our stories are not so very far from those of your own *antepasados*. Maybe if, today, you read this, tomorrow you will find your own Carmen.

---

to realize that by the end of the nineteenth century just about the only estate left to any of our *antepasados* was one situated in the geography of the past" (x).

Works Cited

Anzaldúa, Gloria. *Borderlands: La Frontera*. 1987. San Francisco: Aunt Lute Books, 1999.

Barragán Family Members. *Collected Oral Histories*. Mexico City, April 14-22, 2005.

Battersby, James L. "Narrativity, Self, and Self-Representation." *Narrative* 14.1 (January 2006): 27-44.

Butte, George. "I Know That I Know That I Know: Reflections on Paul John Eakin's 'What Are We Reading When We Read Auto-biography'?" *Narrative* 13.3 (October 2005): 299-306.

Messinger-Cypress, Sandra. *La Malinche in Mexican Literature*. Austin: University of Texas Press, 1991.

Eakin, Paul John. "What Are We Reading When We Read Auto-biography?" *Narrative* 12.2 (May 2004): 121-132.

Freeman, Joseph. *An American Testament*. London: Left Book Club Edition, Victor Gollancz, 1938.

Kurlansky, Mark. *The Basque History of the World*. London: Penguin, 1999.

Messinger, Carmen Barragán. *Collected Diaries: 1945-1977*. Personal Family Archives.

Orr, Elaine Neil. "Inscribing the Daily/Women's Life-Writing: Book Review." *Signs: Journal of Women in Culture and Society* 26.3 (Spring 2001): 5.

Raoul, Valerie. "Women's Diaries as Life-Savings." *Biography: An Interdisciplinary Quarterly* 24.1 (Winter 2001): 140-152.

Padilla, Genaro M. *My History, Not Yours: The Formation of Mexican American Autobiography*. Madison: University of Wisconsin Press, 1993.

Ruiz, Vicki L. *From Out of the Shadows: Mexican Women in Twentieth-Century America*. Oxford: Oxford University Press, 1998.

Rylko-Bauer, Barbara. "Bringing the Past into the Present: Family Narratives of Holocaust, Exile, and Diaspora." *Anthropological Quarterly* 78.1 (Winter 2005): 7-10.

Sheringham, Michael. "Memory and the Archive in Contemporary Life-Writing." *French Studies* LIX.1 (2005): 47-53.

Strawson, Galen. "Against Narrativity." *Ratio* 17 (Dec 2004): 428-452.

Zunshine, Lisa. "Theory of Mind and Experimental Representations of Fictional Consciousness." *Narrative* 11.3 (Oct 2003): 270-291.

Carmen Pearson has taught English at Mount Royal College in Calgary, Alberta and at the University of Houston in Texas. She is currently working on a book-length version of *Searching for Carmen: A Mexican-American Odyssey*, of which this essay is part.

Remembered Community:
Memory and Nationality in Mahmoud Darwish's
Memory for Forgetfulness

Terry DeHay

> *"The State of Palestine is the state of Palestinians wherever they may be. The state is for them to enjoy in it their collective national and cultural identity, theirs to pursue in a complete equality of rights"* (Palestinian Declaration of Independence. November, 1988)

Focusing on *Memory for Forgetfulness*, a memoir written by the Palestinian poet, Mahmoud Darwish, situated on a single day during the Israeli siege of Beirut in August, 1982, this essay explores the role of the autobiographical text in the construction of national narrative in a post-Enlightenment period, what some would call a post-national period. Darwish, in the words of Munir Akash and Caroline Forche, "shar[es] the fate of his people, living in a town under siege, while providing them with a language for their anguish and dreams." Born in the village of Birwe, in the district of Acre in 1942, he was six years old when his family fled to Lebanon after the Israeli Army occupied and destroyed the village. Upon their return a year later, they were labeled "present-absent" aliens by the new Israeli government, and Darwish witnessed "the conversion of the land around him into a 'foreign country' subjected to the power of a new language and new names" (Van Leeuwen 260). Even as a young student in Israel, Darwish's outspoken views on the treatment of Palestinians led to his harassment and imprisonment by the Israeli government, and his early trauma of alienation and exile, coupled with his love for his homeland, has continued to shape his political and poetic voice. In many ways, then, his personal history echoes the collective history of Palestinians, and his personal narrative becomes an important part of the larger narrative of Palestine.

All of Darwish's work can be read as an intervention in the narrative of his people and demonstrates the creation of a national narrative as an on-going process. He has written twenty books of poetry, five books of prose, numerous critical and social commentaries, as well as political documents for Palestinian organizations and governmental bodies— including the Palestinian Declaration of Independence adopted in 1988 and cited above. In 1971, he moved to Beirut, where he worked for the Palestinian Liberation Organization (PLO) and served as editor-in-chief of the Palestinian literary and cultural periodical, *Al-Karmel*, until Israel's 1982 invasion of Lebanon in an ultimately successful attempt to drive out the PLO leadership.

The immediate subject of *Memory for Forgetfulness* is the Palestinian resistance during the Israeli bombing of Beirut from the 13th of June to the 12th of August, 1982; but it also contains a broader historical, political, and personal meditation on the state of exile of the Palestinians from their land since 1948. It is a beautiful and difficult text, that combines poetry and prose, humor and horror, historical documents and the musing of memory into an expression of the Palestinian struggle for statehood. With a kind of Joycean echo of Bloom's wanderings through Dublin, Darwish leads the reader through the maze of West Beirut under a constant rain of shells from Israeli ships and planes, creating an heterogeneous narrative representing the complex history of a people struggling to maintain a national identity, in spite of the dissolution of its geopolitical borders. And similar to Bloom's journey, through external and internal wanderings, Darwish's narrative moves from the personal quest for the perfect cup of coffee to the mythic quest for a homeland, from one person's memories to the collective history of a people, revealing in the events of one day, "their many layers of meaning and their roots in the past" (Van Leeuwen 263). In fact, *Memory for Forgetfulness* uses many of the characteristics of the European modernist text: fragmentation, a poetics of difficulty, and intertextual, crosscultural, and transhistorical allusions, often from a critical, self-referencial position. However, rather than reflecting the critical stance toward national culture attributed to many European modernists' autobiographical texts, Darwish uses these techniques to narrate his personal experience of exile from his homeland and his vision of the troubled nation that is Palestine.

In discussing *Memory for Forgetfulness* as a part of the narration of Palestinian national identity, Benedict Anderson's definition of a nation as an "imagined community" provides a means of understanding the survival of national identity in the face of deterritorialization and diaspora, which are characteristics of most postcolonial nations. This concept of "imagined community" is especially apt for Palestine, a nation whose people have been living in a state of what Homi Bhabha calls "unhomeliness" for over fifty years (10). In fact, the situation of the Palestinian people demonstrates the power of the collective imagination to sustain and revision identity even when the geographic designation of the community is suspended. If there are no "fabricated" or "false" communities and all communities are created, imagined, then a community *can* exist primarily in the minds and wills of the people who identify with it. As Anderson argues, a nation is *"imagined* because the members of even the smallest nations will never know most of their fellow members... yet in the minds of each lives the image of their communion," so that specific geographic proximity is no longer the most important aspect of a nation (6). And in this way, Palestine continues to live in the hearts and minds its people.

In *Memory for Forgetfulness*, as he prepares his coffee with the shelling of the city in the background, Darwish reflects on his own position and that of the fighters in the streets:

> And where is my will?
> It stopped over there, on the other side of the collective voice. But now, I want nothing more than the aroma of coffee. I feel shamed by my fear, and by those defending the scent of the distant homeland—that fragrance they've never smelled because they weren't born on her soil. She bore them, but they were born away from her. Yet they studied her constantly, without fatigue or boredom; and from overpowering memory and constant pursuit, they learned what it means to belong to her. (13)

Throughout the text, he represents those born in exile, in refugee camps, who only know Palestine through collective memory, as perhaps even more closely tied to the idea of the "homeland" than many of those who left it behind in 1948. Edward Said asserts in *The Question of Palestine*, first published in 1979, that because so many Palestinians live in differing conditions of exile, "today Palestine does not exist, except as a memory or, more importantly, as an idea, a political and human experience, and an act of sustained popular will" (5). Supporting this assertion, in her report for the World Refugee Survey, Julia Peteet found that there are several common characteristics for claiming Palestinian identity among the refugees, "including origins in Palestine, a continuing attachment to it and to the right of return as embodied in UN General Assembly Resolution 194, the collective loss and trauma of exile, and calls for justice" (5). When interviewing Palestinian refugees about the possibility of actually resettling in the West Bank if there were a Palestinian state, Peteet got responses such as: "We want our land," or "It's not big enough for all of us, and it's not our land ['our land' refers to their particular villages of origin]." She concluded that "they may be re-thinking selves and communities as national minorities whose citizenship could be tied to a Palestinian authority located in the West Bank and Gaza but whose residence could be elsewhere." From this, Peteet somewhat rhetorically poses the questions of the rethinking of self-identity in terms of "nationality, citizenship, and place," and the "de-linking" of "citizenship, rights, nationality, and territory," as challenging "the correspondence between place, identity, and rights" (9). In other words, if one self-identifies with the Palestinian state, it does not matter that the national boundaries of the state are in question, or that a large part of the population lives in exile.

For this reason, in the postcolonial era, when nations comprise heterogeneous populations and their collective histories, and when geopolitical national borders have become permeable, arbitrary, and unstable, traditional totalizing national narratives no longer serve. The imagination of the nation itself must reflect the heterogeneous nature of the people in whose minds it exists. Partha Chatterjee, in *National Thought and the Colonial World*, argues that the historicizing of the present cultural identity of a nation makes possible a new understanding of the concept of "nationhood" as it applies to the contemporary postcolonial world. Since the modernist urge toward the formation of national identity must be modified in the postcolonial world to what could be called a postmodern nation whose boundaries have been imposed or destroyed by the West, he proposes a dual understanding of nationalism: the western, "the classical, the orthodox, the pure type," and the non-western, "the complex, impure, often deviant" (3). "Classical" nationhood, arising from the desire to create a nation based on some sense of original, natural homogeneity, inevitably clashes with the "disturbed and ambivalent," nationalism of the East and the heterogeneous nature of a postcolonial national identity. Chatterjee offers as a revitalized concept of nationalism, a "regeneration of the national culture, adapted to the requirements of progress, but retaining at the same time its distinctiveness" (2). This regenerated culture will remember the past in a way which points toward the present moment of the nation: "every nationalism has invented a past for the nation; every nationalism speaks through a discourse... which claims to demonstrate the rise, progress and efflorescence of its own particular genius" (9). Indeed, even though a nation has been dismantled by external force, the members of that nation *must and will* continue to imagine that nation through a process which focuses bringing the past history of the "people," into the present moment of the nation.

Darwish's *Memory for Forgetfulness*, a fragmented, even contradictory narrative, reflects this concept of postcolonial nationalism and the importance of reimagining a nation in response to the imperatives of the current historical and political context, but without losing "its distinctiveness," its cultural past. Textual fragmentation, Richard Van Leeuwen argues, is for Darwish, a "deliberate device to convey a sense of confusion and estrangement," the periodic reassertion of his wandering narrative 'I' providing a sense of cohesion for the reader (263). Clearly, in the present historical moment, this fragmented narrative reflects, not only the fragmented experience of the narrator, but also the collective identity of the Palestinian nation: as Said comments, Palestinians must, "tell [their] story in pieces, as it is" (*After the Last Sky* 149). However, that the Palestinian story is in pieces makes it no less a story, and that the nation is fragmented in the present moment makes it no less a nation, again indicating a movement away from the Western concept of nation that corresponds more with a fixed, unified, geopolitical reality.

In his introduction to *After the Last Sky*, a book that combines photographs and a personal narrative of the Palestinian experience, Said describes the difficulty of representing a people whose identity is marked by "dispossession, dispersions, and yet also a kind of power incommensurate with our stateless exile" (6). He rejects any "clear and simple narrative" as a representation the complex history and daily life of the Palestinian people, asserting instead that "essentially unconventional, hybrid, and fragmentary forms of expression should be used to represent us" (5-6). Said describes Palestinians as "a dispersed national community—acting, acted upon, proud, tender, miserable, funny, indomitable, ironic, paranoid, defensive, assertive, attractive" (6), words which could apply as well to *Memory for Forgetfulness*, a text which, again like modernist (or even post-modernist) writing, combines and mixes genres, shifts points of view, and disrupts narrative continuity. As stated above, the narrative outline follows the speaker as he moves through Beirut, but that narrative comprises a series of juxtaposed episodes that read more like prose poems than traditional narrative. As the events of the day elicit his reactions, Darwish moves at will through the cultural history of Palestine, as well as his own memories and critical commentary. Kamal Abdel-Malek describes *Memory for Forgetfulness* as "a discourse that is journal, history, memoir, fiction, myth, and allegory" (175). And Ibrahim Muhawi, who translated the text into English, refers to it as "a multivocal text that resembles a broken mirror, reassembled to present the viewer with vying possibilities of clarity and fracture" (xvi). Clearly establishing the autobiographical voice of the text by inserting details from his own past, Darwish weaves through the narrative references to Arabic classical chronicles, the Bible—Old and New Testaments—the Qur'an exegesis, dreams, conversations between friends and lovers, Palestinans and Jews, newspaper articles, his own poems and political commentary, creating a "crossroads of competing meanings" (Muhawi xvii). At this point of the crossroads, Beruit, August, 1982, it is possible to identify a new idea of national identity, which reasserts the heterogeneity of Palestine from before colonization and the creation of the Israeli state and creates a collective history which includes the on-going suffering and the struggle of a people for their homeland: "A homeland, branded and collapsing in the dialogue of human will against steel; a homeland rising with a voice that looks down on us from the sky—unique voice that unites what can't be united and brings together what can't be brought together" (Darwish 146). In the end the poet uses the voice he creates in his autobiographical narrative to make a whole of the disparate, and sometimes even conflicting parts of a nation struggling to claim its own history and cultural identity: *Memory for Forgetfulness* is "a kind of homeland and reading it represents a return" (Muhawi xvii).

Darwish's narrative, then, is part of the process of regeneration of a national narrative, the production of an alternative narrative toward the re-imagining of national identity; as he states: "whoever writes the story first, owns the place" (qtd. in Enderwitz 42). This statement echoes the frequent assertion that the conflict between Palestinians and Israelis is based on a conflict between two opposing national narratives. As a conflict of two narratives, however, it is an unequal battle. While the central narrative of the state of Israel is one of survival, conquest, and a return to the rightful homeland, Judith Tucker points out, in her analysis of the nature of existing histories of Palestine, that "standard political and diplomatic" histories tend to present that of Palestine "as that of a series of international interventions," a view which negates the reality of an autonomous Palestinian national narrative based on a history and memory associated with the region, severing the relationship between the identity of the people and their land. This challenge to the Palestinian connection to the land forces a reconceptualization of the self-identity of the Palestinian people. As Barbara Harlow writes, 'the historical struggle against colonialism and imperialism... is waged at the same time as a struggle over the historical and cultural record," through what she calls "immediate interventions into the historical record" (116).

This need to intervene in the historical record of Palestine led to a "boom" in autobiographical writing in the 1980s, among the generation of writers, including Darwish, who experienced directly the personal and collective tragedy of the 1948, as well as the on-going conflict. Individuals published their life stories in order to claim "a distinct Palestinianness, a personal attachment to the place, and even a national consciousness" (Enderwitz 37). Suzanne Enderwitz states that for Pales-tinian writers, unlike traditional autobiographers, the autobiographical subject's focus is neither "a philosophical nor a psychological crisis, it is political" (32); as the writer Tawaz Truki states, "just know that for my own generation of Palestinians our last day in Palestine was the first day that we began to define our Palestinian identity" (qtd. in Enderwitz 36). In her analysis, Enderwitz identifies four specific tasks for Palestinian writers and argues for the centrality of the first person narrative in accomplishing them: first, to "set right distorted Palestinian history"; in this sense autobiography serves as "intimate history," a means to "collect the scattered pieces of their historical experience"; second, to revaluate "the distorted image of its people," to supply "a human di-mension"; third to "to raise one's voice, to appeal to the world for acknowledgement, and to bring about lasting justice" — a tall order and one that turns autobiography to testimonial; and fourth, "to create a collective memory" to counter the dominate history focus on Israel (43-45). Because the writer narrates his or her own experience of Palestine, the autobiographical perspective potentially provides the authority necessary to effectively counter the dominate narrative and bring about a change in the consciousness of the reader: "Writing serves as a witness (*shahid*) to the events the author describes... [He] only has words with which to create a memory. He writes to begin a memory of times past. He erects writing as a witness (*shahid*), a testimony to what has already gone" (Abdel-Malek 188). Autobiography, then, is an aspect of post-1948 Palestinian literature which becomes increasing central as a means of preserving Palestinian collective memory as a remedy to "an anxiety about the risk of forgetting a homeland" (Hammer 176). Julianne Hammer argues that "young nations" rely on shared history as expressed and preserved through state institutions—official historiography, education, museums, monuments. The absence of these for Palestinians creates a dependence on individual, subjective memory for formation of collective identity—especially for the young born and raised in exile, in refugee camps (Hammer 177). These are the youth "armed to the teeth," who, as Darwish writes,

> were still being born without a reason, growing up for no reason, remembering for no reason, and being put under siege for no reason. All of them know the story—a story very much like that of a cosmic traffic accident or a natural catastrophe. But they also read a great deal in the books of their bodies and their shacks. They read their segregation, and the Arab-nationalist speeches. They read the publications of UNRWA, and the whips of the police. (14)

For these youth, and all Palestinians, in the absence of an official national history, the politically committed autobiography provides an alternative, personal, immediate narrative that makes sense of national identity at a time when it is most under threat by the discourse of the outside world.

Sidonie Smith also makes a strong case for autobiographical writing's "role in emancipatory politics, stating that "[a]utobiographical practices become occasions for restaging subjectivity, and autobiographical strategies become occasions for the staging of resistance" (156), in what she calls, "autobiographical manifestos." They can provide very self-conscious ways of writing the "new man and woman" that much post-colonial theory asserts as necessary in the process of identity formation in the context of decolonization. This assertion of self-representation "contests the old inscriptions, the old histories, the old politics, the *ancien regime,* by working to dislodge the hold of the universal subject through an expressly political collocation of a new "I" (Smith 157). Since this "universal subject" has historically been a specular representation of the hegemonic center which non-Western subjects can only ever not be, "dislodging its hold" is a major step toward the assertion of self-identity for nonwestern cultures. The individual self of the autobiography, by asserting his or her subject position, begins the process of dismantling the domination of the "universal," not by supplanting one universal subject with another, but by affirming the possibility of multiple subjectivities.

Although Smith develops her ideas of the emancipatory nature of autobiographical manifestos specifically in relationship to women of color in the United States, her basic premises also provide insight into the function of autobiographical practices in other communities struggling to resist the imposition of identity from the outside, such as the Palestinian people. Since the occupation and dismantling of Palestine in 1948, Palestinian national identity has been shaped by the experiences of displacement and dispersion, economic hardship, violence, and repression. Salma Khadra Jayyusi asserts that, somewhat ironically, "Palestinian cultural and literary identity is perhaps more defined and more distinctly concrete than that of other Arabs," precisely because they have been under a literal and figurative siege, from Israel, the West in general, and, at times, from other Arab states (qtd. in Abdel-Malek 171). At the same time, as the dominant western media and governments write the history of the Palestinian State, there seems to be a systematic erasure of the idea of a Palestine that predated the creation of Israel. As Darwish writes in *Memory for Forgetfulness*, "Begin freezes history as of this moment," the early history of the Jewish people in Palestine, which was, however, followed by many centuries of Arab civilization in the area and coexistence of Jews and Arabs on the land. But for the "king of the legend" and his supporters, both internally and externally, since the early habitation of Palestine by the Jewish people, "history has done nothing… except wait for the new king of the legend, Menachem, son of Sarah" (Darwish 144). This silencing of history provides a context for the Zionist slogan, "a land without people, for a people without land," that effectively erases the Arab people from the region. By ignoring the historically situated act of injustice to the Palestinian people, Western powers can concentrate on the present moment, detached from historical contingency and imagined in response to their own self-interests; they can then focus on the creation of an image of Palestine that justifies continued occupation and oppression.

Emancipatory autobiographical writing, by asserting the textual construction of self-identity and permeating the boundaries between the personal and the political, acts as a corrective to these images and provides a model for others who want to identify with the alternative subject position. Palestine is a nation that exists in memory and conflict, in perhaps the most concrete sense of "unhomeliness," a concept which Bhabha adapts from Freud's discussion of the *unheimlich*, "the name for everything that ought to have remained… secret and hidden but has come to light"; he ties "unhomeliness" to narratives which attempt to make "visible the forgetting," to movements which "relate[s] the traumatic ambivalences of a personal, psychic history to the wider disjunctions of political existence" (10-11). Smith argues that the autobiographical manifesto attempts to "bring to light, to make manifest" previously repressed, marginalized experiences, as a means of affecting "an epistemological breakage of repetition" (158). It is also a "public performance," which "insists on the temporalities and spatialities of identity" (160). And according to Smith, with the autobiographical manifesto, "group identification rather than radical individuality is the rhetorical ground for appeal," which she ties to the expression of community and the imagining of nation; she states that "[n]ationalism determines the specific moves through which the manifesto negotiates the landscapes of identity and difference" (162). Again, as distinct from traditional autobiography which projects toward the end of the individual narrative (often gesturing toward death), the autobiographical testimonial "'I' writes under the sign of hope," offering a Utopian vision, and "actively position(ing) the subject in a potentially liberated future distanced from the constraining and oppressive identifications" of the dominant society (Smith 163). The subject of the autobiographical manifesto provides a model for the new, liberated self, even if the immediate historical situation is less hopeful.

Darwish's *Memory for Forgetfulness,* in these terms, can be read as an autobiographical manifesto which provides a very carefully situated, alternative subject position for the Palestinians to that of the hegemonic discourse, re-membering forgotten events and bringing to light that which has been hidden by the hegemonic "memory." In writing his experience of Palestine, rather than becoming the *universal* subject of Palestinian subjectivity, he becomes one subjective voice, inviting other voices to join his. Relating his own trauma and displacement, Darwish provides a narrative form for the trauma and displacement of Pales-tine—the destruction of his own study as he describes it in *Memory for Forgetfulness,* parallels the destruction of the nation as a whole; his pending exile from Beirut reflects the prolonged exile of Palestinians and their on-going search for a homeland. In the process, he never loses sight of his identity as a Palestinian, nor of the relationship of his story to the history of Palestine. He provides his memory, his testimony to his life and to the life of his nation; as Yves Gonzalez-Quijano states: "his personal drama, irreducible to any other, is also a political testimony" (188).

In this sense, Darwish's text fits more closely a definition of a memoir than the more subject-centered writing of the traditional autobiography, in that memoirs privilege the relationship of memory to history, with the subject generally representing him or herself as an observer rather than as the center of the narrative. In the memoir, the subject presents him or herself in relation to other people and events, in a type of metonymic relationship with the community. Gonzalez-Quijano, in his discussion of *Memory for Forgetfulness* defines a memoir as "a narrative which brings out the places and events around the author without giving centrality to the subject, to personal history" (183). In addition, the form of the tradi-tional autobiographical narrative will necessarily be linear, following the subject as he or she moves through key events of life. The structure of the memoir, on the other hand, is generally closer to Nietzsche's concept of genealogy as defined by Foucault in his essay, "Nietzsche, Genealogy, History," in which he states that, in contrast with more static, linear forms of historiography, genealogy:

must record the singularity of events outside of any monotonous finality; it must seek them in the most unpromising places, in what we tend to feel is without history—in sentiments, love, conscience, instincts; it must be sensitive to their recurrence, not in order to trace the gradual curve of their evolution, but to isolate the different scenes where they engaged in different roles. (76)

As Darwish selects the elements of his narrative, from his own and the collective memory, he places them in a seemingly random, fragmented relationship; his memoir is not a linear recounting of events, but rather a collecting and re-membering of feelings, perceptions, documents, conversations around a specific moment in the history of Palestine: his experience, as a Palestinian, of one day during the Israeli siege of Beirut. This technique emphasizes the constructed, fragmented, and historically contingent nature of identity in opposition to the teleological nature of the universal subject's narrative. Darwish is not writing the transcendent origins of the Palestinian national identity, but rather a narrative in which the past and present co-exist in the dynamic present moment of history.

In his discussion of the relationship of the narrative process to the construction of national identity, Bhabha points out the temporal disjunction between the assertion of national origins and the immediate present of nationhood, referring to "the nation's interrupted address, articulated in the tension signifying the people as an a priori historical present, a pedagogical object; and the people constructed in the per-formance of the narrative, its enunciatory 'present'" (147). He then ties this split between the pedagogical and performative aspects of a national narrative to Raymond Williams' "distinction between residual and emergent practices in oppositional cultures," which challenges any metaphysical national identity situated within a dominant culture (148). Although, as Bhabha argues, national unity, especially one that is bounded by conflict, requires the assertion of a strong unified past, "the patriotic, atavistic temporality of Traditionalism," which converts "Ter-ritory into Tradition... the People into One," this same traditionalism opens the liminal space that "provides a place from which to speak both of, and as, the minority, the exilic, the marginal, and the emergent" (149). In other words, national identity is not a homogeneous, meta-physical Subject, but rather "an ambivalent *movement* between the discourses of pedagogy and performance," between the imagined past and the present (Bhabha 149).

This "ambivalent movement" is evident in the structure of *Memory for Forgetfulness*, whose very title underscores the paradox of national identity, the pedagogical memory creating a space for the forgetfulness of performativity. In the text, Darwish examines the complex relationship of the narratives of the past and present, both his own personal narratives and the narratives of the Palestinian people, in the formation of national identity. He has characterized the conflict between the Palestinians and Israelis as a "struggle between two memories," stating that the "Israelis demand from the Palestinians to relinquish their past and adopt instead a new version of the past which is based on totally different experiences and on a cultivation of the memory of the holocaust" (qtd. in Van Leeuwan 260). By selecting and arranging fragments of Palestine's textual past, through his own personal memory and forgetfulness, he provides a narrative of forgetting in relationship to the already received, pedagogical narrative of the West, a forgetting of the "legend" of Israel, of the colonial version of Palestine, to make way for a remembering of Palestine. He seems to assert that, in order to imagine an autonomous national identity, it is necessary actively and selectively to *forget* a past based on a received historical narrative. Leela Ghandi refers to this paradox as the "will-to-forget" or "postcolonial amnesia" that she sees as "symptomatic of the urge for historical self-invention" or the need to make a new start "to erase painful memories of colonial subordination" (4). The danger here is that, if a culture's reconstructed history represses "its own unconsidered and unresolved past," it will be more difficult to reconstruct a social and cultural identity in the present moment (Gandhi 7).

Therefore, in the reconstruction of an autonomous identity, the writer must, "make visible the forgetting," as Bhabha states, and "elaborate the forgotten memories," incorporating them in a constructive way into the national history (10). In fact, the past of a nation must be re-imagined from the present moment of nationhood; as Bhabha asks, "How do we plot the narrative of the nation that must mediate between the teleology of progress tipping over into the 'timeless' discourse of irrationality?" (142). He begins answering this question by asserting that the "language of culture and community is poised on the fissures of the present becoming the rhetorical figures of the national past." By acknowledging that a national past can only ever be reconstructed from "shreds and patches of cultural signification" (142), Bhabha demonstrates the fissures that allow for the possibility of agency in constructing a national identity, for a re-membering of the past that suits the present idea of nationalism. For Palestine, this means moving away from models of history constructed to suit the views of the hegemonic Western values so that the representation of a national history is not controlled by the dominant ideology, and remembering back through the Nakbha of 1948 to the idea of Palestine, to the assertion that the history of Palestine did not begin with the creation of Israel. Van Leeuwan argues that, in *Memory for Forgetfulness*, the "usurpation of history is depicted as a form of violence, which effectively transforms the identity of a spatial history," and he quotes Darwish: "they have also occupied the mental space, the mental disposition and all the relations between you and your homeland" (260-261). Through an analogy between the narrative of the individual and that of nations, Anderson asserts, "[a]ll profound changes in consciousness, by their very nature, bring with them characteristic amnesias." For the individual, the movement from child to adult involves an acknowledgment of this process of forgetting, an estrangement from personal, historical continuity, and then "from this estrangement comes a conception of personhood, *identity*... which, because it can not be 'remembered', must be narrated" (204). This narration generally is bounded by birth and death. With nations, however, there are "no clearly identifiable births," and thus, the national narrative is structured "up time": "in a curious inversion of conventional genealogy... from an originary present" (205) of the individual subjects in time.

This "curious inversion" applies to autobiographical writing as it parallels national narration as the individual constructs his or her own past, and metonymically, the past of the nation through the present act of remembering. With *Memory for Forgetfulness*, the paradox of the title reflects the paradox of a past rewritten, remembered through the perspective of the present. In one of the poems embedded in the narrative of *Memory for Forgetfulness*, Darwish writes:

> Here, I leave behind what's not mine.
> And here I dive into my own soul,

That my time may start with me.
Let Beirut be what it wants to be.
She will forget me,
That I may forget her.

Will I forget? Oh, would, oh, would I could
This moment bring back my homeland
Out of myself!... (153)

He seems to be evoking a process similar to that of "amamnesis," a psychoanalytic process, encouraging individuals "to elaborate their current problems by freely associating apparently inconsequential details with past situations—allowing them to uncover hidden meanings in their lives and their behaviour" (Lyotard, qtd. in Ghandi 8). In postcolonial theory, this translates to "a complex project of historical and psychological 'recovery'" (Ghandi 8). And Nirijana echoes Foucault's insistence on the "heterogeneity of origins" in her analysis of the process inherent to many postcolonial texts of fragmenting 'what was thought unified,'" citing Derek Walcott's call "for amnesia, for the loss of history, which would enable 'imagination' as 'invention'" (138). In other words, forgetting an origin established by an imposed historical narrative and affirming that there is "no single ancestor, no single origin, and therefore no single history," allows one to remember in a freer sense. In this poem, Darwish seems to assert the will-to-forget in relationship to the siege of Beirut, to wish to remember the homeland through his memories and personal experience. The irony, of course, is that the poem itself remembers Beirut, and that Beirut is part of him. But it is not him, nor his origin. He writes the poem—dives into his soul—in order "that [his] time may be [his] own," not the construction of the historical contingency of that moment (153). He must re-member a forgotten past from the perspective of the present brought into existence by a "profound change," clearly identified for Darwish and for Palestine as the Nakhba or the creation of Israel; history, in this sense, is created by the present, a process which in periods of instability, such of that of experienced by Palestine since 1948 or by Darwish in Beirut in 1982, leads to a constant re-membering of the past and a constant re-narrating of identity. As Darwish says, "Poetry is to strive to rewrite or recreate its own book of *Genesis*, to search for beginnings and to interpret myths of creation" (qtd. in Van Leeuwen 266).

Darwish, as a witness to the struggles of his people, fulfils the duties of the Palestinian autobiographical writer that Enderwitz specifies. More than that, though, he provides, in his writing, a sense of the homeland for Palestinians in the present moment. By using his own voice to provide a narrative for Palestine, he creates, imagines in words the homeland for refugees and exiles, both internal and external. At the time of the writing of *Memory for Forgetfulness*, as it is today, the homeland is fragmented and abstracted; as Darwish writes: "homeland is a relation which is expressed between a convergence of material and textual components of land, memory, and history… it should live on in the form of memory and struggle" (qtd. in Van Leeuwen 261). Like many other resistance writers, Darwish stops short of providing a specific picture of the future, emphasizing primarily the openness of possibility. *Memory for Forgetfulness* ends with an image of the sea, which carries multiple significations throughout the text. It is both a barrier, the location from which the Israelis sustain the siege, and it is an opening to escape, to exile. The final lines state:

> The sea is walking in the streets. The sea is dangling from windows and the branches of shriveled trees. The sea drops from the sky and comes into the room. Blue, white, foam, waves. I don't like the sea. I don't want to see the sea, because I don't see a shore, or a dove. I see in the sea nothing except the sea.
> I don't see a shore.
> I don't see a dove. (182)

Darwish's sea does not have a clear definition, a shore, to tell him or us what it is. It doesn't have a symbolic messenger, a dove, a harbinger of a new world. It is only openness and the unknown.

Especially since these final words evoke the betrayal of the Palestinians and the on-going conflict confronting the immediate present of the autobiographical I, it is difficult to read Darwish's text in terms of Smith's concept of the "utopian vision," or to identify the "sign of hope" under which he writes. Perhaps, also, to read the text outside of the ongoing events in Palestine today is difficult. However, in an interview in 2002, Darwish, asked whether a Palestinian state will exist, responded, "A Palestinian state already exists," and was emphatic that there is hope for the Palestinians, stating that "[t]hey do not have another option but to continue to carry the hope that they are going to have a normal life" (Handal). As Smith points out, the hopeful nature of the narrative is in opening to the future, the articulation of "a 'waking dream' of the possible.... which might inspire us to see beyond the constraints of the here and now to the idealized vision of a perfect future" (163). The utopian vision, then, is primarily in the ability to narrate the history from an alternate position, to indicate "a possibly liberating future outside the constraints of the controlling historical narrative of domination" (163). The text as a whole narrates the pedagogical historical identity of Palestine, as well as the performative, immediate present of an individual Palestinian. And as an emancipatory autobiographical narrative, both remembering Palestine and witnessing the emergence of the new, *Memory for Forgetfulness* provides a model for Palestinian subjectivity that is purposefully inconclusive and open to a future.

Works Cited

Abdel-Malek, Kamal, and David C. Jacobson. *Israeli and Palestinian Identities in History and Literature*. New York: St. Martin's Press, 1999.

Akash, Munir, and Carolyn Forche. "Introduction." *Unfortunately, It Was Paradise*. By Mahmoud Darwish. Berkeley, CA: University of California Press, 2003. http://www.ucpress.edu/books/pages/9973/9973.intro.html (Viewed on March 24, 2006).

Anderson, Benjamin. *Imagined Communities: Reflections on the Origin and Spread of Nationalism*. London: Verso, 1991.

Bhabha, Homi. *The Location of Culture*. London: Routledge, 1994.

Chatterjee, Partha. *Nationalist Thought and the Colonial World*. Minneapolis: University of Minnesota Press, 1984.

Darwish, Mahmoud. *Memory for Forgetfulness: August, Beirut, 1982*. Trans. Ibrahim Muhawi. Berkeley, CA: University of California Press, 1995.

Enderwitz, Susanne. "The Palestinian Autobiographer." *Crisis and Memory*. Ed. Ken Seigneurie. Wiesbaden: Reichert Verlag Wiesbaden, 2003. 29-50.

Ghandi, Leela. *Postcolonial Theory: A Critical Introduction*. New York: Columbia University Press, 1998.

Gonzalez-Quijano, Yves. "The Territory of Autobiography in Mahmud Darwish's *Memory for Forgetfulness*." *Writing the Self: Autobiographical Writing in Modern Arabic Literature*. Eds. Robin Ostle, Ed de Moor, and Stefan Wild. London: Saqi Books, 1998. 183-191.

Handal, Nathalie. "Mahmoud Darwish: Palestine's Poet of Exile." *The Progressive* 66.5 (2002). http://progressive.org/node/1575 (Viewed July 12, 2006).

Hammer, Julianne. "Crisis of Memory: Homeland and Exile in Contemporary Palestinian Memoirs." *Crisis and Memory*. Ed. Ken Seigneurie. Wiesbaden: Reichert Verlag Wiesbaden, 2003. 177-198.

Muhawi, Ibrahim. "Introduction." *Memory for Forgetfulness*. By Mahmoud Darwish. Berkeley, CA: University of California Press, 1995. xi-xxx.

Niranjana, Tejaswini. "History, Really Beginning: The Compulsions of Postcolonial Pedagogy." *Journal of English and Foreign Literature* 7&8 (June-December 1991): 132-146.

Peteet, Julie. "Identity Crisis: Palestinians in Post-War Lebanon." *Worldwide Refugee Information*. 1997. 1-9.
http://www.refugees.org/world/articles/palesti_lebanon_wrs97.htm
(Viewed on June 17 2003).

Said, Edward. *After the Last Sky: Palestinian Lives*. New York: Columbia University Press, 1999.

—. *The Question of Palestine*. New York: Vintage Books, 1979.

Seigneurie, Ken, ed. *Crisis and Memory*. Wiesbaden: Reichert Verlag Wiesbaden, 2003.

Smith, Sidonie. *Women's Autobiographical Practices in the Twentieth Century*. Bloomington: Indiana University Press, 1993.

Van Leeuwan, Richard. "The Poet and his Mission: Text and Space in the Prose Works of Mahmoud Darwish." *Conscious Voices: Concepts of Writing in the Middle East: Proceedings of the Berne Symposium, July 1997*. Eds. Stephan Guth, Priska Furrer, and Johann Christoph Bürgel. Beirut: Orient-Institut der Deutschen Morgenländischen Gesellschaft, 1999. 255-275.

Terry DeHay is a professor in the English and Writing department at Southern Oregon University where she teaches courses on postcolonial literature, critical theory, and modernism.

"No Nation Woman" Writes Her Self: War and the Return Home in Meena Alexander's Memoirs

Lavina D. Shankar

> "Returning makes a turmoil of its own." (Meena Alexander, *Fault Lines* 2003, 254)
>
> "All water has a perfect memory and is forever trying to get back to where it was. Writers are like that: remembering where we were, what valley we ran through, what the banks were like, the light that was there and the route back to our original place. It is emotional memory—what the nerves and the skin remember as well as how it appeared." (Toni Morrison, "The Site of Memory" 119)
>
> "2nd May... I write the date, because I think that I have discovered a possible form for these notes. That is, to make them include the present—at least enough of the present to serve as platform to stand upon. It would be interesting to make the two people, I now, I then, come out in contrast. And further, this past is much affected by the present moment. What I write today I should not write in a year's time." (Virginia Woolf, *Moments of Being* 75)

In his essay "Autobiography as De-facement," Paul de Man asserts that it is the unreliability of autobiography as self-knowledge that makes it worth studying:

> The interest of autobiography, then, is not that it reveals reliable self-knowledge—it does not—but that it demonstrates in a striking way the impossibility of closure and of totalization (that is the impossibility of coming into being) of all textual systems made up of tropological substitutions. (922)

For nearly two decades, Meena Alexander has written obsessively about herself and her lifelong search for home—in her semi-autobiographical novels *Nampally Road* (1991) and *Manhattan Music* (1997), the personal essay collection *The Shock of Arrival: Reflections on Postcolonial Experience* (1996), a memoir *Fault Lines* (1993, 2003), and her recent lyric poetry collections, *Illiterate Heart* (2002) and *Raw Silk* (2004). Her writing has been published in (or translated into) multiple languages, as she has lived on four continents—Asia, Africa, Europe, and North America. Hence, she named herself as a "No Nation Woman," in her 1996 essay collection *The Shock of Arrival* (116). Similarly, in her memoir *Fault Lines* (1993), she declared herself as a "nowhere creature," who "babbles in a multitude of tongues: Malayalam, Hindi, Tamil, Arabic, English, French" (30), "living in a place where I have no history" (182). In the revised and expanded 2003 version of the same memoir, she continues her musings on feeling homeless (256) and her sense of self being torn by the "seizures of dislocation" (260). However, in the second edition, the author questions the previous version of her own memoir and rewrites her past so drastically that Paul de Man's view about the unreliability of autobiography as self-knowledge seems particularly relevant.

This essay examines Meena Alexander's constantly shifting sense of her self and her relationships to her homes through the initial writing and then re-writing of her memoir *Fault Lines*. Specifically, it analyzes the diasporic writer's evolving relationship to "claiming America" as home, and her return to her childhood home in India, to search for a past self that she had not remembered when she wrote the first memoir. Drawing on the epigraph to this essay, from Virginia Woolf's posthumously published memoir *Moments of Being*, I argue that Meena Alexander uses the lens of her violent present in post-9/11/2001 New York City to "re-vision," in Adrienne Rich's sense, her past longing for her idyllic ancestral home in Tiruvella, and tentatively claims Manhattan as home. Finally, I suggest that because of the physical destruction of global terror and wars and the psychological turmoil of memories of childhood incest that the New Yorker Alexander confronts, both publicly and privately after 9/11, the only home she can thus seek refuge in is Art–the sanctuary of words leading to healing and wholeness.

The essay raises questions such as: (How) does the art of life-writing change because the memories of a personal history depicted in an earlier version of the memoir have been transformed by the flow of life itself? How is subjectivity altered when new memories of the past self surface? Does the ethnic subject merely recount memories of lost homelands in her life writing, or does the narration of evolving memories necessitate a return to the lost home to claim a new/old self and create a new subjecthood? How does the present self return to a past "home" following public wars that force the subject to recollect its private history of the war with/in itself?

The complex interweaving of multiple—often conflicting—identities, affiliations, and homelands began even before the diasporic writer's birth. Born Mary Elizabeth Alexander, a Syrian Christian of South Indian ancestry, in the North Indian Hindu city of Allahabad, she moved at age five to Sudan, and shuttled every six months between her father's workplace in Africa and her maternal grandparents' home in Kerala, South India. Choosing to be known publicly by her private (ironically Hindu/Indianized) name "Meena" instead of the Christian/westernized "Mary Elizabeth," she moved as a teenager to England for college, back to India through her twenties, to teach British Romantic poetry, and immigrated to the U.S. at age twenty-nine, married to a Jewish American studying medieval Muslim Indian history.

In her memoir *Fault Lines*, describing herself as "a woman cracked by multiple migrations… writing in search of a homeland" (1993, 3-4), Alexander thus explains the predicament of having claimed multiple continents as home before immigrating to the U.S. The first edition of the memoir (1993) began with Alexander outlining her alienation and dislocation in New York City and ended with her feeling a sense of peaceful rootedness in her maternal grandparents' house and garden in Tiruvella, Kerala. Ten years later, in 2003, at the age of fifty-two, Alexander published a new, revised version of her memoir, uncovering a traumatic past that would have been impossible for both reader and writer to imagine in the first edition.

In *Crucial Conversations: Interpreting Contemporary American Literary Autobiographies by Women*, Jeanne Braham observes that historically "the autobiographical act" within Anglo-American male writing has been "connected to and defined by a sense of place" (67). She cites Thoreau's *Walden*, Emerson's journals, *The Education of Henry Adams*, and Whitman's *Specimen Days*, where an individual male autobiographer's private experience intertwines with the public crises of his time: "the personal record intersects history. The window on a life, as recorded by a sensitive and gifted perceiver, also reveals a window on an 'age'—one usually characterized by crisis or profound change." Hence, the auto-biographer speaks not just for and about himself but transforms into "a seismograph of the times" (67). In contrast, female autobiographers' "sense of place" initiates "self-assessments or insights into interior consciousness [rather] than to engage the public world's moral or historical issues" (67).

Synthesizing Braham's theory, I suggest that Alexander's second memoir, written after 9/11, follows both the traditional male and female autobiographer's models. The transnational poet simultaneously observes and comments on the external world of political public events, and goes inward, searching deep inside her soul to uncover her most intimate, confidential life story, thus undertaking "The Voyage In," to use Marianne Hirsch's term. As soon as she records the public grief she witnessed in NYC, Alexander's writing becomes imbued with what Toni Morrison calls "emotional memory" (in the epigraph above), as the memoirist re-collects the fragments of her childhood to form a new self by returning to "what the nerves and skin remember" (Morrison 119).

In his introduction to *Multicultural Autobiography: American Lives*, James Robert Payne refers to James M. Cox's essay "Autobiography and America" (1971)—which discusses the intimate relationship between self-writing and America—and observes that an "astonishingly large proportion of the slender shelf of so-called American classics" comprises autobiographies (qtd. in Payne xii). Payne also discusses G. Thomas Couser's *American Autobiography: The Prophetic Mode*, where Couser finds a "coherent tradition" from the Puritans onwards (including narratives by Jonathan Edwards, Benjamin Franklin, Henry David Thoreau, Walt Whitman, and others) depicting American autobiographers' inclination to "assume the role of prophet" (xiv). Couser views this tradition as situated within writers' "Puritan attitudes toward themselves and their history" (qtd. in Payne xiv).

In a critical response to scholars focused on Puritan writers as the sole creators of American life writing, Frances Smith Foster chides early literary historians and critics who viewed autobiography as an Anglo-American male genre. These scholars "established a canon which privileges the life histories of white men," even though well-known African American autobiographies included Richard Wright's *Black Boy*, Maya Angelou's *I Know Why the Caged Bird Sings*, and *The Autobiography of Malcolm X* (34). She is skeptical about William Dean Howells' claim that the genre of autobiography in America was accessible to "any age, or sex, creed, class or color" (qtd. in Forster 35). Foster cogently summarizes the arguments of multi-ethnic feminist literary scholars including Paula Gunn Allen, Estelle Jelinek, Amy Ling, Sidonie Smith, and Domna Stanton, who examined the "female autograph" and argued that since literacy was based on race and gender restrictions not all Americans had equal access to writing their life-stories (35).

Foster's valid arguments notwithstanding, and despite Meena Alexander's self-delineated marginalization in mainstream American society due to gender and race, her family's socio-economic advantages provided her the opportunity to write her ethnic American life story. Although a female subject from the once-colonized worlds of Asia and Africa, Alexander's class and educational privilege empowered her to become a globe-trotting polyglot in childhood, to publish in multiple languages as a teenager, complete a Ph.D. at age twenty-two, and be invited by a renowned American Press to write the story of her life as a transnational feminist poet. The privileged access to a global audience of multi-ethnic American life writing, then, helped her publicly claim a new private history for herself and re-create a new self. In the second memoir, telling the most intimate history of her life as set against the context of the worldwide tragedy since 9/11/01, immediately gained Alexander a strong, articulate writing voice and a global listening and reading audience.

I. To Claim or Not to Claim America?

The tradition of "Claiming America" has been a major trope in Asian American literature as discussed by, among others, Frank Chin et al., Sau-ling Wong, Jinqui Ling, and David Leiwei Li. In an earlier essay, "Postcolonial Diasporics 'Writing in Search of a Homeland': Meena Alexander's *Manhattan Music, Fault Lines* and *The Shock of Arrival*," I argued that Alexander was using her tormented autobiographical writings to "claim psychic and literary space while searching for and trying to define herself" (288). Unlike her Asian American predecessors Maxine Hong Kingston and Carlos Bulosan—and some South Asian American women writers like Bharati Mukherjee, Jhumpa Lahiri, and Chitra Divakaruni—who are identified with the trope of "Claiming America," in her earlier works, Alexander seemed more invested in claiming her-self and not necessarily her-self *as an American*.

Claiming her-self rather than claiming a nation does remain No Nation Woman's perpetual struggle as evident in her newer writings, too. Alexander's turmoil at examining herself as "She not I" (*Fault Lines* 2003, 301)—or in Virginia Woolf's words "I now, I then" (75)—suggests that identity is always shifting and is a far more delicate, "fragile, precarious" thing (*Fault Lines* 2003, 289) than being, or claiming to become, American, or not. Or as Stuart Hall articulates, instead of conceptualizing identity as a finished product, we should view identity as "a 'production,' which is never complete, always in process" (222).

Not surprisingly then, Alexander's views on life-writing and on her American-ness—as expressed in interviews and the two editions of her memoir—are filled with contradictions, perhaps due to the constantly shifting homes and overlapping transnational identities she inhabits. At times she exhibits what she claims is an American impulse towards self-examination and "auto-voyeurism" (Bahri 36) that is, the self-reflexive gaze at oneself looking at oneself. So, ironically, Alexander's turn home, a reconnection with her childhood and her Kerala roots, is a direct result of her being a feminist poet-activist in the U.S. When she was invited by her friend Florence Howe of the Feminist Press to write a memoir of lost homelands (like another postcolonial diasporic Asian American feminist Shirley Geok-lin Lim), the thirty-five year old Alexander initially considered it "ridiculous," an "American thing" (Duncan 23), and the memoir a genre appropriate only for the aged or the dying. Cautioned by her own mother against self-disclosure in the first edition of *Fault Lines*, and knowledgeable about the fate of earlier Indian women writers like Kamala Das who "got into a lot of trouble" for writing her autobiography *My Story*, Alexander claims she consciously "tried to walk a delicate line between self-disclosure and self-knowledge" (Bahri 37). She recognized immediately that it "is a very American thing to try to define one's self" and that had she "lived in India I would never have written a book like *Fault Lines*" (Bahri 36-37).

Despite her earlier having considered autobiographical life writing a uniquely American attribute, Alexander herself exhibits an Emersonian and Whitmanian struggle at finding and defining a self. Yet, in the first edition, her self is usually not confined to the American present, but rather obsessed with understanding her private transnational pasts. She knows she cannot be like Emerson as she pointedly critiques the archetypal "American Scholar" poet's—and America's—obsession with the present:

> Was this the price to be paid for living in the American present, in a world that Emerson felt had no need of memory, where, "history is an impertinence and an injury" (Emerson, "Self-Reliance"), where autobiography had to be inscribed, "in colossal cipher"? (Alexander, "In Whitman's Country" 191)

Nevertheless, Alexander does not quote the rest of Emerson's sentence where the prophet rejects history as ineffective and inexpedient if anything more than an "apologue or parable of my being and becoming" ("Self-Reliance" 141).

In sharp contrast to the New England sage, the narration of her own being and becoming, her past history, obsesses the New Yorker Meena Alexander. However, the ethnic female writer is unable to participate in the convention Sacvan Bercovitch terms "auto-American-biography: the celebration of the representative self as America, and of the American self as the embodiment of a prophetic universal design" (qtd. in Reaves 3). Unlike her fellow-South Asian male diasporic memoirist, the physician Abraham Verghese, who stakes a claim to suffering with and healing the AIDS-stricken American Southern small towns in the 1980s by naming his memoir *My Own Country*, Alexander writes an article trying to find herself called "In Whitman's Country." She explains why and how much she feels the New Yorker Walt Whitman to be her kindred soul and a poetic inspiration, and that she "cannot imagine myself in America without Whitman" (186). Ironically, or perhaps intentionally, Alexander begins the essay by physically and politically locating herself as an American citizen standing in line to vote on election day November 4, 2004, clutching pages from Whitman's *Leaves of Grass* in her coat pocket, hence claiming both Whitman and her rights as an American ("In Whitman's Country" 187). And yet, sadly, even after living in the U.S. for over a decade, in the first memoir, she feels like an interloper in Whitman's city and country because of her brown body "exotic, Asian, border-line black" (*Fault Lines* 1993, 188). Ironically, perhaps, she chooses Whitman as her muse because despite his apparently ebullient "Song of Myself" and his celebration of the body and soul, his anxiety about his homosexual body made him not fully belong in a heteronormative nineteenth century American society.[1]

Longing to belong to American society, then seems to motivate these two poets who, a century apart, have written about themselves and about New York city. In *The Shock of Arrival*, Alexander explains how the 1993 edition of *Fault Lines* inspired her to think about history as she inscribed her account of "borders shifting inside [her]—languages, gestures, memories of places" just to acquire a sense of belonging in America:

> I felt that having this book out in the world might give me the right to be in America… I started to muse on what we call 'history'. Did it mean a space memories can flow into, a depth of shared sense, of matters invisible that pierce our ordinary lives?
>
> Having entered this world as an immigrant I felt I was living in a place where I had no history. Who was I? Where was I? When was I? (63)

Thus trying to claim a history for herself and her passage to America, to inscribe herself into American history, was Alexander's unstated but implied project even when she wrote the first *Fault Lines*. Claiming that "In America you have to explain yourself, constantly. It's the confessional thing. Who are you? Where are you from? What do you do?" she answers hesitantly. The barrage of questions that follow her reply, in turn, reveal her anxieties about both her poetry and her Americanness, "As much as anything else I am a poet writing in America. But American poet? What sort? Surely not of the Robert Frost or Wallace Stevens variety?" (*Fault Lines* 1993, 193). So, Alexander remains acutely aware that her ethnic life story has no historical precedent in the Anglo-American male literary intelligentsia with whom she implicitly and explicitly wishes to identify—Emerson, Whitman, Frost and Stevens—as she defines both herself and her new home, America.

Nevertheless, ten years later, as Alexander's life-writing results in a new version of the memoir, her identity as an American poet evolves, too. When she depicts the "uncommon light" ("Aftermath"), the

---

[1] As Paul John Eakin points out in another context, Whitman's ebullient "Song of Myself" was followed four years later by the despair of "As I Ebb'd with the Ocean of Life" (*Fictions* 222).

"altered light" ("Pitfire") in the blue sky of NYC on 9/11/2001, and the
burning towers in the section "Lyric in a Time of Violence," or when she
stands aligned with the NYC fire department bagpipers when her poem
"Pitfire" follows their elegiac music, in that most American of cultural
institutions, Radio City Music Hall, Meena Alexander *is* an American
poet describing an American reality and moment in history. It is un-
doubtedly a watershed moment in a nation's own self-definition—and
its place in world history—that it is now obsessed with not forgetting; a
moment where the initial violence has been repaid with multiple wars,
on diverse populations, on the other side of the world, creating both
domestic and global history. As Inderpal Grewal astutely observes in
Transnational America: Feminisms, Diasporas, Neoliberalisms, this historic
moment has ironically forced a renewed, re-nationalization of patriotic
American identities among South Asian Americans. Afraid of being
misidentified as Arabs, many prominently display American flags on
their front yards, on their storefronts and houses, and on their bodies, in
the form of baseball caps and t-shirts (Grewal 212, 214). Hence, since
9/11/01, South Asians have begun Claiming America and Americanness
as never before in their hundred-year-old history in the US.[2]

Alexander's poetry about Manhattan, and the Wasteland that was
Ground Zero, written in the days and weeks following 9/11—and
published in the revised memoir—seems as quintessentially American
as Walt Whitman's ebullient or Allen Ginsberg's trenchant visions of
America–both gay poets whom she admires.[3] Perhaps, it is significant
that although Whitman and Ginsberg are now both identified with
America and valued for their prophetic visions, as homosexuals, they
were also outsiders who—like Alexander—observed, admired, cri-
tiqued, and defined the America of their time and location.

Simultaneously, Alexander seems to draw on T. S. Eliot for inspiration for her apocalyptic vision of a burning city. With unusual restraint
Alexander's lyrical lines evoke the shared emotional trauma of her

---

[2] For varied perspectives on the history and evolving positions and identities
of South Asians in the U.S., see the essays in Shankar and Srikanth, eds. *A Part,
Yet Apart*. Also, see Samir Dayal's essay in the same collection for early critical
views on Alexander's memoir.

[3] See especially Whitman's "Crossing Brooklyn Ferry," Ginsberg's
"America," and Alexander's poem "Indian April," a tribute to Ginsberg.

fellow New Yorkers who witnessed the "Bruised trees" the "color of sand" ("Invisible City"), and the ravaged bird's heart-rending cry among the burning hell-fires of the Wasteland that Eliot termed "Unreal City" ("The Fire Sermon," *The Wasteland*). Alexander portrays the ironically "Falling towers ... Unreal" (Eliot, "What the Thunder Said," *The Wasteland*): "By the pit, tor of metal, strut of death/ ... Flesh in fiery pieces, mute sediments of love" ("Pitfire"). In the lyric "Aftermath," written and dated "New York City, September 13-18, 2001," Alexander evokes the Eliotesque "objective correlative" ("Hamlet and His Problems"), as she describes how "Pale petals are scored into stone," or "Syllables of flame stitch the rubble." She takes the reader on a Prufrockian journey where like the sickly, paralytic "evening [that] is spread out against the sky/Like a patient etherised upon a table" (T. S. Eliot, "The Love Song of J. Alfred Prufrock"), surrounding the burning Twin Towers, the oxymoronic "Sweet and bitter smoke stains the sky" (*Fault Lines* 2003, 284-286).

Thus, like the polyglot T. S. Eliot, who quoted from Sanskrit *Upanishads* in his *Wasteland*, who felt a misfit in America, yet whose poetry functions as among the best "seismographs" of post-World War I Europe, and who is ironically claimed by America as among its foremost national poets, Alexander creates beauty from painting the devastation of her American home. Unlike Emerson, who wanted to escape history, Alexander thus wishes to represent history in her poetry. She explicitly clarifies the integral relationship between her poetry and history in an interview: "Unfortunately, the histories that we are part of are often brutal and violent. In making a poem, one mustn't turn one's face away, I feel that very strongly. I think the beauty has to exist within that history" (Basu 32).

Having been a witness to the violence surrounding 9/11, not only to those who died at Ground Zero, but also those immigrants and American citizens who became victims of hate crimes as they were assumed to be or resemble Muslims, the pacifist Christian Alexander emerges as an American poet as she poignantly describes her empathy for the varied individuals and groups she chooses to belong with. In her poem "Kabir Sings in a City of Burning Towers" (*Raw Silk*), Alexander invokes a weaver, an Indian Muslim Medieval saint poet, Kabir (ca. 1398-1518), known for preaching religious tolerance among both Hindus and

Muslims. As her friends warned her of being mistaken for "an Arab" due to her "dark skin" (*Fault Lines* 2003, 282), she expresses how she felt her innermost core as a racialized body too threatened to travel on the NYC subway in a sari, to expose her ethnic self. With tightly controlled emotion and taut imagistic precision, Alexander has Kabir address the frightened ethnic American poet, in short, urgent lines and dense, tense couplets: "What a shame/they scared you so" to hide the sari and "spread it/on the toilet floor," as "Sparks from the towers/fled through the weave of silk." Bringing the two disparate locations together on the same landscape and timescape, Alexander admits she wrote the poems "quickly, to survive" (*Fault Lines* 2003, 288). In Whitman's city, haunted by multiple forms of terror, she feels consoled, pacified, and inspired by Kabir's voice reminding her to accept herself since "With your black hair/and sun dark skin/you're just a child of earth" (*Fault Lines* 2003, 288).

In the second *Fault Lines*, then, not only does the Christian poet ironically turn to a medieval Indian Muslim poet for inspiration on how to live her life in a postmodern American world torn by historic religious wars, but Meena also gives voice to her half-Jewish daughter's pain on 9/11 at being singled out by her Jewish-American classmates at the Bronx High School of Science as she ironically looked "Middle Eastern" and therefore on the wrong side of the American war. In the teenage Svati's cryptic words, "My skin was screaming at me, Mama" (*Fault Lines* 2003, 280). Despite her otherwise obsessive insistence on feeling homeless and her focus on the past, here Meena Alexander locates herself physically and psychically, in the present tense, in that liminal space—her home and not home—sharing the couch with her daughter, witnessing on television "the devastation in this island city we love" (*Fault Lines* 2003, 280). Thus, Alexander delineates a poignant moment shared by the mother and child who were divided by skin color in the memoir's first edition—in the color-conscious American child's words as "peach Svati" and her "brown Mama" (*Fault Lines* 1993, 170)—but are seen now united by their ironically Indian skins in their Manhattan home.[4] Perhaps moved by the tragedy looming over her

---

[4] For a discussion of Alexander's self-consciousness about Svati's comment, see my "Postcolonial Diasporics."

biracial American-born children's world right after 9/11, Alexander unequivocally confesses a desire to live in the present, write about it, and temporarily let go of her own childhood history:

> I turn to my first love, poetry. I do not want to write about childhood. I do not want to be swallowed up in the past with so much molten and flowing. I need to bear witness to what is now, and the poem will allow me to do what I can... I feel the lyric poem will allow me to catch the edginess of things, the sharp nervosity, the flaming, falling buildings. (*Fault Lines* 2003, 284)

Moving away from her private, personal history, then, Alexander becomes a public "seismograph" of her historic times (to use Braham's term) as she witnesses and records the "flaming, falling buildings." Her locational and emotional intimacy with *"our floating life, this peril, this sweet island with its southern tip burning"* (*Fault Lines* 2003, 283; Alexander's italics) seems to ground the No Nation Woman who until then had not felt rooted in America. When urged during a 2005 interview to claim one geographical space as home, Alexander admitted, after much resistance, that since 9/11 she considers New York city as her home, primarily because it is the place she has raised her children:

> I think actually, to be very honest, Lavina, since you are pushing me on this, I think that now I feel that my home is New York City. Such as it is; I don't think I felt that when I wrote *Fault Lines*, and it may just be simply a matter of time. But also I think that 9/11 shocked me in a way that I really felt it was my home, in a way that I just haven't before. So in that sense, and this is where I've given birth to my children, and what can be deeper than that, and where they're growing up? (Alexander to Shankar, November 8, 2005)

So, home, for Alexander as for many immigrants, becomes not one's birthplace, but where one's children are born. New York represents Adam's and Svati's childhood and their roots, even though Meena's own roots still seek sustenance in the multiple homelands and transit lounges of the world she has wandered before settling in Manhattan. New York is Meena's home because of her children, the place she has given birth, therefore, a sort of home, but it still doesn't determine for her a fixed or stable national identity as someone claiming America per se. Thus, unanswered questions remain: does Alexander's claiming of

New York as home automatically also entail her claiming of America? Why did the public tragedy she witnessed from her home in New York make her return to the personal historical trauma of her childhood home in Tiruvella?

II. "Nurturing and Violent" Homes and Homelands

> The destruction visited on the island where I make my home, a second home, tore open the skin of memory, made me start to write again. But to close this book I had to go back to India. I had to return to the house of childhood. (Meena Alexander, *Fault Lines* 2003, 229)

In *Shattered Subjects: Trauma and Testimony in Women's Life-Writing*, Suzette Henke explains Cathy Caruth's reading of Freud's idea that "history, like trauma, is never simply one's own, that history is precisely the way we are implicated in each other's traumas" (qtd. in Henke 22). Alexander's revised and expanded memoir is testament to this sentiment and demonstrates how shared public trauma of catastrophic historical events can trigger the personal trauma of private memories to the extent that the individual self is at risk of dissolution from the intertwined trauma.

Even though after living in the U.S. for over two decades, Meena Alexander does not simply (or simplistically?) claim the American nation per se, her revised memoir expresses a strong sense of different homes where she has a history of being violated, or has not felt secure, in places where one expects to be safe. The extremely public, globally televised, spectacle of violence that had torn the fabric of normalcy in her present home, Manhattan, on 9/11/2001, and the ensuing global wars, shattered Meena's sense of her private self—fragmented though it had always been. As the epigraph to this section states, it forced her to return to the ancestral home of her childhood, Tiruvella, Kerala, to understand her tormented private history and re-claim her self.

The ironies of a fifty-year old woman who had always felt homeless, returning "home" to fight a war with and within herself and her memories, are so cruel that re-reading the first edition of the memoir becomes painful. Hence, it becomes easier to understand why for Alexander, language (especially lyric poetry) seems to be the only sanctuary, the only home where she can find refuge. Towards the end of the second version of the memoir, in the section "Lyric in a Time of Violence," Alexander ponders how to reconcile the real with the conflicting views of the imagined, felt, seen and remembered that is then translated into the literate/literary in life-writing:

> How can these violent versions of the real that cut into memory be translated into art? Art in a time of trauma, a necessary translation... can incorporate scansion of the actual, the broken steps, the pauses, the blunt silences, the brutal explosions... a recasting that permits our lives to be given back to us, fragile, precarious. (*Fault Lines* 2003, 289)

Hence, commenting on the relationships between art and life, for Alexander, art—even if conceived from violence—not merely mirrors life, but in the reflection, life-writing re-allows life, re-authorizes living.

As Alexander understood even when she had just begun her life writing in the first *Fault Lines* and in *Shock of Arrival*: "Tale telling is like breathing. If you try to hold it in, it explodes outwards" (*Shock of Arrival* 118). Through her brutally honest life story, Meena Alexander thus allowed herself in the revised memoir to articulate the excruciating memory of a private history that would otherwise have been too traumatic to let her live. Thus, as she said in a recent interview with me, instead of writing a couple of pages to introduce a tenth anniversary edition of her memoir that her publisher requested, she wrote a "a book that is eating itself up from the inside and revising itself" (Interview with Shankar). Since in Meena Alexander's own words, "Memory knows but knowing cannot remember," the remembering self is divided from its past self that was violated: "I do not like to say I... She not I. Not I, not I" (*Fault Lines* 2003, 301). The insistent refrain of the personal pronoun "I"—juxtaposed with a denial of itself—sounds simultaneously hollow and plaintive, a desperate clamor to assert the self. The distressed cry to claim the self is, perhaps, a result of what Homi Bhabha defines as "unhomeliness," the violent disjunction between the self, the home, and the world: "the estranging sense of the relocation of the home and the world in an unhallowed place" (141).

Alexander uses the concluding section of her second memoir "The Book of Childhood" to re-turn to a past idyllic home—that has turned "unhomely"—to re-claim herself, almost as if at war with(in) her own sense of her-self and her repressed memories of the violent past in the idealized home. Alexander's two memoirs thus result in very different artistic forms based on the writer's constantly evolving memories separated by another decade of living. Ironically, in the first edition of her memoir, the only place Meena felt at peace in the universe was in her beloved maternal grandfather Ilya's house and in his saintly presence learning about his encounters with Mahatma Gandhi, the non-violent Indian independence struggles, and other intellectual subjects that Meena's traditional mother didn't think were appropriate for women.

Focused on the freedom, magic, and Edenic qualities of a blissful childhood in her beloved grandfather's home, in the first edition, Tiruvella is the only location in the universe where Alexander describes herself as happy and at peace with herself, and with both her interior and exterior worlds, as being at home in the world. In her chapter "No Nation Woman" in *The Shock of Arrival*, too, she describes being exiled to North Africa at age five torn from the "radiant love of my grandparental home" (116). As she unambiguously states in the first *Fault Lines*, homesickness by definition meant being separated from Ilya's love: "Pothos, a homesickness that is never sated. When I think of homesickness, the Tiruvella house where Ilya lived rises up for me" (30). Ironically, Meena nostalgically describes Ilya's idyllic home, with its mango and golmohur trees where "my childhood was *free*... In Tiruvella I could run as fast as I wanted... places I could hide in and *find myself* again, utterly transformed in the *magic* of childhood... the closest we get to any possible *paradise*" (38; emphasis added). The first edition, which focused on the No Nation Woman's sense of rootlessness, ends with the mother of two adult children leaving Manhattan and returning home to her grandmother's garden, where she finds "the peace of a place" by literally lying down on the native soil. At the end of the first edition, Alexander literally and symbolically touches her cheeks to the "incense roots," tastes "raw earth," displays a proud sense of belonging "in our southern town," and feels a temporary "peace" (226).

Hence, Meena's world collapsed when, at age eleven, she faced Ilya's death: "As for me, I could not conceive of life without Ilya. I drew nourishment from him... Sometimes in my dreams I cry out his name... and wake up confused at so much longing welling up out of a grown woman" (36). Losing her savior-like Ilya was like losing herself: "the torment of his death plunged us into grief and rage. I think neither amma nor I have ever gotten over it... A whole world shivered and cracked" (38).

Thus it is shocking and traumatic for the reader, too, when in the revised edition of the memoir, the idealized and idolized Gandhian Socialist intellectual Ilya is exposed as having wreaked sexual violence on six-year old Meena. In "The Book of Childhood" the adult writer revisits the "dark door to grandfather's library" where her life itself is at stake: "Breath stops when I think of that door." Ironically, Alexander who has until then expended a lot of words writing her life, suddenly becomes telegramatic, cryptic. She does not describe what happened in the library to "a child in a white dress... She not I" (301). The awkward sentence construction, the concrete images of torture, and the short, poetic lines in the prose memoir, leave the unspeakable to the reader's imagination:

> Her eyes were burnt holes for the sun to shine through.
> I do not like to say I.
> I do not like to say I picked up my skirts and skipped into that doorway. For then I would be forced to say: sometime later I came out...
> What happened in grandfather Kuruvilla's library me makes float [sic].
> No before, no after.
> No up, down, down, up.
> Who will save me?
> Who will save Meena mol? (301)

The savior-like figure whom Meena affectionately termed "Ilya" in the first memoir is renamed as the unemotional relational, matter-of-fact "grandfather Kuruvilla" by the adult survivor learning to write her life one word at a time.

As Chandra Mohanty and Biddy Martin have explained in their 1986 essay "Feminist Politics: What's Home Got to Do With It?" (George 26), home is not always a safe space. In *The Politics of Home: Postcolonial Relocations and Twentieth-Century Fiction*, Rosemary George reminds us that homes are "not neutral places. Imagining a home is as political an act as is imagining a nation" (6). Homes are "places of violence and nurturing," "a place to escape to and a place to escape from" (9). In the traditional Victorian constructions, such as in John Ruskin's *Sesame and Lilies*, a home by definition was a haven, where one must belong, and feel safe, a "place of Peace; the shelter not only from all injury, but from all terror, doubt, and division... a sacred place, a vestal temple, a temple of the hearth watched over by Household Gods" ("Of Queen's Gardens," qtd. in George, 71). But for six-year old girls like Meena Alexander, Shirley Lim (as seen in her memoir *Among the White Moon Faces*), and Virginia Woolf, childhood homes were places of physical and psychological torment.

Like Virginia Woolf who, in her late forties, after witnessing the violence of World War II, recalled repressed memories of incest at age six (DeSalvo), the war in her backyard on 9/11/01 Meena's American home, New York, the resultant worldwide "War on Terror," and the unspoken war on brown bodies in the U.S., evoked memories of her childhood terror and forced Alexander to remember that which she did not dare to earlier. Perhaps, the doubleness of "violence and nurturing" (to use George's phrase) in Manhattan evoked the forgotten doubleness of her Indian and African childhoods.

The ironies of Alexander's brutally honest self-awareness about her lack of self-knowledge in the first edition of her life writing seem poignant. Overwrought by questions and self-doubt, while trying to claim a sense of self, the memoirist questions the shaky foundations her figurative "house" of memory has earlier stood on, almost as if proving Paul de Man's dismissal of autobiographical reliability:

> What foundations did my house stand on? What sort of architect was I if the lowest beams were shredded? If the stones were mouldering, fit to fall apart? What was the worth of words?
> A woman who did not know herself, how could I have written a book of my life and thought it was true? I was tormented by the feeling that I had written a memoir that was not true. (*Fault Lines* 2003, 241)

The once-confident sophisticated, intellectual, worldly author of the first edition here presents herself as humble, vulnerable, unsure, and child-like in the second edition.[5] Notwithstanding the writer's self-doubt

---

[5] Here, Alexander echoes Sylvia Fraser's self-doubting sentiments in *My Father's House: A Memoir of Incest and Healing* which seems to parallel Alexan-

about her inaccurate sense of her own life history, as Paul John Eakin states succinctly, autobiography is "a privileged bridge of discourse of the self with itself across lapsing time" (36). Hence Alexander's two memoirs are two versions of her-story, reflecting her own self in conversation with itself, rewriting its own history.

Alexander's relationship to witnessing wars, returning home and claiming homelands is, thus, complicated by her being haunted by the "unquiet space of memory" (*Raw Silk*) and the personal familial violence of childhood that is not just hard to forget, but also hard to remember. A line from Alexander's sensuous and evocative poem "Pitfire"—about the fires raging at Ground Zero in Manhattan—sums up the internal and external wars of both her present and her past and the poignant songs she has created from the pain of her voyages back and forth between homes and homelands throughout the globe. The enigmatic, rhetorical questions apply to the poet's own life writing: "Shall a soul visit her mutilated parts? /How much shall a body be home?" (*Fault Lines* 2003, 287). At the end of the second edition of her memoir, Alexander questions whether there ever can be a single, fixed home for those like her to turn —or return—to:

> Home for me is bound up with a migrant's memory and the way that poetry, ... permits a dwelling at the edge of the world.
> I use that last phrase since the sensuous density of location, the hold of a loved place can scarcely be taken for granted. The making up of home and, indeed, locality, given the shifting, multiple worlds we inhabit, might best be considered part and parcel of an art of negativity, praise songs for what remains when the taken-for-grantedness of things falls away. (*Fault Lines* 2003, 260)

Since even the most sacred of places can be, become, or be re-membered as a site of war, of violation, Alexander's memoir is a reminder that no home can ever be taken for granted and that for postcolonial migrants every home is always, already, at the edge of the world. So, the only abode No Nation Woman can take refuge in is art—the language and

---

der's expanded memoir of survival: "In retrospect, I feel about my life the way some people feel about war. If you survive, then it becomes a good war. Danger makes you active, it makes you alert, it forces you to experience and thus to learn... My pride of intellect has been shattered. If I didn't know about half my own life, what other knowledge can I trust?" (Fraser 253).

poetry, that allow her to create through words (and reconcile with) the worlds she could not otherwise control.[6]

Works Cited

Alexander, Meena. *Fault Lines: A Memoir*. New York: Feminist Press, 1993.

—. *Fault Lines: A Memoir*. Preface by N'gugi wa Thiong'o. Revised and expanded edition. New York: Feminist Press of the City University of New York, 2003.

—. *Illiterate Heart*. Evanston, IL: TriQuarterly Books, 2002.

—. "In Whitman's Country." *Virginia Quarterly Review* 81.2 (Spring 2005): 186-192

—. *Manhattan Music: A Novel*. San Francisco: Mercury House, 1997.

—. *Nampally Road: A Novel*. San Francisco: Mercury House, 1991.

—. *Raw Silk*. Evanston, IL: TriQuarterly Books/Northwestern University Press, 2004.

—. *The Shock of Arrival: Reflections on Postcolonial Experience*. Boston: South End Press, 1996.

Bahri, Deepika and Mary Vasudeva. "Observing Ourselves among Others: Interview with Meena Alexander." *Between the Lines: South Asians and Postcoloniality*. Eds. Deepika Bahri and Mary Vasudeva. Philadelphia: Temple University Press, 1996. 35-53.

Basu, Lopamudra. "The Poet in the Public Sphere: A Conversation with Meena Alexander." *Social Text* 20.3 (Fall 2002): 31-38.

Bercovitch, Sacvan. *The Puritan Origins of the American Self*. New Haven: Yale University Press, 1975.

Bhabha, Homi. "The World and the Home." *Social Text* 31-32 (1992): 141-153.

Braham, Jeanne. *Crucial Conversations: Interpreting Contemporary American Literary Autobiographies by Women*. New York: Columbia University Press, 1995.

Caruth, Cathy. *Unclaimed Experience: Trauma, Narrative, and History*. Baltimore: Johns Hopkins University Press, 1996.

Chin, Frank et. al., eds. *Aiiieeeee! An Anthology of Asian-American Writers*. Washington, D.C.: Howard University Press, 1974.

[6] I would like to thank Rocío Davis and the reviewers of this volume for their suggestions for revision. I am grateful to my thesis student Lauren Kawana, and the students in my seminar on Asian American Women Writers for their feedback on an earlier version of this paper presented at Parents and Families Weekend at Bates, October 2006. I also appreciate the support I received from Dean of Faculty Jill Reich for this research.

Couser, G. Thomas. *American Autobiography: The Prophetic Mode.* Amherst: University of Massachusetts Press, 1979.

Cox, James M. "Autobiography and America." *Virginia Quarterly Review* 47 (1971): 252-77. Rpt. in James M. Cox, *Recovering Literature's Lost Ground: Essays in American Autobiography.* Baton Rouge: Louisiana State University Press, 1989. 11-32.

Dayal, Samir. "Min(d)ing the Gap: South Asian Americans and Diaspora." *A Part, Yet Apart: South Asians in Asian America.* Eds. Lavina Dhingra Shankar and Rajini Srikanth, Philadelphia: Temple University Press, 1998. 235-265.

De Man, Paul. "Autobiography as De-Facement." *Modern Language Notes* 94.5 (December 1979): 919-930.

DeSalvo, Louise. *Virginia Woolf: The Impact of Childhood Sexual Abuse on Her Life and Work.* Boston: Beacon Press, 1989.

Duncan, Erika. "A Portrait of Meena Alexander." *World Literature Today* 73.1 (Winter 1999): 23-28.

Eakin, Paul John. *Fictions in Autobiography: Studies in the Art of Self-Invention.* Princeton, NJ: Princeton University Press, 1985.

Emerson, Ralph Waldo. "Self-Reliance." *Selected Writings of Emerson.* Ed. Donald McQuade. New York: Modern Library, 1981. 129-153.

Foster, Frances Smith. "Autobiography after Emancipation: The Example of Elizabeth Keckley." *Multicultural Autobiography: American Lives.* Ed. James Robert Payne. Knoxville: University of Tennessee Press, 1992. 32-63.

Fraser, Sylvia. *My Father's House: A Memoir of Incest and Healing.* New York: Harper and Row, 1987.

George, Rosemary Marangoly. *The Politics of Home: Postcolonial Relocations and Twentieth-Century Fiction.* Cambridge: Cambridge University Press, 1996.

Grewal, Inderpal. *Transnational America: Feminisms, Diasporas, Neoliberalisms.* Durham, NC: Duke University Press, 2005.

Hall, Stuart. "Cultural Identity and Diaspora." *Identity: Community, Culture, Difference.* Ed. Jonathan Rutherford. London: Lawrence and Wishart, 1990. 222-237.

Henke, Suzette A. *Shattered Subjects: Trauma and Testimony in Women's Life-Writing.* New York: St. Martin's Press, 1998.

Hirsch, Marianne, Elizabeth Abel and Elizabeth Langland, eds. *The Voyage In: Fictions of Female Development.* Hanover and London: University Press of New England, 1983.

Li, David Leiwei. *Imagining the Nation: Asian American Literature and Cultural Consent.* Stanford: Stanford University Press, 1998.

Lim, Shirley Geok-lin. *Among the White Moon Faces: An Asian-American Memoir of Homelands.* New York: Feminist Press at the City University of NY, 1996.

Ling, Jinqui. *Narrating Nationalisms: Ideology and Form in Asian American Litera-
    ture*. New York: Oxford University Press, 1998.

Martin, Biddy and Chandra Talpade Mohanty. "Feminist Politics: What's Home
    Got to Do With It?" *Feminist Studies/Critical Studies*. Ed. Theresa de
    Lauretis. Bloomington: Indiana University Press, 1986. 191-212.

Morrison, Toni. "The Site of Memory." *Inventing the Truth: The Art and Craft of
    the Memoir*. Ed. William Zinsser. Boston: Houghton Mifflin, 1987. 101-124.

Payne, James Robert. *Multicultural Autobiography: American Lives*. Knoxville:
    University of Tennessee Press, 1992.

Reaves, Gerri. *Mapping the Private Geography: Autobiography, Identity, and Amer-
    ica*. Jefferson, NC, & London: McFarland & Co., 2001.

Rich, Adrienne. "When We Dead Awaken: Writing as Re-vision." *Arts of the
    Possible: Essays and Conversations*. New York: Norton, 2001.

Rose, Susan. "Naming and Claiming: The Integration of Traumatic Experience
    and the Reconstruction of Self in Survivors' Stories of Sexual Abuse."
    Trauma and Life Stories: International Perspectives. Ed. Kim Lacy Rogers,
    Selma Leydesdorff, Graham Dawson. London, New York: Routledge,
    1999. 160-179.

Ruskin, John. "Of Queen's Garden." *Sesame and Lilies*. Ed. Agnes Spofford Cook.
    New York: Silver, Burdett and Co., 1900.

Shankar, Lavina Dhingra. "Postcolonial Diasporics 'Writing in Search of a
    Homeland': Meena Alexander's *Manhattan Music, Fault Lines*, and *The
    Shock of Arrival*." *LIT: Literature Interpretation Theory* 12.3 (September
    2001): 285-312.

—. "Re-Visioning Memoirs Old and New: A Conversation with Meena Alexan-
    der." Unpublished Interview under review. Lewiston, Maine, USA.
    November 8, 2005.

— and Rajini Srikanth, eds. *A Part, Yet Apart: South Asians in Asian America*.
    Philadelphia: Temple University Press, 1998.

Verghese, Abraham. *My Own Country: A Doctor's Story of a Town and its People in
    the Age of AIDS*. New York: Simon & Schuster, 1994.

Wong, Sau-ling Cynthia. "Denationalization Reconsidered: Asian American
    Cultural Criticism at a Theoretical Crossroads." *Amerasia Journal* 21.1 & 2
    (1995): 1-27.

Woolf, Virginia. 1985. *Moments of Being*. Ed. Jeanne Schulkind. San Diego, New
    York, London: Harvest/HBJ, 1976.

Lavina D. Shankar is Faculty Associate Dean of Admissions and Associate Professor of
English at Bates College in Maine. She is coeditor of *A Part, Yet Apart: South Asians in
Asian America*.

At Home in the Diaspora?
Abraham Verghese's and Mira Nair's *My Own Country*

Pin-chia Feng

> As I got to know more gay men, I became curious about their life stories, keen to compare their stories with mine. There was an obvious parallel: society considered them alien and much of their life was spent faking conformity; in my case my Green Card labeled me a 'resident alien.' New immigrants expend a great deal to fit in: learning the language, losing the accent, picking up the ritual of Monday Night Football and Happy Hour. Gay men, in order to avoid conflict, had also become experts of blending in, camouflaging themselves, but at a great cost to their spirit. By contrast, my adaptation had been voluntary, even joyful: from the time I was born I lacked a country I could speak of as home. My survival had depended on a chameleonlike adaptability, taking on the rituals of a place I found myself to be in: Africa, India, Boston, Johnson City. I feel as if I was always reinventing myself, discovering who I was. (Abraham Verghese, *My Own Country* 53)

Abraham Verghese's first book, the memoir *My Own Country: A Doctor's Story of a Town and Its People in the Age of AIDS*, was published in 1994 and was credited as one of the five best books of the year by *Time* magazine ("Profile"). Four years later *My Own Country* appeared as a Showtime TV film, produced and directed by Mira Nair. Both literary and filmic texts, however, have received little critical attention. Rajini Srikanth, for instance, is vocal about this neglect of Verghese's text. She argues that the text is rich in "cross-ethnic and cross-racial encounters" yet "only a small handful of scholars and educators treat this text for its implications for American ethnic literature, despite the far-reaching impact of the book" (434). Perhaps one of the reasons for this scholarly silence is that Verghese's text is hard to categorize. Is this a text about a South Asian ethnic self in the making or is it about his predominantly white patients? Can we call *My Own Country* a text of ethnic self writing if it is read as a collective story?[1] The subtitle of Verghese's book implicitly suggests that this memoir is a recording by a medical specialist of the collective experience of a rural American community encountering a lethal disease. The title itself shows no identifiable ethnic marker except the idea of a strong desire to belong. The fact that the author is an Indian immigrant who was born in Ethiopia seems to be purely accidental. Or is it?

In addition, as part of Mira Nair's film oeuvre, *My Own Country* has attracted almost no discussion. One possible reason for this maybe because it is has been labeled a TV drama and can be easily overlooked when one wants to discuss the South Asian American filmmaker's "serious work."[2] And yet what can be more serious than the struggles of life and death while faced with a yet unknown and incurable disease, the "black death" of the late twentieth century, and the desire to find a place to call home? What *My Own Country* has questioned and made problematic, I argue, is precisely the politics of representation in extreme situations. This paper therefore, aims to discuss the problem associated with writing and visualizing the ethnic self in *My Own Country*. My reading of the literary text will focus on an ethnic self vis-à-vis a questionable group identity constructed out of an alternative blood relation, while my analysis of Nair's filmic text attempts to probe the ways in which diasporic ethnicity is accentuated through cinematic practices.

I. Writing the Ethnic Self and Finding a Home in the Diaspora

Abraham Verghese's text opens in 1985 with the story of a young white man driving home from New York City to Johnson City, Tennessee for Thanksgiving but who ends up in the emergency room of the Johnson City Medical Center and is later diagnosed with AIDS. This is the rural town's first case of AIDS, which is soon "suppressed like a shameful

---

[1] Srikanth also mentions an anecdote about how the book did not receive an Association of Asian American Studies book award because it "was deemed not to illuminate sufficiently the Asian American experience" and "was primarily about Southern white patients" (447).

[2] That was the comment from the audience when I attended a conference in India. *Salaam Bombay!* and *Monsoon Wedding* are the films that the Indian audience are most familiar with, as in the rest of the world. With Hollywood stars like Reese Witherspoon on the cast, one may perhaps add *Vanity Fair* to the list.

memory" (46). Two months after the young man's death, Dr. Verghese, an "African-born-but-of-Indian-parentage-naturalized American" ("Profile of a SAJAer"), becomes the director of the infectious diseases division of the same medical center and spends four years helping patients and their families to live with the disease. At that time, with very limited knowledge of the virus that causes a general failure of the human immune system, Verghese resorts to a treatment with a personal approach. His close intimacy with his patients, however, creates tremendous stress for himself and his family. Despite the fact that he regards Johnson City as his "own country," on New Year's Eve of 1989 he moves away for a new beginning.

This memoir, framed by a homecoming and a departure told by a narrator with the experience of multiple migrations and thus an identity of multiple hyphenations, is problematic in terms of where to locate home and selfhood. From the beginning the author ignores the ostensible autobiographical priority of narrating his own story in order to talk about a stranger he never met in person. And this anecdote in which "the hometown boy was now regarded as an alien" (6) after he was found with AIDS ironically challenges the very title of Verghese's book. This act of self-effacement in memoir-writing is further complicated by the interweaving narrative of the various personal and case stories of Dr. Verghese's patients; these stories in turn become an integral part of his self-writing and self-formation. Verghese talks about how he is interested in collecting patients' stories transcends clinical interest: "But I was also interested in the patients' stories for their own sake. I was fascinated by the voyage that had brought them to my clinic door. The anecdotes they told me lingered in my mind and became the way I identified them. Most of the stories I kept in my head. Some I recorded in a journal that I kept faithfully and that became very important to me as time went on" (119). The writing of the narrative appears to parallel the way Verghese treats his patients—they both involve great empathy. Verghese confesses that he offers his empathy since he cannot offer a cure: "In the absence of a magic portion to cure AIDS, my job was to minister to family and his social situation. I would have to make more home visits, make more attempts to understand the person I saw in the clinic, be sure I understood the family dynamics by meeting all its members" (259).[3] Thus, this autobiographical work appears to be not only rather "self-less," but also a collective story of a doctor and his patients, who share an extraordinary bond because of the unspeakable disease and the status of being "outsiders." It is at once a story of a community as well as of those not completely included in that community. These paradoxes and tensions eventually lead to a questioning of the politics of representing the ethnic self and of the complex insider/outsider dynamics in the text.

This act of collectivity in fact confirms to the generic description of memoirs. As Lee Quinby points out, "Whereas autobiography promotes an 'I' that shares with confessional discourse an assumed interiority and an ethical mandate to examine the interiority, memoirs promote an 'I' that is explicitly constituted in the reports of the utterances and proceedings of others. The 'I" or subjectivity produced in memoirs is externalized and, in the Bakhtinian sense, overly dialogical" (299). The "dialogical" or even heteroglossic way of life writing in fact counterpoints the monologic and unified selfhood as presented in traditional autobiographies.[4] Through the haunting stories of the AIDS patients and their families that constitute Vergese's memoir, therefore, we encounter an excellent example of collective identity in memoirs and ethnic life writing. Yet while such a collectivity is often celebrated in the theorization of ethnic self-writing, it is also problematic when we consider the collective stigma associated with AIDS. Diseases, as Susan Sontag perceptively observes, are always understood in society through metaphors.[5] For the metaphoric meaning of AIDS, Sontag pinpoints the

---

[3] To his credit, Dr. Verghese is still promoting this empathetic treatment. In his 1998 interview with Barnesandnoble.com, he states that "I suspect the challenge for doctors in the next century will be to discover why the profession was once called the 'ministry of healing,' to rediscover why medicine was at one time a calling and not a particularly lucrative one at that. People who visit doctors are looking for more than a cure, they are looking for 'healing' as well" (Laxmi).

[4] "The Enlightenment 'self,' ontologically identical to other 'I's, as Sidonie Smith and Julia Watson contend, "sees its destiny in a teleological narrative enshrining the 'individual' and his 'uniqueness'" (xvii).

[5] Sontag states that "nothing is more punitive than to give a disease a meaning—that meaning being invariably a moralistic one. Any important disease

emphasis on a particular group identity: "Indeed, to get Aids is precisely to be revealed, in the majority of cases so far, as a member of a certain 'risk group,' a community of pariahs. The illness flushes out an identity that might have remained hidden from neighbors, jobmates, family friends" (112-113). This membership is revealed because of the symptoms shown on the patients' faces, which are not only the tell-tale signs of the disease but may also be aesthetically disturbing.[6] Luther Hines, the patient who insists on demonstrating his own AIDS-induced bodily decomposition in public, is the only character in Verghese's text who can strike back at the socially constructed monstrosity with his own body. And yet having to watch Luther on his deathbed is precisely what has prompted Verghese to leave Johnson City. As he watches Luther lying in a coma, Verghese confesses, "All the stories that I have painfully collected have come to haunt me with their tragic endings, as if I am the author and must take full responsibility. In a new place I can begin from a wiser and more careful vantage" (408). The collected/collective stories weigh the doctor down with the responsibility of authorship and he is seeking a way out of the tremendous burden.

In her cultural analysis of the creation of AIDS patients as "a new class of lifetime pariahs" (121-122), Sontag keeps on going back to this collective aspect in terms of social judgment: "Plagues are invariably regarded as judgments on society, and the metaphoric inflation of AIDS into such a judgment also accustoms people to the inevitability of global spread. This is traditional use of sexually transmitted diseases: to be described as punishments not just of individuals but of a group ('generall licentiousnes')" (142). Verghese's book shows that not only the AIDS

---

whose causality is murky, and for which treatment is ineffectual, tends to be awash in significance. First, the subjects of deepest dread (corruption, decay, pollution, anomie, weakness) are identified with the disease. The disease itself becomes a metaphor. Then, in the name of the disease (that is, using it as a metaphor), that horror is imposed on other things. The disease becomes adjectival" (58).

[6] "Underlying some of the moral judgments attached to disease are aesthetic judgments about the beautiful and the ugly, the clean and the unclean, the familiar and the alien or uncanny," Sontag remarks, "the marks on the face of a leper, a syphilitic, someone with AIDS are the signs of a progressive mutation, decomposition; something organic" (129).

patients are stigmatized, so are their families: even their doctors can feel "tainted." Working as an AIDS doctor, Verghese has indeed acquired membership into a community. However, for many such an inclusion is a stigma as it involves a "risk group." Thus in a way he is forced into a group identity; and yet at the same time Verghese is also actively courting an affective bond with his patients to make himself feel "at home." This becomes an "imagined community" created through an affiliation based not on blood but on a blood disease and through which the circulation of "blood narrative" in theorizing ethnicity is revised and re-routed.

There is of course another membership that Dr. Verghese can actually enjoy. He not only has cultivated intimacy with his patients and their families through empathetic treatment, but he has also achieved an elite status in his profession. Yet this kind of "heroism" requires him to put his own life on the line. That is why Verghese's immediate family, his wife and parents, are constantly worried about the potential risk to his health. Verghese himself also has a recurrent nightmare about the danger of being infected. It is his "'infection' dream" that makes him acknowledge the superficiality of his conscious empathy and affiliation with his patients. As Verghese states, "in my waking hours I never understood the absolute terror of finding out you have HIV; in my dreams I understood all too well" (361). Moreover, although Verghese ostensibly combats the stigmatization and metaphoric imagination of AIDS, he himself is shown to be not above judging his patients by their deeds. He reflects on the reasons why he treats a couple with AIDS differently from other patients because the husband has contracted the virus through blood transfusion during a heart surgery and then passes it on to his wife: Will and Bess Johnson are regarded as "innocent victims" and, accordingly, receive special treatment from the doctor. Moreover, he is highly aware of the fact that the Johnsons are highly respected in their own community, which requires them to seek treatment outside their own town. Even Verghese himself suspects that he has a "blind spot" in his treatment of the Johnsons—"After all, how many other patients had I personally escorted up to their hospital rooms? When had I ever carried luggage for patients, spent hours of my evening listening to them and settling them in, allowing them to dictate the pace of the interview, leaving only when I thought they would not mind my departure?" (238-239).

Thus by merit of his medical specialty and by choice Verghese acquired a certain membership in the "risk group." And yet ironically his position as an observer-narrator never allows him to be a full member of any group. In his first interaction with the gay community in the local gay bar the Connection, for instance, he is very ill at ease and very afraid of being linked to the gay community. This fear is real because of the possibility of being sighted near or in the gay bar. As his wife Rajini pragmatically puts it, "You can easily get labeled. It's bad enough that it is a small town; we are a very visible Indian community and it's tough to miss someone like you" (55). His satirical description of the social gathering of the South Asian expatriate community further reveals his sense of alienation from this race-based community. The small South Asian community of professionals Verghese describes has its own caste system based on professional specialties and property ownership: he is like "a bathroom sweeper" in the rank of medical specialists and has committed a "crime" by renting instead of owning a house (195).[7] Thus, he is always out of place and even appears to be an outsider in his own memoir.

On the other hand, there is a persistent desire for home in the text, starting from the title of the memoir itself. Early on in the narrative Verghese voices this longing to be re-territorialized: "Stateless and roaming for so long, I wanted to put down roots... I wanted my son to have a permanent home, something I never had. Johnson City was going to be my own. I felt at peace in this corner of east Tennessee. Finally, this was my own country" (41). In his longing for permanence and roots, Verghese adopts a rural American town as his own; and with his text, he has put this town on the map of American public awareness. In Srikanth's analysis of the complex interplay of the positions of insider/outsider in Verghese's text, she points out that rural Johnson City "lies

---

[7] Verghese writes, "the pecking order of these functions was clear: doctors ruled over engineers, who lorded over everyone else... surgeons—particularly thoracic surgeons—were treated as the maharajahs... Needless to say, on this ranking, being an infectious disease specialist was equivalent to being a bathroom sweeper.... In the competition to build a larger and fancier house, I was not even in the race: I was *renting* from the VA—a heinous crime from the perspective of an Indian community that saw land acquisition as a primal necessity" (195).

outside the consciousness of most Americans," thus Verghese's insider position in this rural community "may represent a dubious kind of belonging to America"; and yet "the particular nature of his doctoring enables him to move from the privilege of being an insider in Johnson City to being an insider nationally" (440). Verghese, the foreign doctor, discovers his "own country" by reconstituting the social landscape of the town: "He leads a community to examine itself in its capacity to create a home for its sons. In this sense, once read his memoir as an act of reshaping the landscape. He uncovers new landmarks to the locals, laying bare to their own eyes the previously unseen parts of the social landscape: the hidden communities of gay men and those suffering from AIDS" (Srikanth 441). Thus, Srikanth argues, "What gives to this autobiography its particular value is its inversion of insider-outsider positions" (441). For Srikanth, clearly Verghese's effort to chart the routes through which AIDS has been "imported" to Johnson City embodies a "trope of map" that "leads us to an examination of constructed categories, i.e. to new ways of 'reading' the landscape" (442). This recharting of the American landscape, one may add, is exactly an act of "claiming America" in a way many of Verghese's Asian American predecessors have attempted.

And yet at the end of the text the Vergheses, instead of setting down their roots in Johnson City, are on the road again and on route to a new town at the beginning of a new year. The location and meaning of "home," therefore, is constantly under revision in *My Own Country*. The question of the location of home is not simply a problem for the diasporic author. More than once Verghese writes about how the patients and their families find themselves as outcasts of the community because of the stigma of AIDS. From the first case of the young man who returns home from New York City to Gordon, the prodigal son who comes home to die, the association of homecoming and death is persistent throughout *My Own Country*. This association has become a part of Verghese's finding and a clue to the spread of the AIDS virus in the rural areas of the United States. At a symbolic level, however, it is highly ironic that a text which is ostensibly seeking to find a place called "home" is permeated with this shadowy association of home and death. Verghese, a diasporic subject, manifests a desire for re-territorialization through his autobiographical writing, as exemplified by the title of his book.[8] Paradoxically he has to engage in yet another de-territorializing journey at the end so that he can recover from his professional burn-out and to keep his family from disintegration—to "reinvent" himself again, so to speak, as is suggested in the epigraph. Thus *My Own Country*, a text full of paradoxical desires, ends on an ambivalent note and one which never fully answers the question about whether an ethnic subject can really find a home in the diaspora.

II. Visualizing *My Own Country*

When questioned in an interview about her "particularity as a film-maker," Mira Nair replied, "I like to amplify every frame with life. The film, whether it's tragedy or comedy or whatever, should be exploding with life" (15). Life is what permeates her rendition of *My Own Country*, a drama overshadowed by death. Scripted by Sooni Taraporevala, who has written the screenplays of Nair's two other films, *Salaam Bombay!* and *Mississippi Masala*, *My Own Country* is unique among Nair's projects in that it is her only film to date that is adapted from the life writing project of a fellow South Asian American.[9] In a sense, *My Own Country* can be regarded as a mixture of documentary, the genre Nair began working in and through which she has repeatedly focused on Indian society, especially the underclass, and fictional film, one that Nair has moved into with her acclaimed *Salaam Bombay!* so that she could "make things happen."[10] Whereas Nair is well-known for handling the subject

---

[8] Lisa Diedrich analyzes the route of voyage out and back in Deleuze and Guattari's terms of de-territorialization and re-territorializaiton: The voyage out is marked by what Deleuze and Guattari would call "a de-territorializing desire for other individuations and other pleasures, while the voyage back is marked by a re-territorializing desire for the hoped-for safety of home and a nostalgic past as conservative response in the face of inevitable death" (241). Dietrich observes that Verghese writes with a hope to repair the rupture created by AIDS and therefore the book is "a reparative narrative" or "a reterritorializing narra-tive" that notably fails "to repair or to reterritorialize" (249).

[9] Nair has recently adapted Jhumpa Lahiri's novel *The Namesake* and the film was premiered on September 11, 2006.

[10] In the director's commentary on *Salaam Bombay!* Nair confesses that the reason she moved from making documentaries to feature films is because she was tired of waiting for things to happen.

matter of South Asian immigrants in the United States, interracial conflicts, and the complicated politics of home in the diaspora, adapting Verghese's autobiography became a fresh attempt at interpreting the South Asian diaspora from the perspective of the lived experience of a real person. In this case, visualizing this autobiographical text was an act of "transposition" that takes a literary text "and delivers it to new audiences by means of the aesthetic conventions of an entirely different generic process" (Sanders 20).

Instead of enumerating the differences of the literary and filmic texts while discussing Nair's adaptation of *My Own Country*,[11] it is more fruitful to look into Nair's own interpretation of the diasporic condition through her cinematic practices. I argue that, on the one hand, Nair wants to continue Verghese's narrative desire of belonging in her film version by representing Verghese's close relationship with his patients and their families and his integration into the American landscape by resorting to a discourse of mobility. On the other hand, Nair is trying to extract Verghese from both the voluntary and involuntary group identity and to reintroduce the personal dimension of Abraham Verghese into the digesis by strengthening the African and South Asian "accents."[12] While Verghese insists on introducing medical discourse into his memoir as a marker of profession and as a sign of the impotence of medical research confronted by the newly discovered disease, Nair also places emphasis on the doctor as an individual with personal emotions and problems. The doctor is not only the central intelligence through whom readers come into contact with a network of other characters (as in the original memoir), but he also stands out as a multiply-displaced South Asian victim of the diaspora in search of a home and an answer to the meaning of life. AIDS still has its metaphorical significance in the film, but more as a strategy that reveals human dignity and courage. Finally, Nair's film has a stronger humanistic vision and a greater hope for the future than are found in Verghese's text. Furthermore, in its own way the film also confirms Michael M. J. Fischer's

---

[11] For instance, the film was shot in Toronto in the fall of 1997, a location much removed from the southern American town. Yet this does not discredit the "realistic" aura of the film.

[12] I am referring to Hamid Naficy's term "accented cinema" (68-70). Nair is one of Naficy's examples of an accented filmmaker.

argument that ethnic autobiographies often use "retrospection to gain a vision for the future" (198).

While transposing Verghese's written text into a visual one, Nair follows the basic storyline of the narrative and thus in the diagesis of the film, the personal is always intimately linked with the communal and the ethnic with the marginalized. However, compared to the original memoir, Nair's film has placed much more emphasis on Verghese's personal experience and daily life. This reorientation of narrative focus on the memoirist on the one hand helps to extract Verghese from the entrapment of medical discourse and the group identity he has acquired; on the other hand, the numerous negotiations and struggles in Verghese's daily life give nuances to the cinematic depiction of the formation of his Asian American identity. As Jun Xing observes, "History teaches us that while personal and cultural identities can be externally imposed, they are usually negotiated successfully in our daily lives. The movies help illuminate the process and strategies by which Asian Americans construct and articulate their personal sense of identity" (142). Furthermore, the added personal details in Nair's film imaginatively fill in the gaps or absences in Verghese's text. "Asian American identity," Peter X. Feng argues, "is defined not by history, but by gaps in history: the absence of information bespeaks a historical trauma that defines Asian Americans" (17). Hence while Verghese is relatively laconic about his past before coming to America, Nair insists on opening her film from the "proper beginning"—Verghese's African and Indian past—to bring into relief her focus on Verghese's "identities in motion" as a diasporian.[13]

To visualize Abraham Verghese's personal and cultural *Bildung*, therefore, Nair takes pains to personalize him by emphasizing his diasporic background and by providing details about his personal life. Nair's interest in Verghese's status as a South Asian of multiple migrations is, of course, no coincidence. Sharing a similar immigrant status and a middle-class/professional background with Verghese, Nair is able to bring a particular diasporic perspective to the visualization of the

---

[13] Here I am alluding to Peter X. Feng's concept of "identities in motion" in his monograph on Asian American film. Yet my focus is mostly on Verghese's constant re-location as a diasporic subject.

good doctor's story.[14] Verghese, who was born to Kerala Christian parents in Ethiopia in 1955 and who studied medicine there until he was forced to "return" to India because of the Ethiopian revolution and who then immigrated to the United States to continue his medical training, is a "twice displaced" character like the protagonist Mena in *Mississippi Masala*.[15] And yet he is not a "typical" Indian because of his parents' Christian background. In his memoir, Verghese does not dwell much upon his Ethiopian past. He simply explains that his parents went to teach in Africa because when Emperor Haile Selassie visited Kerala he was so impressed by the high literacy of the Christian state in India that he decided to man schools in Ethiopia with expatriate teachers from Kerala (11). The three pages about Africa in Verghese's text are meaningfully expanded to create the African "accent" that opens the film. Nair alludes to Verghese's African "origin" by playing an African song during the opening credit sequence. Then the film starts with a voice-over narration and a clip showing young Verghese happily taking photographs in a studio in his African outfit. Next there is a series of still photographs from a scene in an Ethiopian pub on September 12, 1974, when news about the dethronement of the emperor and a curfew were being announced on the radio. The monotonous and jarring metal sound, a single gun shot and Verghese's nervous panting punctuate the soundtrack. Together with the three documentary photographs of the civil war, the audio and visual elements of the opening sequence suggest a memory of violence that should preferably remain buried, or be transformed into a souvenir in the shape of Africa, as shown in the film. The composition of fragmentary imagery in the film also concretely expresses a sense of dislocation. As Verghese comments in the voice-

---

[14] Jun Xing makes the same point about how Nair's "own diasporic experience informs her film works" while discussing her *The Perez Family* as one of the Asian American cross-over films (201).

[15] In her essay on Nair's *Mississippi Masala*, Binita Mehta talks about how the Indian characters in the film are "twice displaced" (218). Mehta writes, "The Indian family depicted in *Mississippi Masala* has migrated via England from Uganda, East Africa, to Greenwood, Mississippi. Expelled from Uganda by General Idi Amin in 1972, they are twice displaced: Indians by culture and tradition, Uganda by birth, they move to the United States to live in a motel owned by their relatives, themselves immigrants from India" (218).

over, "When you are forced to leave a country you once called home, it changed everything. You can't appreciate the simple pleasures of life. You envy people around you who can." Furthermore, the African motif is maintained throughout the film by the use of "Malaika" ("Angel")—a love song by a Kenyan musician—as the theme song to open and end the film.

Thus, Nair deploys the musical component and visual images to uncover and underscore the African layer of Verghese's personal history. The few singing scenes in the film also dramatically personalized the doctor. He sings to release his emotions, be they tender or angry. After the hospital administrator has suggested that Verghese's reputation has attracted unwanted AIDS patients to the medical center, the doctor is seen getting drunk, playing the guitar, and singing with a zest in the company of his buddy, the white mechanic Allen. That moment of interracial male bonding also bespeaks Verghese's intense sense of alienation. Whereas he sings the African song "Malaika" to his family in moments of intimacy, when he is distressed the lyric that he keeps on repeating is "Do you love me?": a line which interestingly frames Verghese's relationship with the place that he would like to call home into one that is of uncertain and, most likely, unrequited love.

Nair also adds a section about Verghese's medical training in Madras to further contextualize his diasporic background. Before Verghese moved to the United States, the talk about how a foreign medical graduate is regarded as a "transplanted organ" that is "life-saving, but rejected because of foreign tissue" is jokingly passed around among the Indian medical students. This reference activates the series of metaphors that link the medical profession with politics of identity. The additional section on Verghese's medical training in Madras in the film extends the central metaphor of *My Own Country*. A mutual space of belonging is constructed for both the expatriate doctor and his group of patients: both parties are marginalized and "diseased," either racially or physically. This allows the immigrant doctor to excel in a certain way. Hence when questioned by the interns as to why he has chosen infectious diseases as his specialty, Verghese replies that treating AIDS patients is his "only chance to play hero." And yet he has to admit that his predominantly white patients tend to tell him things they will not normally reveal to white doctors because they feel that as a "foreign doctor" he has no right to judge them. Thus the potentially close doctor-patient bonding also paradoxically forces Verghese to confront his own ethnicity and racial difference.

Besides adding the Madras section, Nair also changes the character of Verghese's wife Rajani from a business major in Verghese's memoir into a dancer. Ellora Patnaik, the actress who plays Rajani in the film, is also a professional Odissi dancer. Nair conveniently adds a few scenes of Odissi dance to the script and effectively makes Rajani into a symbol of "authentic, educated India"[16] with a secure national/cultural identity. Thus when they first move to Johnson City Verghese talks about how he envies people like Rajani, who can always go back home to India which is always there for her. Rajani, conversely, talks about how limited her world is with only Verghese and the baby as her family in the United States. By contrast, Verghese can be at home wherever he goes. The couple is thus set to contrast with each other right from the beginning in the film in which cultural rootedness and "authenticity" are pitted against a kind of "flexible citizenship," in Aihwa Ong's phrase. And they are torn apart when Verghese's search for a sense of belonging to his own country through his medical profession threatens Rajani's sense of security. Later on in the film Nair uses Rajani's failed attempt at practicing Odissi dance in her house at Tennessee to highlight a sense of cultural uprooting. As Rajani explains to the inquiry from a fellow Indian shopper, who incidentally is played by Nair herself, the American town produces the wrong aura, making it hard to practice. Thus, dislocation severs her from her art and from her close connection with India. As with the emphasis on Verghese's African and South Asian past, Nair's rendition of Rajani's deep sense of dislocation has made her a more personal character than the somewhat flat character in the memoir.

In addition to individualizing her characters, Nair effectively uses the visual quality of cinema to bring her audience face to face with the fear of AIDS. The stunned faces of the medical team when they find out that the Code Blue patient they have helped to resurrect has AIDS vividly represent the intense fear associated with this disease. The sequence

---

[16] This is quoted from Patnaik's remark in a Screenindia.com article "From Odissi Dancer to Doctor's Wife," which introduces her in the role of Rajini in Nair's film.

depicting Verghese's "infection dream" in the film version also embodies Verghese's inner terror. Whereas in Verghese's text the infection dream recurs many times to haunt his waking and sleeping hours, the film only shows this dream sequence once. It also connects Vickie's heartbreaking experience of losing her husband, Clyde, one of Verghese's patients, to AIDS with Verghese's own imminent fear of being infected by the virus and his anxiety about being alienated from Rajini. Nair opens the sequence by showing Rajini dressed in bridal splendor and stabbing herself in the stomach with a branch of the swamp dogwood or *"hearts-a-bustin,"* presented by Vickie to Verghese when he pays her a visit at her trailer home.[17] The violent act that begins Verghese's nightmare underlines the association of blood with AIDS. When later in the dream sequence a nonchalant Rajini announces that Verghese has "got it now," his worst nightmare is confirmed: he has contracted AIDS and lost Rajini at the same time. As suggested in the memoir, in his effort to build his "own country" through his intimate connections with his patients, Verghese has lost his wife. Nair's film ends with a hope of new life for the couple; however, the marital stress is emphasized with a dramatic revision of how Verghese fails to be present when Rajini is in labor with their second child. This drama of absence stresses the point that Verghese's devotion to his patients has prevented him from being a responsible husband and family man, a point that is frequently deployed in the genre of medical drama, but which has a special inflection in this case. As Verghese confesses through voice-over, he fails to realize how much Rajini feels deserted while he is out there playing hero and that he has become "a stranger to his own family" in the process.

While Nair has added in distinct African and South Asian accents to the film, she also carefully places Verghese in relation to America. As Sau-ling Wong points out, "Since its birth as a political and social entity, it is safe to say, America has customarily defined its uniqueness in terms of the enhanced mobility it can offer: the opportunity to go where one wants, do what one wants, shape life anew" (119). Whereas Verghese

---

[17] In the memoir, Vickie introduces the floral plant to Verghese as a way to express her grief about the coming death of her husband and her state of being infected with HIV: "Oh yes, 'Hearts-a-bustin' It's also called 'swamp dogwood,' but I don't care for that much. 'Hearts-a-bustin': That's pretty much how I feel sometimes about what's happening to me" (336-337).

has risen up in the social ladder from a hospital orderly to the head of the infectious diseases division, with his motorbike and leather jacket, Verghese is visually presented as an American character on the road out of the discourse of mobility. In the film, Verghese is often seen paying home visits to his patients by riding on a motorbike. In fact, when he first reports to the medical center as the new director of the division of infectious diseases, Verghese is seen rushing to the clinic on his motorbike. The motorbike, in a way, replaces the image of the horse in a western on which the hero rides out into the sunset. By repeatedly showing Verghese as a biker, Nair visually emphasizes Verghese's integration into the American landscape and his constant movement at the same time. This paradox concerning Verghese's mobility nicely brings out his dilemma as a diasporic character. A brown hero riding out into the distance, he is visually incorporated into the landscape and yet in the end he always has to leave for somewhere else. Verghese thus embodies the clashes between a desire for belonging and an experience of the constant movement of a diasporic character. For Mira Nair, therefore, visualizing Abraham Verghese's life writing also allows her to present her own reflection on the constant tension between the desires for roots and routes in the South Asian diaspora.

Perhaps it would be useful to conclude with a brief note about the problem of representation itself. This analysis focuses on the ways in which Verghese's and Nair's texts navigate around the entanglement of the personal and the collective in life writing. In Lisa Diedrich's analysis of doctors' stories of AIDS, she takes up the patient's position and questions: "who gets to tell AIDS narratives?" (250); "Do these doctors' narratives occult their patients' lives? Are these representations, in effect, doctors' self-portraits in which the subjectivity of the patient is effaced? Is Verghese's position voyeuristic in relation to his patients' stories" (256)? Diedrich's questions about "the limits of representation" (256), it can be said, are also for us as readers of Verghese's memoir and as spectators of Nair's film. Does our visual pleasure at watching this medical drama, for instance, originate in a voyeuristic position of watching suffering at a safe distance? What is the ethical responsibility of writing/filming diseases, and by extension, reading/watching them as texts? At the same time, it is also imperative to remember that *My Own Country* appeared at a point when AIDS research was still not mature enough to provide a cure and AIDS education was still in its early stages. Both the literary and filmic texts, therefore, serve not only to introduce the personal life of a South Asian American doctor, but also to raise public awareness concerning the experience of AIDS patients and their families. Thus, the complex interweaving of the personal and the collective in this doctor's story continues beyond the ending and challenges our own consciousness as readers and spectators.[18]

Works Cited

Anbarasan, Ethirajan and Amy Otchet. "Mira Nair: An Eye for Paradox." http://www.unesco.org/courier/1998_11/uk/dires/tet1.htm. (Viewed on March 2, 2005).

Badt, Karin Luisa. "I Want My Films to Explode with Life: An Interview with Mira Nair." *Cineaste* XXX.1 (Winter 2004): 10-15.

Diedrich, Lisa. "AIDS and Its Treatments: Two Doctors' Narratives of Healing, Desire, and Belonging." *Journal of Medical Humanities* 26.4 (Winter 2005): 237-257.

Feng, Peter X. *Identities in Motion: Asian American Film and Video*. Durham, NC: Duke University Press, 2002.

Fischer, Michael. M. J. "Ethnicity and the Post-Modern Arts of Memory." *Writing Culture: The Poetics and Politics of Ethnography*. Ed. James Clifford and George E. Marcus. Berkeley, CA: University of California Press, 1986. 194-233.

"From Odissi Dancer to Doctor's Wife." *Screenindia.com*. http://www.screenindia.com/feb27/films3.htm (Viewed on March 2, 2005).

Laxmi, John. "The Delectable Doctor." *SAJA (South Asian Journalists Association)*. http://www.saja.org/verghese.html (Viewed on March 2, 2005).

Mehta, Binita. "Emigrants Twice Displaced: Race, Color, and Identity in Mira Nair's *Mississippi Masala*." *Between the Lines: South Asians and Postcoloniality*. Ed. Deepika Bahri and Mary Vasudeva. Philadelphia: Temple University Press, 1996. 185-203.

Nair, Mira. *Mississippi Masala*. SCS Films, 1991.

—. *Monsoon Wedding*. USA Films, 2001.

—. *My Own Country*. Showtime Networks, 1998.

---

[18] This paper is a partial result of a research project supported by National Science Council and National Chiao Tung University, Taiwan (NSC 94-2411-H-009-005; 95W811).

—. *The Namesake*. Fox Searchlight, 2006.

—. *The Perez Family*. Samuel Goldwyn, 1995.

—. *Salaam Bombay!* Cinecom, 1988.

—. *Vanity Fair*. Gramercy, 2004.

Naficy, Hamid. *An Accented Cinema: Exilic and Diasporic Filmmaking*. Princeton, NJ: Princeton University Press, 2001.

Ong, Aihwa. *Flexible Citizenship: The Cultural Logics of Transnationality*. Durham, NC: Duke University Press, 1999.

"Profile of a SAJAer: Abraham Verghese Distinguished Writer and Physician." *SAJA (South Asian Journalists Association)*. http://www.saja.org/verghese.html. (Viewed on March 2, 2005).

Quinby, Lee. "The Subject of Memoir: *The Woman Warrior's* Technology of Ideographic Selfhood." *De/Colonizing the Subject: The Politics of Gender in Women's Autobiography*. Eds. Sidonie Smith and Julia Watson. Minneapolis: University of Minnesota Press, 1992. 297-320.

Sanders, Julie. *Adaptation and Appropriation*. London: Routledge, 2006.

Smith, Sidonie, and Julia Watson, eds. "Introduction." *De/Colonizing the Subject: The Politics of Gender in Women's Autobiography*. Minneapolis: University of Minnesota Press, 1992. xiii-xxxi.

Srikanth, Rajini. "Ethic Outsider as the Ultimate Insider: The Paradox of Verghese's *My Own Country*." *MELUS* 29.3-4 (Fall/Winter 2004): 433-450.

Sontang, Susan. *Illness as Metaphor and AIDS and Its Metaphors*. New York: Doubleday, 1990.

Verghese, Abraham. *My Own Country: A Doctor's Story of A Town and Its People in the Age of AIDS*. New York: Simon and Schuster, 1994.

Wong, Sau-ling Cynthia. *Reading Asian American Literature: From Necessity to Extravagance*. Princeton, NJ: Princeton University Press, 1993.

Xing, J. *Asian America Through the Lens: History, Representations, and Identity*. Walnut Creek, CA: AltaMira Press, 1998.

Pin-chia Feng is Dean of Academic Affairs and Professor of the Department of Foreign Languages and Literatures, National Chiao Tung University, Taiwan. Her publications include *The Female Bildungsroman by Toni Morrison and Maxine Hong Kingston* and *En-Gendering Chinese Americas: Reading Chinese American Women Writers*.

Looking Back:
Diasporic Longing in *Citizen 13660* and *Persepolis*

Min Hyoung Song

Few tropes in contemporary theory are as familiar, or as vivid, as the one Louis Althusser conjures in "Ideology and Ideological State Apparatuses": a man is called from behind by the police, or by some similar figure of authority, and responds by turning around to look back. By doing so, the man recognizes immediately that the call is meant for him. As Judith Butler has pointed out, this figure of the man looking back is foundational to understanding the paradox of subjectivity, being at once "dominated by a power external to oneself" and "dependent upon that very power" to give meaning to "one's very formation as a subject" (1-2). Butler continues, "The form this power takes is relentlessly marked by a figure of turning, a turning back upon oneself or even a turning *on* oneself. This figure operates as part of the explanation of how a subject is produced, and so there is no subject, strictly speaking, who makes this turn. On the contrary, the turn appears to function as a tropological inauguration of the subject, a founding moment whose ontological status remains permanently uncertain" (3-4). In her meditations on these opening thoughts, Butler focuses on the call itself, an act which foregrounds language as speech. Language is where the "power external to oneself" is located, and as such makes the figural gesture of the body turning around to look behind the very moment at which, and the very trope for, the subject being called into being.

But what happens to this understanding of the gesture of looking back as a "tropological inauguration of the subject" when the conditions assumed by both Althusser and Butler can no longer be assumed? What happens, in other words, when the intimation of violence latent in this famous trope becomes more explicit? What does the looking back signify in such an altered context? If the turning is tropologically subject-making, almost by definition, what does it mean when a turn refuses the call of power rather than submits to it? What happens to the subject when the turning back gazes upon the abuses of the state, its regression from subjection to explicit oppression? My own understanding of the trope of looking back concentrates on the notion of a centralized state authority that lends credence to Althusser's trope of subject-making.

What seems clearly at stake in this trope is the power of the state, and its ability to penetrate into the psyche of the subject to the point where the subject depends wholly on it for its meaning as a subject. Indeed, the force of the police hail only remains implicit, and therefore ideological, when the state is confident in its ability to maintain order, when it assumes an unguarded relationship with its subjects so that being hailed by the police would not necessarily be a threatening gesture (even if threat is latent in the gesture), and when the subject's relation to the state is an unquestionably constitutive one. In what follows, I query the rich theoretical discussion surrounding the trope of looking back with questions of my own motivated by historical moments when the state is not so confident, and when the subject rather than being interpellated through ideology is oppressed by a brute exercise of state power. In short, I am interested in moments when the state undergoes a trans-formation in its strategies of governance and of producing national identity. At such moments, states may resort to oppression rather than subjection to maintain its power; the subject produced out of such a moment may often find him- or herself constituted as what falls outside the state's domain, a subject interpellated as what is actively excluded from the state's uncertain definition of itself at a moment of change, purification, and added valuation of conformity.

This topic has felt especially urgent to me in reading Miné Okubo's *Citizen 13660* side-by-side with Marjane Satrapi's *Persepolis* and *Persepolis 2*, especially at our shared present defined, as Rajini Srikanth succinctly puts it, by "tense geopolitics and interlinked economics" (1). A more unlikely pairing might be hard to imagine, so let me say something about what makes them different before proceeding to explain why they are so interesting to read next to each other. In addition to the disparity in chronology and geography that characterizes these two works, I especially want to call attention in the earlier sections of this essay to the ways in which each work marks itself off in relation to the respective nation's population. In short, Okubo is interested in a numerically small class of people whose differences from the rest of the United States are intensified as the Second World War catalyzes a change of govern-mentality at home while Satrapi is interested in making her experiences indicative of what is endured by the entire people of Iran as the shah is replaced by a supreme religious leader. Despite these differences, which lead to differences in narrative strategies, both illuminate—especially in their melding of prose narration with graphic depiction—the ways in which the trope of looking back during times of transition in state power gains a markedly different meaning from the one Althusser so famously described.

I.

Citizen 13660, published in 1946, was the first personal account of the Japanese American internment to have found a general audience. Each page contains a line drawing Okubo made while at Tanforan and Topaz, and a block of text that provides extremely factual exposition. *Citizen 13660* is thus unwilling to say more than is necessary. We learn little about the narrator's personal background, family life, or future beyond the camps. We are forced to read between the lines, or perhaps literally in the lines of her drawings, for meaning that goes beyond what is too plainly stated. In these ways, the qualities found in the text make the work emblematic of Nisei (second-generation Japanese American) women's autobiographies from the mid-twentieth century in general. As Traise Yamamoto has pointed out, "they are frustratingly *unauto-*biographical, not given to personal disclosure or passages of intimate self-reflection" (103). Such surface characteristics have exacerbated the tendency to treat these works as "sociological and/or historical documents" (104) and therefore not to extend to their first-person protagonists the full range of "discursive agency" (105). But what is the agency to which their writings might give witness? In the case of *Citizen 13660*, the response to this question seems most interestingly explored in the drawings themselves, and much less in the text, which seems intentionally self-effacing. The more the text feels unemotional, withdrawn, the product of a person hiding behind rhetorical distance to protect against the anger that still lingers against people of Japanese ancestry in mid-century America, the more the drawings spring to life, demand attention, seem ever more artful in the way they convey a rich range of emotional responses to being driven away from one's home, placed under armed guard, and penned into crude camps because of race.

In almost all of the drawings in this book, the narrator is prominently positioned in the foreground and she is mute. She therefore becomes a notable figure of witness who sees with her own eyes what she has committed to paper. Her position in the drawings also provides dual composition of prominent foreground and, another important feature of her drawings, a determined detailing of background that sweeps beyond the individual subject. The latter makes us aware at all times of the larger story that is taking place told through the many bodies that crowd the page and the specificity of the location that the drawings insist upon. As Elena Creef observes, the composition of Okubo's drawings makes "it virtually and visually impossible to forget the crowded conditions of the camps that were built to house ten-thousand Japanese American prisoners in one square mile" (83). In depicting the condition of the camps as one of constant bodily awareness, awareness that is of both one's own body and the many bodies of others confined to the same, and particular, fenced spaces, Okubo asks us to consider that she is not the only one looking, alive with a consciousness of the crowds that surrounds her, lips closed in grim determined silence. All the other figures in her drawings are similarly looking at each other, crowds that refuse to be undifferentiated even as their mouths remain tightly shut, not speaking either because they cannot or because they will not. The contrast between drawings and text is further reinforced in the drawings themselves as at once a visual awareness of bodies and a mute refusal to articulate this awareness in speech. This further demands the focusing of attention on the act of looking itself.

Deep into the narrative, when the narrator has already been at Topaz for some time, we are told that clothing ordered from the "Sears, Roebuck summer catalog" when they were all still at Tanforan have begun to arrive "with many substitutions" (152). These clothes help complement what the U.S. government has allotted them, primarily remnants of uniforms from the First World War. "Everyone was dressed alike," the narrator testifies, "because of the catalog orders and the G.I. clothes" (153). Above this simple sentence, the drawing reveals three women all wearing the same outfit, yet at the same time when we look at the drawing it is apparent that none of the women look alike. Their body shapes are different. In the middle foreground, there is a thin, older woman wearing eyeglasses. To her right, there is a younger woman with a round face staring down at her. On the other side of the page, there is the thick but trim figure of Okubo herself looking wearily at the round-faced woman. Behind Okubo there are two men, also apparently internees, one looking down at her and another, immediately behind and above her, with his back to everyone, including us. Together, the two men enact the hard work of seeing and, perhaps more difficult of all, refusing to see. This drawing as a whole, then, is a dynamic if static commentary on the official power of the state to claim that it cannot differentiate between any of these bodies, that they are indeed, at least from the state's perspective, all the same by reason of race. Looking but not speaking infuses the look itself with greater meaning and draws us, the viewer of this drawing, into an economy of sight that works within the official discourses of race and state security that has made looking alike a reason for internment.

On the one hand, this drawing is occasion for laughter as it reveals in its masked way how the official discourse of race fails to see what is obviously apparent to us when we look at these figures. On the other hand, the drawing—like the figures it portrays—remains mute, hiding behind a silent mask of humor a fierce but impotent indignation at the obvious that cannot be seen by the state because of its own willed blindness. Even if they see the differences that are so obvious they become humorous, they cannot comment on these differences and they must, as a result, through their silence, acquiesce to the official gaze that sees no difference between them. This is why the man with his back turned to us, a gesture of refusing to look, draws our attention in this drawing, since there is in this refusal a troubling ambivalence. Is this gesture a gesture of defiance, a refusal to participate in an economy of looking that must ignore what is obviously presented to view, or is it a gesture of further acquiescence, a participatory refusal that reenacts that state's unwillingness to see? We might pose a similar question to the others in this drawing: are they seeing the difference that seems so obvious to us or are they startled to find that everyone looks alike? To put this another way, are their looks registering the blatant oppression of a racial logic that has imprisoned them because they look too much alike to differentiate between loyal subject and saboteur or are their looks participating ideologically in this same racial logic, a form still of subjection despite the conditions in which they find themselves?

The difficulty of answering these questions, the ambiguity drama-tized by this drawing, suggests the vexed problem many Japanese Americans faced during the internment period. Do they go along with what is asked of them in the hopes that their condition will improve? Do they resist openly and risk giving up all that makes them who they are (as so many did at Tule Lake)? How can they express feelings of indig-nation, annoyance, anger, despair when to do so might not mean anything that might materially improve their conditions, but might cost them dearly? In addition to the compositional features of the drawings I have already highlighted, we can note the ways in which human figures are drawn, almost as if in response to the problems they have no simple way of resolving. There are a few bold dark lines that define the perimeters of an individual. This individuality, however, is undercut by the rendering of patterns on cloths of various kinds. These patterns are uniform and vertical, never showing any wrinkle or deformity. This perhaps most obviously suggests a comment on the ways in which bod-ies are covered over by uniform expectations, an official discourse that reduces individual characteristics to a pattern that covers everything. But another way to think about the use of patterns in these drawings is to think of them as suggesting contiguity between bodies, the ways in which the internees are connected by their most elemental needs, such as for warmth, for protection from wind, for modesty. There is also a wide variety of patterns in these drawings, which further emphasizes a kind of heterogeneity in the population that the state, in putting them in camps, fails to see. Thus, the patterns might point to a particularly interesting duality of heterogeneous designs and uniform placement that captures the willed blindness of state knowledge to the complexity of the bodies it has consigned to imprisonment.

Other parts of the internees' bodies—hands and faces in particular—add greater nuance to what their forms convey. The hands are almost always prominently on display, indicating their importance as a signifier of agency, since hands are important for a subject's ability to manipulate one's environment. At the same time, the hands are drawn curved, almost shapeless at times, and easily the most vulnerable aspect of any person's body, suggesting how their agency is under a constant and intense threat that seems literally to leave their hands shriveled, weak, and fatigued. The faces emphasize this point further in their detailed expressiveness, the choppy thin lines cross-hatched against the bold contours of their body's outline to render detailed nuances of heavy-set eyes, glaring intelligence, and worried wrinkles almost permanently etched into place. Anger, resentment, resignation, hunger, annoyance, and so forth are all registered in this way on their faces, gesturing toward the range of unspoken emotional experiences that accompany the daily indignities of camp life.

II.

The ambiguity, the silences, the looks full of barely suppressed feelings found in such abundance in Okubo's drawings are also apparent in *Persepolis* and *Persepolis 2*, but the latter are more explicit about where the narrator's agency is located. They insist that such agency continues to exist in the Iranian population at large, even if not ideally, despite a regime that seeks to crush it into a pietistic conformity: "The more time passed, the more I became conscious of the contrast between the official representation of my country and the real life of the people, the one that went on behind the walls. Our behavior in public and our behavior in private were polar opposites... This disparity made us schizophrenic" (*Persepolis 2*, 150-151). While this passage attests to the outward conformity demanded by the state, one worn like a rigid mask, there is no question of any kind of rhetorical masking. Unlike the drawings in *Citizen 13660*, in other words, there is no need for subtle ironies, reading between the lines, disjunction between the coolness of the text and the fierce indignation of the drawings since what is at stake is not the feelings of a minority population at odds with a dominant race but a split between the "real life of the people" and the state that has taken them hostage in its pursuit of an alien national ideal. There is, therefore, no question about what kind of document Satrapi's paired volumes are. They are an emphatic assertion of subjective will in the face of deepening state oppression, and as such a coordinated contestation between drawings and text against an emergent nation-state that has secured its power on the restriction of women and their bodies.

Hence, compared to *Citizen 13660*, *Persepolis* and *Persepolis 2* are much more intimate portraits of a childhood and young adulthood spent in the shadow of the Iranian revolution and the subsequent protracted war with Iraq, the moral meaning of which and the righteous indignation they engender—both against the current state in power and the foreign powers whose self-interested meddling has enabled such a state to come into power—are never in dispute. Such a comparison, therefore, asks us to read Satrapi's paired texts as inhabiting an in-between space that is full of surprising clarity and sharpness of vision. Even as individual subjects must dissimulate and lie to protect their private selves against the fierce encroachments of the state, and even as the narrator's eventual dislocation and exile in Austria and later France attests to the difficulties of engaging in such a protracted war of position, the private self of the narrator as it blooms into maturity and seeks to find more liberated expression abroad is one of privileged insight. While there is psychic pain in physical dislocation, for instance, there is also—as Amy Malek explains in her superb essay—the "position of liminality" which "allows [Satrapi] to use a third space position from which to complete her cultural translation, in which she addresses issues of identity, exile, and return" (369). The "third space" carved out by Satrapi's graphic memoir, in short, is vested with a great deal of moral authority and privileged understanding. The physical condition of exile has not meant for Satrapi an undermining of her right to speak about conditions in her homeland. Rather, such removal enables her work to fulfill "a special potential": "she has questioned authorities and identities, such as the negative images of Iran that have often been incorporated into second-generation diaspora collective consciousness, while creating via exile culture new spaces and creative frontiers from which to examine the exilic condition" (Malek 379).

In keeping with the privileged stance the books will eventually find for themselves as they become translated into multiple languages and celebrated by numerous reviewers, the drawings announce the author's earnest determination to assert a subjectivity besieged by a state in violent change, a state seeking to purify its rule at home while maintaining isolation from the impurities of the world beyond. Each drawing is encased in a panel with ruler-strait borders and the meaningfulness of what the drawing is meant to illustrate seems accentuated by the black-and-white coloring. No shades of grey are here, obviously, but because the drawings are meant to look like ink blocks, there are also many moments when black is the background and white the foreground. In this way, the drawings gesture to a world where everything is at once black and white, and simultaneously dueling in moral absolutes: what is claimed by one party as right and wrong is refuted by another as being exactly opposite to the truth. The arbitrariness of absolutist moral pronouncements is allegorized in the first few pages of *Persepolis*. The narrator tells us: "in 1979, we were in a French non-religious school. Where boys and girls were together. And then suddenly in 1980... We found ourselves veiled and separated from our friends" (4). Just like that, what was once perfectly acceptable (co-education) has become morally reprehensible.

The reversals of moral absolutism, *of course*, should not lead us to believe that Satrapi is somehow a relativist. From her anger at her parents for not being able to live up to their secular ideals of class-leveling and democracy to the scorn she heaps on those who gain social privilege by donning their new piety like a robe they can put on at will, it is obvious throughout the narrative that Satrapi is committed to a consistent political ideal. This ideal is inspired by Marxism, mediated through a social liberalism, and founded on a Persian tradition of cultural achievement that is explicitly contrasted (even by the title of the two volumes and by the style of the drawings that is reminiscent of ancient Persian art) against the relatively late introduction of Shia Islamic beliefs. While excess, especially when it leads to selfish behavior, is criticized at some length in *Persepolis 2*, on the whole Satrapi welcomes sexual experimentation and spurns religious proscriptions on individual liberty, explicitly because these embrace the liberalism that the state abhors. As she explains in the first volume, "In spite of all the dangers, the parties went on. 'Without them it wouldn't be psychologically bearable,' some said" (106). In the second volume, Satrapi is much more explicit that such prohibited behavior has become in a highly oppressive environment a form of resistance that was also constitutive of their personhoods: "It's only natural! When we're afraid, we lose all sense of analysis and reflection. Our fear paralyzes us. Besides, fear has always been the driving force behind all dictator's repression. Showing your hair or putting on makeup became acts of rebellion" (150-151). What I want to call attention to in quoting these two examples is the ways in which they shore up an ideal of subjectivity that is whole, that is consistent between public and private, that reaffirms something morally lucid that has been betrayed by an oppressive state ruling with a shameless hypocrisy. If, as Rocío G. Davis claims, "Marji's story is one of contradictions, of a child finding herself between cultural, political, religious, linguistic, and social demands and impositions" (273), such contradictions are largely traceable to the state's heavy-handed use of power. This literally forces an unhealthy splitting of the subject between what is professed in public and what is lived as an open secret in private. The drama of Satrapi's narrative, then, is the refusal to wear the masks, often accompanied by grave dangers and severe punishments, that the state would have them wear.

No wonder that in bringing this drama to life in her work, Satrapi refuses a modernist subtlety that would feel too much like the games of truth she feels compelled to play in Iran. Unlike *Citizen 13660*, Satrapi freely expresses as a narrative strategy tailored to the specificity of her historical situation a prescriptive moral didacticism in her narrator's maturity into young womanhood. In *Persepolis 2*, Satrapi recalls being accosted by Guardians of the Revolution who might take her away for wearing lipstick in public. In a panic, she accuses a man who happens to be sitting near her on some steps of saying something indecent to her. Satrapi later recounts this story to her grandmother to brag about her quick thinking, but instead of being praised she is admonished. Her grandmother tells her, "I think you're a selfish bitch! That's what I think!!!... What have I taught you? Hunh? 'Integrity'!!! Does this word mean nothing to you?" (137). The struggle of the narrator is not so much to find a way to express an anger that circumstances demand be stifled as it is to maintain a consistency of moral behavior, an "integrity," against the exhaustion of an everyday revolt against an oppressive state power. This struggle emerges as a synecdoche of the wider struggle found in the "real life of the people," something Okubo, stuck in a different kind of in-between space defined by the overlapping of oppression and subjection and by the hyper-awareness of her marginality in American society, cannot claim.

III.

Despite the obvious differences between *Citizen 13660* and the two-volume *Perspolis*, they nonetheless share a common concern about the subject's relation to a state that feels at once under attack by a formidable foe from without its borders and at risk of dangers emanating from within its population. If Althusser sought to understand how subjectivity is formed through an ideological, as much as material, connection to the state, then Okubo and Satrapi both concern themselves with how subjectivity responds to a change in state governance brought about by a rupturing historical event. In Okubo, it is the Second World War, and more explicitly the way in which Pearl Harbor suddenly rendered West Coast Japanese Americans alien enemies. Just after the attack, Okubo recalls: "The people looked at all of us, both citizens and aliens, with suspicion and mistrust" (12). The accompanying drawing shows the narrator riding a bus. She is at the center of the page. All the other passengers are bodily turned toward her, and the few faces we see are wearing sharp disapproving frowns. We see them in this pose from outside the bus, through the bar that runs horizontally across their figures and the frame of the window studded with rivets, further emphasizing the ways in which the narrator is imprisoned by these looks. In Satrapi, it is the overthrow of the shah and the ways in which the rise of an Islamic Republic made secular women abruptly suspect. To emphasize this point, *Persepolis* begins with a self-portrait of a young Satrapi wearing a veil and a black dress accompanied by the explanation: "In 1979 a revolution took place. It was later called 'the Islamic Revolution.' Then came 1980: the year it became obligatory to wear the veil at school" (3). On the next page, there is a drawing of a bearded man in what looks like a military uniform standing between two doors: through one, boys are shown entering, and, through the other, girls (all wearing veils, of course).

Beyond the surface similarity, it is also worth noting the ways in which the drawing of Okubo on the bus and Satrapi entering a separate doorway both emphasize looking, whether it is other passengers or a figure of repressive authority. In both cases, the eyes look juridically, judging against some newly dominant moral code about what presentations of bodies are acceptable and unacceptable. Such bodies, as the ones being looked at in these examples, need to be covered or removed physically. This leads to another reason why I want to read Okubo's and Satrapi's works side-by-side. They are both what are called today graphic novels.[1] That is, their narratives take place in the visual play between drawings and text. The experience of reading a graphic novel thus entails a greater self-awareness of the act of looking. Davis, again, writes, "Graphic narratives contain more gaps than a traditional auto-biography —even those written in as separate stories—and we must therefore read the design and intention behind the textual destabiliza-tions and the cultural implications of such fragmentation" (270). More than in prose narratives, then, graphic novels require the reader to consider what the relationship is between a given image and the words that accompany them. The form of the graphic novel, to put this another way, requires us to consider more self-consciously what the relationship is between the image and its surrounding discourse, a lingering over each page that deepens meaning rather than linearly presents it. In a different but still relevant context, Laura Junka has recently asked in a photo-essay about Palestinians going to the beach in Gaza, "if represen-tation is... always conditioned by discourses against which utterances are interpreted and given meaning, how is it possible to move beyond this discursive poverty?" (349-50). This is the question, it seems to me, that both Okubo and Satrapi demands us to consider in the way they tell their life stories through the form of the graphic novel. Both authors eloquently call attention to the "discursive poverty" surrounding the historical experiences they are trying to represent through this form.

In *Citizen 13660*, Okubo attempts to capture what life was like at Topaz by depicting different aspects of their lives there. In most of these drawings, as has already be pointed out, Okubo represents herself somewhere in the drawing, usually in the foreground and often facing to her left. In the middle ground, there are almost always numerous bodies crowding against each other and getting in each others' way; Okubo herself is usually a part of this crowd. In the background, there is

---

[1] Graphic novels have received a great deal of attention in the U.S. press as recent works continue to demonstrate the range of expression of which this form is capable, and while more popular fare have become adapted into major motion pictures. For popular press coverage, see Foroohar, Lanham, Schkel-dahl. It is customary to trace the flowering of this form to the awarding of a special Pulitzer Prize to Art Spiegelman for his two-volume *Maus*, and on several occasions Satrapi points to these latter works as her inspiration. See O'Connor, Guthmann, Sante, Jones.

usually some distant buildings or landscape that reminds us of where these bodies are located. But in one drawing, there is a man in the foreground and identical-looking buildings in the background. In the middle, there is one lone figure suggesting the starkness of the landscape. The absence of bodies usually found in her drawings is striking, almost unnerving, and the look in the man's eyes (his face is covered by his right hand and a hat is pulled way down) is expressive of fear, confusion, and shock. The accompanying text merely says, "All residential blocks looked alike; people were lost all the time" (136).

Near the end of *Persepolis*, after the Iran-Iraq War has begun and Tehran finds itself the target of massive aerial bombing, a building near Satrapi's home is destroyed. Inside, there lived a childhood friend who could not get out in time. As the young Satrapi approaches the ruined building, she sees in the rubble a shining object that looks like her friend's bracelet. On closer inspection, it turns out to be the bracelet, but the bracelet is still attached to something. And, just as the narration is about to tell us what we know but don't want to hear—the identification of the "something" that the bracelet is still attached to—the drawings close in on Satrapi's face, first with mouth covered and eyes wide open in horror, each panel slowing down the eventual revelation. The head is shown bowed and covered in grief. The last panel is black. Underneath, there are the words: "No scream in the world could have relieved my suffering and my anger" (142).

In both of these examples, the focus of the drawings is on what is missing, the absence that refuses to be represented in language. At the same time, even as the drawing themselves refuse to represent, the text ironically speaks about what it is that's missing in the drawings. This reverses the usual relationship between drawings and text, as the former are almost always the most expressive in both works. By reversing an expected relationship, these examples call attention to the ways in which what can be articulated in language and what can be graphically depicted are often at odds with each other, the two not working to weave greater nuanced meaning but often quite the reverse: the stripping of discourse into something crude, demeaning, and ugly, a blunt instrument for making the other into the Other (with a capital O).

If there is thus a counter-discursive richness in these works, one which is drawn out by the play between graphic images and prose narration, what should we make of the fact that both *Citizen 13660* and *Persepolis* end on almost exactly the same graphic trope? In the former, the final drawing shows the narrator looking backward as she enters the front of a bus that will take her away from Topaz. The bus is rendered in little detail. The composition of the picture contains the same features that all the other drawings in the book share, but with the exception of the narrator's face turned back, pointing to the left and over the shoulder (instead of forward and to the right), and toward a crowd that is now firmly held back by a low gate (rather than being depicted as part of the crowd). Hence, even as the text faces forward—"There was only the desert now. My thoughts shifted from the past to the future" (209)— the drawing compels us to remain fixed by a backward looking gaze, to consider the vivid but now distant image of human figures, old and very young, penned behind fence and barbed wire, guards standing on duty in a gatehouse determining who may stay and who may go. In the further distance, the barracks continue to stand in their uniform regularity, the power of the state summarily to imprison and hold without trial a whole people unrestrained but not forgotten.

Similarly, on the last page of *Persepolis*, the narrator is boarding a plane that will carry her to Austria and presumably to greater freedom than the one she has enjoyed in Tehran. Her parents have decided that given the way she has been raised, she is likely to endanger herself too much if she remains. At the airport she turns around to face the family she is leaving behind: "I couldn't just go. I turned around to see them one last time. It would have been better to just go" (153). Next to these final words is a picture of the narrator's father, his face and torso cast in black shadow, holding her mother in his arm. The mother is supine, limp, and practically unconscious. Her face is a rictus of sorrow. Like Okubo's narrator, the young Satrapi is transfixed by the image, her body turned a complete one-hundred-eighty-degrees, her hands pressed flat against the glass partition that divides parents from departee.

IV.

Whatever prior difficulties I might have had with Althusser's trope of subject-making have been amplified by these twin endings. What does the looking back signify here? What hailing are they responding to? I am tempted to argue that there is another story of looking back that might be more applicable than the one Althusser tells. I am thinking of the story of Lot's wife, a story with which Christians, Jews, and Muslims will be familiar. Selected by God as the only bloodline worth saving from His wrath against the wickedness of Sodom and Gommorah—the Christian version of this story affirms—the patriarch Lot, his wife, and two daughters are guided by two angels to safety with strict instructions not to look back. Lot's sons-in-laws do not go with them because they think it impossible that their city will be destroyed. Along the way to safety, however, unable to resist, Lot's wife does what is forbidden. The Bible is terse: "But Lot's wife looked back, and she became a pillar of salt" (Genesis 19:26). The simplicity of the punishment suggests the absoluteness of the authority she has defied. God's will, or the police hail as expression of authority (and whose authority is more to be re-spected than God's?), demands she looks resolutely forward, to the future, to the prospect of a new life and the regeneration of a male line undone by the refusal of Lot's son-in-laws to flee with them, to the rejection of all that she and her family leave behind, a city of corruption that has nothing to offer in exchange for redemption.

The caution this story dramatizes seems interesting to consider (even as I wish to emphasize that there is no moral corollary between the city Lot's family leaves behind and the one Satrapi leaves). Do not look back. Think only of the future. Accept one's permanent separation from a country of origin, almost as if that country no longer exists—which probably it doesn't since the country that is left behind will inevitably be different from the country that one can return to. But Lot's wife cannot help herself. She looks back. And in looking back, she becomes stuck in place, turned literally into a substance which can bear no life, and her subjectivity is thus stripped from her completely. The act of looking back in this instance turns out to have the exact opposite effect of the looking back in Althusser's allegory. Rather than accepting power's call, it is a gesture of defiance, the refusal to heed the call of power. Rather than being interpellated as a subject, the act of looking back turns the subject into a thing, the very most antithesis of subjecthood imaginable. By looking back and answering a mysterious call—perhaps out of sentimental attachment? curiosity? a desire for the familiar in the midst of embarking upon the uncertain?—the subject undoes herself.

Does the transformation of Lot's wife as a subject into a thing provide some clues as to how to interpret the looks that end both *Citizen 13660* and *Persepolis*? I wish to say it does, at least to the point that it highlights the ambivalence of the scene that ends both books, an ambivalence that Althusser's allegory of subject-making has no room for. There is no going back, but there is little to look forward to. In such a situation, our subjectivities are paralyzed, unsure of what powers beacon us and what our attachment to others mean. The looking back in this instance dramatizes the predicament of the subject without a state—or, better still, the subject who has been betrayed by a state seeking to found itself more securely at a moment of danger on the bodies of those it does not care to accommodate. At the risk of undoing oneself, the diasporic who refuses the call of power and looks back at what has been left behind bears witness to what should have never been in the first place. In doing so, such a diasporic expresses a longing for what no longer exists, a form of nostalgia, and a desire to think anew relations of power that do not have to revert almost by default to oppression when the state's sovereignty is endangered. The latter is more than a form of nostalgia because it dares to wish something better for the future.[2]

Works Cited

Althusser, Louis. *Lenin and Philosophy and Other Essays*. Trans. Ben Brewster. New York: Monthly Review Press, 1971.

Butler, Judith. *Psychic Life of Power: Theories in Subjection*. Stanford, CA: Stanford University Press, 1997.

Creef, Elena Tajima. *Imaging Japanese America: The Visual Construction of Citizenship, Nation, and the Body*. New York: New York University Press, 2004.

Davis, Rocío G. "A Graphic Self: Comics as Autobiography in Marjane Satrapi's *Persepolis*." *Prose Studies* 27.3 (2005): 264-279.

Foroohar, Rana. "Comic Relief." *Newsweek* (August 22, 2005): 58.

Guthmann, Edward. "Weed, Sex, Paranoia—Iranian Graphic Novelist Marjane Satrapi Lets It All out in *Persepolis* Sequel." *San Francisco Chronicle* (October 2, 2004): sec. E: 1.

Jones, Vanessa. "A Life in Graphic Detail: Iranian Exile's Memoirs Draw Readers into Her Experience." *Boston Globe* (October 4, 2004): B8.

---

    [2] I thank Patricia P. Chu for her careful reading of this essay, and her many thoughtful comments.

Junka, Laura. "Camping in the Third Space: Agency, Representation, and the Politics of Gaza Beach." *Public Culture* 18.2 (2006): 348-360.

Lanham, Fritz. "From Pulp to Pulitzer; How the Underground Comic Finds Its Way to the Mainstream." *The Houston Chronicle* (August 29, 2004): 6.

Malek, Amy. "Memoir as Iranian Exile Cultural Production: A Case Study of Marjane Satrapi's *Persepolis Series*." *Iranian Studies* 39.3 (2006): 353-380.

O'Connor, Anne-Marie. "Unveiled, Unvarnished; in Marjane Satrapi's Graphic Novels, Stereotypes Unravel." *Los Angeles Times* (November 20, 2005): sec. E: 1.

Okubo, Miné. *Citizen 13660*. 1946. Seattle: University of Washington Press, 1983.

Sante, Luc. "She Can't Go Home Again." *New York Times* (August 22, 2004): sec. 7: 7.

Satrapi, Marjane. *Persepolis 2: The Story of a Return*. Trans. unknown. New York: Pantheon-Random House, 2004.

—. *Persepolis: The Story of a Childhood*. Trans. unknown. New York: Pantheon-Random House, 2003.

Schjeldahl, Peter. "Words and Pictures: Graphic Novels Come of Age." *The New Yorker* (October 17, 2005): 162-168.

Spiegelman, Art. *Maus: A Survivor's Tale. My Father Bleeds History*. New York: Pantheon-Random House, 1973.

—. *Maus 2: A Survivor's Tale. And Here My Troubles Begin*. New York: Pantheon-Random House, 1986.

Srikanth, Rajini. *The World Next Door: South Asian American Literature and the Idea of America*. Philadelphia: Temple University Press, 2004.

Yamamoto, Traise. *Masking Selves, Making Subjects: Japanese American Women, Identity, and the Body*. Berkeley, CA: University of California Press, 1999.

Min Hyoung Song is an Associate Professor of English at Boston College. He is the author of *Strange Future: Pessimism and the 1992 Los Angeles Riots* and the co-editor of *Asian American Studies: A Reader*.

Reconstructing the Woman behind the Photograph: Denise Chong's *The Girl in the Picture*

Eleanor Ty

> "what unrealized possibilities lie unnoticed behind the silence of women's lives in the outback of history, biography, and memoir, the standard records of the past?" (Lyndall Gordon, "Women's Lives: The Unmapped Country")

Denise Chong's biographical account of Phan Ti Kim Phuc, the South Vietnamese girl whose picture captured the world's attention in 1972, is a work of creative non-fiction, a term which also best describes her first bestselling book, *The Concubine's Children.* The book, a project suggested by two editors from Penguin Canada, is constructed from interviews with the subject, Kim Phuc, her family members, reporters who covered the Vietnam War some twenty-five years ago, and from newspapers, books, and film sources. While the book is classified as a biography, it provides a good illustration of a number of problems that relate to writing lives of women who are not considered "great" in the traditional sense. It reveals the tightly woven intersection of biography, politics, and history, the fluidity of global subjects in an age of transnational crossings at the same time as it raises questions about competing discursive forms of image and text in contemporary society. My paper looks at these issues, and explores the way *The Girl in the Picture* exceeds its biographical framework to become a kind of immigrant narrative, a contemporary hagiography, a form of trauma narrative, a disability narrative, and an elegy for a generation of Vietnamese people caught in perpetual warfare.

Kim Phuc running away from the napalm bomb, stripped of her clothing, crying naked and in pain is more than an image; it is emblematic of the rest of this woman's life, and, in some ways, the generation of Vietnamese people who later became known as "boat people." I suggest that Kim Phuc has been and is continually stripped, and continually has to run away—from Communist propaganda, from reporters, from well-meaning charitable folks, from politics, and from curious readers like ourselves. She was a victim of the war, but is also trapped incessantly as an object of scrutiny, and by the master trope of victimhood that her story necessarily evokes. Ira Bruce Nadel writes that "for the biographer the attempt to unify the life becomes a quest for metaphor which has a dual meaning: metaphor simultaneously acts as the guiding or controlling trope of the subject's life while also embodying or projecting the biographer's conception of that life" (158). In order for Chong's narrative to make sense to Western audiences, in order for the biographical account of an unknown Vietnamese girl to capture her readers' sympathies, she had to use this familiar trope of the victim to frame the story. Yet, the use of this trope reveals the ways in which women, particularly ethnic or racial others, are still circumscribed by Western notions of subjectivity, delimited by the gaze of Western culture, and caught by the problematic myth of the white capitalist knight who comes to rescue yellow women.[1]

Denise Chong's Foreword suggests the incompleteness of photographs as a reason for her to write the book: "And so came a chance, by way of this book, and with the added clarity of time, to revisit through the lens of her life what the war was for an ordinary peasant in South Vietnam and what the end of it wrought, *and* to examine the impact of the picture on her life" (xvi). For Chong, words and narratives are necessary supplements to the image. This view echoes that of Susan Sontag, who believes "that the photograph cannot by itself provide an interpretation, that we need captions and written analysis to supplement the discrete and punctual image, which can only affect us and never offer a full understanding of what we see" (paraphrased by Butler 823). However, in contemporary society, images are no longer supplementary to narrative; they frequently become the thing itself. As the photograph is not posed, but rather un-staged or "natural," the picture tends to be viewed as an eyewitness account and is taken to be more reliable than verbal accounts and narratives of the same event. Sontag remarks, "Their credentials of objectivity were in-built. Yet they always had, necessarily, a point of view" (*Regarding the Pain* 26). The photograph has been misinterpreted, adapted and juxtaposed with others, and even misused. It has provided Western viewers with the kind of spectacle that

---

[1] Here I am deliberately echoing Gayatri Spivak's "White men are saving brown women from brown men" in "Can the Subaltern Speak?"

is familiar to us: the female body as object of the gaze, and Third World suffering as a display or show.

Part of the problem comes from the visuality of Vietnam. For Euro-American culture after the 1970s, Vietnam has become more than a country or a location in Southeast Asia. It has acquired a pseudo-mythic status. As Trinh T. Minh-Ha notes, "Vietnam as spectacle remains passionately an owned territory ... Every spectator owns a Vietnam of his or her own" (101, 99). Similarly, film scholar Michael Anderegg says, "the Vietnam War was the most visually represented war in history, existing, to a great degree, as moving image, as the site of a specific and complex iconic cluster. As even the novels and memoirs insist, the Vietnam War was itself a movie. Certainly, the war became a television event, a tragic serial drama stretched over thousands of nights in the American consciousness" (2). Tony Williams, who has surveyed Holly-wood Vietnam films of the 1970s and 1980s, notes that "all Vietnam films attempt to impose some form of narrative order upon a conflict that refuses, both historically and fictionally, any form of convenient definition... Many films tend conveniently to focus upon a predomi-nantly individualized personal tragedy or adolescent bildungsroman" (116, 118). Rather than "accurate depictions of the broad social and historical picture, they focus instead on fantastic displacements," and involve familiar patterns of anachronistic cultural myths and narratives" (Williams 118). These narratives "allow no complexity, only an abstract ahistorical interplay of Manichaean opposites. The enemy now becomes a symbolic reincarnation of those alien nineteenth-century blacks, Native Americans, and women. They exhibit traits of irrationality, hys-teria, and madness, as opposed to those strong virile heroes who will restore American supremacy" (Williams 120). The women in films such as *Rambo*, *Missing in Action*, and their sequels are problematically represented. They are uses mainly as sexual lure, seen as villains, and those who violate their assigned patriarchal roles are recuperated only by fatherly intervention (Williams 127). These are some of the challenges confronting Chong as she attempts to supplement the picture with her narrative.

Another problem facing Chong as she embarked on this project was the ubiquity of this particular photograph. The picture had become a kind of iconic photograph representing trauma over the last thirty years. Most recently, it was used after the attack on the World Trade Center by a British newspaper, *The Mirror*, which juxtaposed "the famous photo of Kim Phuc with another woman, who appears to be Asian, escaping from the burning towers, covered in dust" (Miller 278). Before that, it had been reprinted in an article "reporting on the plight of the 'terrified Catholic schoolgirls' in Belfast, connecting their picture with those of Kim and the little boy from the Warsaw ghetto with his hands in the air, as well as the baby being carried out of the Oklahoma bombing and the father trying to protect his son during the Intifada" (Miller 279). Kim Phuc, the child in the picture, becomes symbolic of the assault on the innocent, the brutality of war or terrorism or horror. In media and visual history, the specific identity of Kim Phuc is less important than what she stands for: the victim of senseless violence, the horror of twentieth-century weapons, and the apparent casualness of the military's attitude toward suffering. The picture is not always Kim Phuc's story; it has become an every child story. In a similar manner, the real Vietnam is of no interest to Americans: Trinh says, "For general Western spectatorship, Vietnam does not exist outside of the war. And she no longer exists since the war has ended, except as a name, an exemplary model of revolution, or a nostalgic cult object for those who, while admiring unconditionally the revolution, do not seem to take any genuine, sustained interest in the troubled reality of Vietnam in her social and cultural autonomy. The more Vietnam is mystified, the more invisible she becomes" (100).

Denise Chong's wish to tell or reconstruct the full story about the "girl in the picture," as she did with the story of her grandmother from China, who became a teahouse waitress in Canada, is thus full of challenges. She has to write about someone who was, at one point, highly visible, yet who does not conform, to the trajectory or *Bildung* of a traditional hero. She has to counter prevalent images of the Third World and Vietnam War found in film and popular media; and yet avoid the sentimentality and pity of a World Vision appeal. In her biography, she uses some of the same techniques she employed successfully in *The Concubine's Children*: the even-handed and un-exotic account of her subject's life and work; resisting the sensationalizing of the woman's body—the prostitute's body in *Concubine's Children*, and here, the disabled body of Kim Phuc; breaking down the boundaries between private and the public in order for readers to see a nuanced historicized perspective.[2] The obstacles to her revealing the "truth" in this case are many and somewhat different. Unlike her grandmother, Meiying, Kim Phuc is a public figure whose story is known to the West. Vietnam and the Vietnam War have been written about, filmed, and mythologized. While Denise Chong can claim to have an insider's knowledge of her grandmother's story, a story which she partly heard from her mother, she cannot claim to be a "native informant" in Kim Phuc's case. Though Chong and Phuc are both Asian, they are from vastly different backgrounds. Chong's information about Vietnam and Vietnamese culture and traditions has been gleaned from research and in some instances may be erroneous.[3] For Chong, the biography of Kim Phuc is a work which entailed a transnational and global effort, as she writes in her Foreword that she conducted interviews and did research in Vietnam, in the U.S., in Cuba, and in Canada (xvii, 372-373).

Chong's biography performs a reversal of an Asian woman's paradoxical invisibility, as she revisits scenes, people from the 1970s, and introduces the story of Kim Phuc to a generation of readers who may

---

[2] See my chapter "Writing Historiographic Autoethnography: Denise Chong's *The Concubine's Children*" in *Politics of the Visible* for a discussion of Chong's autobiography.

[3] Trung Tam in the *Vietnamese Bulletin vietnamien*, writes, "Since this book is about an incident in history, some historical comments were inevitable. It is here that the readers are cautioned about some of the author's views on some events. For example, she believed that the Ngo Dinh Diem's regime was brought down in 1963 because—inter alia—of its inept handling of the Buddhist crisis. Nowadays, nearly everybody knows that the CIA was behind the coup because Diem refused to submit to the American will. Also, it is no longer a secret that the so-called 'Liberation Front of South Vietnam' was nothing but a farce! The armed resistance movement in the South would have never come into being in 1960 without active orders and support from Hanoi. In addition, it is unfair to criticize the Armed Forces of South Vietnam for lack of fighting will. How can one talk about will when all important strategic and even some tactical decisions (like the air support in this incident) were made by the Americans?"

not have heard of her before.[4] In her book which is subtitled, *The Story of Kim Phuc, the Photograph, and the Vietnam War,* she generates interest not only in Phuc, but in the Vietnamese people, their daily lives, their ways of worship, their food and family life by giving details and textures of everyday life. By resituating Kim in the specificities of history, in South Vietnamese culture, politics, and religion, Chong gives voice and sub-jectivity to Kim Phuc, who had largely become as still and silent as her photograph, in spite of her apparent public presence. Mary Evans suggests that "the reclamation of the past by those outside the circle of the great and good has been one of the more striking features of the cultural history of the twentieth century. That reclamation is, of course, ideally not just a voyage back into the history of a particularly group, but equally, a reclamation of the present. Whatever we may wish to say about the past, it cannot be relieved, whereas the reinterpretation of history, the recognition of marginal, disenfranchised and powerless groups can serve to empower in the present" (9-10). *The Girl in the Picture* then reclaims both our understanding of the past and also the situation of Vietnam in the present for the present generation of readers.

Chong begins her story by presenting details of Phuc's parents' and grandparents' lives before the bombing. Her technique follows Samuel Johnson's admonition that "the business of the biographer is often to pass slightly over those performances and incidents, which produce vulgar greatness, to lead the thoughts into domestic privacies, and dis-play the minute details of daily life, where exterior appendages are cast aside, and men excel each other only by prudence and by virtue" (2739). Johnson encourages biographers to pay attention the "many invisible circumstances" which he felt were "more important than public occur-rences" (2739). The private occurrences include Grandfather Kiem's way of worship, his strong allegiance to his family and the Caodai religion, a combination of Taoism, Buddhism and Confucianism, as well as Christianity. Chong tells us of Grandfather Kiem's "presiding over weddings and funerals and mediating local disputes," and his donation of one-third of his land "for a temple in Trang Bang" (15). He had a big house with seven entrances built for his family. This information about

---

[4] I discuss Asian people's visibility and invisibility in North America in *Politics of the Visible.*

the spiritual life of Phuc's grandparents, as well as the economic pros-
perity of Phuc's parents, present a different perspective on Phuc. Instead
of simply seeing Phuc, an Asian woman, in a desolate country road
running like a homeless refugee, Chong's details give us a semblance of
a "normal" and even semi-prosperous world of South Vietnam before it
was hit by the napalm bomb.

Other details Chong includes in her book include seemingly unre-
lated information about the rituals of daily life of Phuc's extended
family. In particular, Chong focuses on the minutiae of women's lives
which, though insignificant to the war or the event of the bombing,
make the Vietnamese culture come alive for her Western readers. She
writes of Phuc's mother, Nu, who ran a successful restaurant: "At half
past one, after about three hours' sleep, Nu would ease herself out of the
van, ... would head for the market to buy her day's requirements of *banh
canh*, ... water chestnuts, bean sprouts, tofu, carrots, cucumbers and
lemon grass, before heading for the shop back along the highway.
Grandmother Tao joined her in the predawn, helping to chop and cut"
(24-25). Chong's list of ingredients for the noodle dishes, as well as her
attention to the hundred fruit trees on the family property, "forty-two
were guava trees; their crunchy, tart fruit, sprinkled with salt, was a
local favorite–pomelo, jackfruit, sapota, mango, pineapple, coconuts,
longan, green-skinned oranges, lemon and lime" (25), give a sense of the
exotic tropical to their existence without an Orientalizing effect. *Rau mau*
the herb that "went well with cooked chick embryos" is mentioned
along with warm "baguettes, sweet egg breads, and a favorite, sticky
rice mixed with grated coconut, sugar and grilled sesame seeds" (26).
The tastes, smells, and textures create a sensual immediacy that supplements the starkness and emptiness of the visual image of the naked
Phuc.

Another way of adding a layer of richness to the aridity of the photograph is to provide historical context for 1972, the year when the picture
was taken. Writing for a transnational readership, Chong assumes that
her readers know little of the history of Vietnam, even with the visibility
of the Vietnam War in American popular culture. She presents the story
of the photograph from multiple perspectives: from the viewpoint of the
"average peasant," from the American government, and also from the
perspective of the photographer, Nick Ut. These perspectives supple-

ment the captions that had accompanied the picture when it appeared, and add different angles and layers not only to the napalm bomb incident, but to the Vietnam War itself. Hence through the biography, Chong participates in the rewriting of cultural memory, which, as Marita Sturken has noted, "is a field of cultural negotiation through which different stories vie for a place in history" (1). In their book that remembers the Vietnam War from the oral stories and the language of the combat veteran, Paul Budra and Michael Zeitlin write, "in the broadest sense, the Vietnam War oral history project proceeds from the deeply felt recognition that there is something unfinished and incomplete, perhaps even something false, about the official accounts of the war" (2). Similarly, Chong's book completes the sometimes sensational readings of the photo and of the Vietnamese people. Instead of portraying them as enemy aliens or crazed ideologues, she says, "the average peasant cared nothing for politics and wanted only to be left alone. At most, he leaned to whichever side harassed him less" (36). She repeats the saying that he was "caught between the two, between the sticky rice and the bean–a favorite daily fare made by steaming inside a banana leaf glutinous white rice with black beans, which, once cooked, are inseparable. And so it was for the peasant, living entrapped and beholden to both sides" (36). Chong familiarizes the unfamiliar and the strange by her domestic and culinary metaphors. The comparison of the Vietnamese peasant to the sticky sweet renders him no longer a mysterious and threatening other. In addition, Chong describes incidents which reveal the vulnerability and humanity of the enemy other. She recounts the way Viet Cong visitors would come to Tung and Nu's family home and ask for help at night: "Mother… we are so hungry. Please can we have some rice?" (39). Instead of a fierce enemy, there was usually a "teenage boy standing there, looking horribly thin" (39). Other times, they would bring the wounded to Phuc's house, and these Viet Cong soldiers would be hidden from the government authorities.

Chong's account of the American government's involvement under President Richard Nixon includes an unbiased summary of Nixon's successful as well as unsuccessful effort to wage war and seek peace. She briefly recounts the atrocities of Mylai village in 1969, the Cambodian offensive, the demonstrations at Kent State University, and the slow withdrawal of troops by 1971. She notes that "by the spring of

1972, scheduled American troop withdrawals had cut the total at year's end in 1971 by half, leaving fewer than seventy thousand in Vietnam" (44). This fact is important because some of the later reports credit Kim Phuc's picture with stopping the war. However, as Chong points out, the U.S. was already beginning its withdrawal of troops before the famous photograph. Chong also gives a brief biography of Nick Ut, the Vietnamese photographer who is credited with saving Kim Phuc's life because it was he who drove her to the hospital after taking her picture. Nick Ut's story comes after Chong's brief historical overview of the U.S. position in Vietnam. Chong gives a short background of some of the reporters working for the Associated Press (AP) and the United Press International (UPI). Twenty-four year old Huynh Cong Ut, better known as Nick Ut, had become an apprentice or errand boy for Pulitzer prize-winning combat German photographer, Horst Faas. Nick's brother, Huyn Cong La, had also been a photographer and had been killed in 1965 at the age of 28. Chong writes of Nick, "From the start, Nick believed that his older brother's fate, an early death, awaited him. That belief drove him to go where the action was, to not come back until he had a picture he was happy with" (50). This personal story of an eager young photographer who has suffered a loss in his family because of the war contrasts with the impersonal statistics about the U.S. government's involvement in Vietnam. It reveals the real and human cost of the war, not just in economic, political, and military terms, but also highlighting the way it has affected virtually every family in Vietnam.

In the same way, Chong provides an account of not only Kim Phuc's situation but of the reaction of a number of people present at the temple right after the bombing in order to give the photograph a fuller frame or greater depth. She gives several horrific vignettes: "There was a deafening pop. Auntie Anh's baby was thrown from her arms, and she buckled at the knees. Instinctively she clutched at the back of her left leg. The fingers on that hand instant fused, from coming into contact with the gob of jellied napalm burning there" (66). She also notes the indignant reactions of the journalists, the Peace Corps workers, and the soldiers who helped carried injured children and babies out of the temple. Kim Phuc herself suffered severe burns on her left side, on the upper part of her body, almost all of her back and her left arm. Chong writes, "As if a spirit leaving her body, Phuc saw herself burned and pitied" (67). In order to make sure her readers fully understand the horror of Kim Phuc's accident, Chong later even gives a pseudo-technical or scientific explanation of napalm:

> napalm, first used in flame-throwers during the Second World War, is a highly lethal weapon when dropped from an airplane. The bomb explodes and fragments, and the burning jellied napalm (the name comes from its combination of naphthenic and palmitic acids) sticks to whatever it lands on. It burns at 800 to 1,200 degreed Celsius (by comparison, water boils at 100 degree Celsius) and for a long time. A big enough mass of burning napalm will consume the full thickness of skin; gone instantly are hair follicles, sweat glands and sensory nerve endings. (89)

Here she is relying on the affective power of her words to supplement the already shocking photographs that have become world famous. Referring to shocking and harrowing photographs, Susan Sontag says, "Narratives can make us understand: photographs do something else. They haunt us"(89).

Included in the center of the book are about fifteen photographs of Kim Phuc and her family over the years. The first is of Grandmother Tao carrying a three-year-old burned child, Danh, a picture also taken by Nick Ut. This photograph is one of those that "haunts us," as Sontag says. However, not all the photographs are from this day. Some depict Kim Phuc a year later. One shows Phuc standing with her family, and another standing on Route 1, approximately at the same location as the initial photograph. Some show her in front of a Caodai temple, or show her when she is older, in various locations, such as Bangkok, Havana, and Canada. Most of the photographs, except for two, show Kim Phuc clothed, without visible burn marks. Though these photographs make Kim Phuc look more like an "average" girl with a family and a life, rather than just a war victim, they can also be deceptive in their seemingly normalizing effect. As Chong notes over and over, Kim Phuc's burns affected her back and left side, "so that her scars could be hidden under clothing" (xvi). She "was an *acceptable* living symbol of wartime suffering" (xvi) and was later used for propaganda by the government. The photographs, mostly posed and taken during travel or especially for reporters and foreigners, show Kim smiling, as a happy woman, rather than one plagued by pain and bad dreams throughout her life.

Chong's narrative supplements the impression of normalcy given by these photographs by revealing the painful sequence of events that led to Phuc's healing and integration into society. A large section in the middle of the book reads somewhat like a survival narrative, and also echoes trauma and disability narratives, as Chong describes the ways Kim tries to live with the agonizing pain from her burns, and from the numerous surgeries she had to undergo. Offering medical, technical, and socio-cultural details, she presents a vivid rendition of Phuc's suffering at various stages:

> Phuc remained in critical condition for thirty to forty days. More than 80 percent of severely burned patients succumb to infection or other complications before that. For weeks, the main concerns were to keep up her strength as her body battled progressive malnutrition (brought on by the leakage of body proteins) and to rid her body of the toxic poisons of infection from charred tissue circulating in her body… The daily cleansing of burn patient inflicts pain that defies description… the physical pain of the daily procedure… [is] the most intense known to human beings… It inflicts a 'wound to the soul' and is akin to being 'flayed alive'. (94)

Through her use of medical facts and statistics, her metaphors of battles and wounds, and the particular consequences of the treatment, Chong succeeds in rendering in language and words the pain that says "defies description" (94).

The strict regime of rehabilitation and care followed by Kim Phuc and her family after the incident reminds one of Michel Foucault's notion of the "care of the self" that has become standard practice in medicine in the modern age. From the moment Phuc entered the hospital as a burn victim, her life becomes regimented; her body an object of scrutiny and care. Foucault notes that medicine defines "in the form of a corpus of knowledge and rules, a way of living, a reflective mode of relation to oneself, to one's body, to food, to wakefulness and sleep, to the various activities, and to the environment. Medicine was expected to propose, in the form of regimen, a voluntary and rational structure of conduct" (100). Kim Phuc, her parents, the medical staff who tended her, and Chong all participate in the representation of Phuc as the ideal patient, as someone who had a "happy and uncomplaining personality" (116), and who follows orders. At the same time, the horrific pain of the procedure remains, "the daily burn bath,… Phuc's life-saving treatment was itself traumatic. No matter how much time passed, mere mention of the burn bath would send Phuc into a wordless darkness. However, with the care of the nurses, she emerged from that haze of pain, prolonged agony and isolation, re-born" (116). The language Chong uses emphasizes endurance and patience for Phuc and her mother, Nu:

> Only Nu was able to withstand Phuc's cries at tight skin stretching and stiff joints pulling. Pain is a necessary part of a burn victim's rehabilitation; the more movement and flexibility gained, the more there is. A victim's rejuvenation can take as long as two or three years. Nu was firm with Phuc. 'It is very painful,' she agreed, 'but you must do your exercises now if you don't want to be ugly forever. You must do them if you want to help yourself to live the rest of your life'. (121)

By implication, the narrative attributes the slow recovery of Phuc to this regimentation and discipline: "While she would never again have the stamina or physical ability to keep up with others her age, within a year she appeared to be like any other child, running in play, riding her bicycle to school" (121). The narrative suggests that Phuc is rewarded because of her suffering, regimentation, and sacrifice, which follows a familiar discourse in medicine and religion.

One of the consequences of the photograph being circulated all over Europe and North American through newspapers is that Phuc forever loses her privacy. She becomes the subject of interest to the world almost continually after it was discovered that she survived her ordeal. An additional tragedy of her life is that she never had a chance to follow her dream, that of becoming a medical doctor, because of the constant interruptions to her schooling at various stages in her life. Journalists and dignitaries from all over the world come to Vietnam to interview her and to photograph her. She is placed in the difficult situation of always having to relive and to narrate her trauma for a public. As she is of interest only because of her suffering, she can only have the attention of the world only as long as she maintains the subjectivity of victim. Symbolically and physically, she is always having to reveal herself, pull up her sleeve, show her burned back, her disabled self, to reassure people that she is indeed the "girl in the picture" (190). Yet, at certain points in her life, she longed to shed the subjectivity of victimhood, and yearned simply to be an average girl. In addition, since the takeover of South Vietnam by the communist led by President Duong Van Minh in 1975, the family's fortune and domestic circumstances deteriorated. Phuc's mother and father no longer could live together: Nu had to return to what remained of the noodle shop in Trang Bang, while the father, Phuc, and the rest of the family stayed in the war-free region of Tay Ninh. The economic downturn affected Phuc as she "suffered from a persistent soreness in her left forearm," which was only treated by a wrapping of banana leaves or ice rather than medication which she needed (161). In front of journalists, reporters, and Westerners, she was allowed to speak of her pain from her burns, but not about life in postwar Vietnam, not about her family nor about the fact that there were times when "there had not been enough to eat" (201): she was "not to portray the people as having suffered under the new regime" (201). Chong's biography captures with sympathy the multiple ways in which Phuc is oppressed and imprisoned during these years—by the physical pain and limitations of her body, by her family's difficult socio-economic position, by her frustrations at her inability to pursue the career she dreamed of, and by the censorship of her speech and activities by the communist government.

Since the narrative thrust of the biography is towards Phuc's immigration to Canada, the impression that one receives as one reads of Phuc's difficulties is that there is no way out of her misery except through Western intervention. At one point around 1984, Phuc becomes very ill, is very low in spirit, and has no money or job. She prays to God for a "someone to rescue [her], a savior" (228), and writes a letter to Perry Kretz, the German photojournalist who had returned to Vietnam to take pictures of her a year after the bombing. Because she had converted to Christianity by then, Phuc thinks in Christian terms of Kretz as her savior, as "God's way of opening a door to a better future" for her (230). Kretz does come and take her to Bonn for treatment, offering her a temporary respite from her physical and emotional captivity. But he does not rescue her permanently. Phuc later travels to other places—to Moscow, to Germany, and later to study in Cuba, but in all these places she is carefully and closely watched by her minder, a designate of the government who ensures that she behaves properly and does not embarrass the Vietnamese government. In Cuba, where she started to study Spanish in 1986, she receives better health care and education than she did in Vietnam. It is also here that she meets her husband, Bui Huy Toan, who came from "the desperately poor fishing village of Vi Thanh, thirty miles from Hanoi" (292-293) and who often helped her when she was not well. They become friends, but Chong plays down the romantic aspects of the relationship saying that Phuc was determined to "save herself for the night she married" (294). In spite of Toan's helpfulness and the advantages of education, their lives in Cuba are difficult, with daily electricity shutdowns and lack of reliable public transportation. Chong, who used to be an economist, methodically links Phuc's experiences in Cuba to the larger world of international politics, explaining that by 1986, Cuba's economy would turn for the worst because, unlike Vietnam, it refused to shift to a market economy. By 1992, Phuc "continued to feel herself losing ground in Cuba and dreading her future in Vietnam, the all-too-familiar suffering returned" (338). The only solution was to defect to Canada, a country that would later accept Phuc and Toan on "humanitarian grounds" (356). The narrative thus inevitably reinforces the notion that the "happy" end is finally only to be found in the West, a common theme in immigrant narratives.

Living in Canada, Kim Phuc becomes an emblem of reconciliation. Like fellow Vietnamese Le Ly Hayslip, who immigrated to the U.S., she represents "those anonymous millions of Vietnamese in whose name the Vietnam War was fought by both sides" (Nguyen 108). As Viet Thanh Nguyen says of Hayslip, "through her extraordinary personal story, she not only symbolically bears their collective pain but also bears the victim's burden of forgiveness" (108). She has transformed herself from an ambassador for Vietnam, to an ambassador for world peace. In 1994, she was appointed Goodwill ambassador for UNESCO, and has partici-pated in conferences and colloquia in Canada, the United States, Colombia, Mexico, Brazil, Spain, and Italy for the promotion of peace and pardon ("Phan Thi Kim Phuc"). The themes of her talks are peace and forgiveness. At her Address at the United States Vietnam War Memorial Veterans' Day in 1996, Kim Phuc said, "Even if I could talk face to face with the pilot who dropped the bombs, I would tell him we cannot change history but we should try to do good things for the present and for the future to promote peace" (Phuc, Address). In a bizarre turn of events, this willingness to forgive inspired or provoked a small-town Methodist minister, John Plummer, to come forward and claim responsibility for the bombing, though it was later proven that he was not actually involved (362-363). He had been harboring an illusion since his Vietnam days and feeling guilty about having killed an innocent woman in Vietnam. His guilt had been displaced onto Phuc when he saw her picture in the papers. This incident illustrates the numerous pervading fantasies about Vietnam that live both in one's personal mind and in the collective memory. It also shows the power of the image and media in the creation of a popular icon or symbol. In addition, since the end of the war, the pervasive theme about Vietnam has been to heal, to forget, and to forgive. The Methodist minister sought relief, and the fantasy of absolution from someone who was giving it, whether he was actually guilty or not. In the popular imagination, through her suffering, endurance, and strength, she has, in essence, been elevated to a kind of priestess or saint. The discourse of reconciliation and healing is so compelling in our society that some people willingly adopt it, even at the expense of historical truth. Denise Chong's book, however, keeps us rooted in history, reminds us of the power of memory, of stories, or at the very least, a well-reconstructed and well-researched version of the truth.

Works Cited

Anderegg, Michael, ed. *Inventing Vietnam: The War in Film and Television.* Philadelphia: Temple University Press, 1991.

Budra, Paul and Michael Zeitlin. "Introduction." *Soldier Talk: The Vietnam War in Oral Narrative.* Bloomington: Indiana University Press, 2004. 1-25.

Butler, Judith. "Photography, War, Outrage." *PMLA* 120.3 (May 2005): 822-827.

Chong, Denise. *The Concubine's Children.* Toronto: Penguin Books, 1995.

—. *The Girl in the Picture: The Kim Phuc Story.* Toronto: Penguin Viking, 1999.

Evans, Mary. *Missing Persons: The Impossibility of Auto/Biography.* New York & London: Routledge, 1999.

Foucault, Michel. *The Care of the Self: The History of Sexuality.* Vol. 3. Trans. Robert Hurley. New York: Vintage Books, 1988.

Gordon, Lyndall. "Women's Lives: The Unmapped Country." *The Art of Literary Biography.* Ed. John Batchelor. Oxford: Clarendon Press, 1995. 87-98.

Johnson, Samuel. "On Biography." *Rambler No. 60. The Longman Anthology of British Literature: Vol. 1C The Restoration and the Eighteenth Century.* 2nd Ed. Ed. Stuart Sherman. New York: Longman, 2003. 2738-2740.

Miller, Nancy K. "The Girl in the Photograph: The Vietnam War and the Making of National Memory." *Journal of Advanced Composition* 24.2 (2004): 261-290.

Nadel, Ira Bruce. *Biography: Fiction, Fact, and Form.* New York: St. Martin's Press, 1984.

"Phan Thi Kim Phuc - The Human Suffering."
http://www.vietnamwar.com/phanthikimphuc.htm. (Viewed on December 21, 2005).

Phuc, Kim. "Address At The United States Vietnam War Memorial Veterans' Day 1996." November 11, 1996. Washington, DC.
http://gos.sbc.edu/p/phuc.html. (Viewed on December 21, 2005).

Review of "Kim Phuc Story: *The Girl in the Picture* by Denise Chong." *Vietnamese Bulletin vietnamien.* 15.6 (Nov.-Dec. 1999).
http://www.vietfederation.ca/newsletters/BLT99F.html. (Viewed on January 1, 2006).

Sontag, Susan. *Regarding the Pain of Others.* New York: Farrar, Straus and Giroux, 2003.

Spivak, Gayatri Chakravorty. "Can the Subaltern Speak?" *Colonial Discourse and Post-Colonial Theory: A Reader.* Ed. Patrick Williams and Laura Chrisman. New York: Columbia University Press, 1994. 66-111.

Sturken, Marita. *Tangled Memories: The Vietnam War, the AIDS epidemic, and the Politics of Remembering.* Berkeley, CA: University of California Press, 1997.

Timberlake, Ronald. "Vietnam Napalm Strike: The Myth of Kim Phuc, The Girl In The Photo." November 1997.
http://www.warbirdforum.com/vphoto.htm. (Viewed on December 21, 2005).

Trinh, Minh-ha T. *When the Moon Waxes Red: Representation, Gender and Cultural Politics.* New York: Routledge, 1991.

Ty, Eleanor. *The Politics of the Visible in Asian North American Narratives.* Toronto: University of Toronto Press, 2004. 33-53.

Williams, Tony. "Narrative Patterns and Mythic Trajectories in Mid-1980s Vietnam Movies." *Inventing Vietnam: The War in Film and Television.* Ed. Michael Anderegg. Philadelphia: Temple University Press, 1991. 114-139.

Eleanor Ty is Professor and Chair of English & Film Studies at Wilfrid Laurier University in Ontario. Her books include *The Politics of the Visible in Asian North American Narratives,* and *Empowering the Feminine: The Narratives of Mary Robinson, Jane West, and Amelia Opie, 1796-1812.*

"Ejemplos Metafóricos": Self-Presentation and History in Chicana Autobiography and Life-Narrative

A. Gabriel Meléndez

I. Introduction

A great debt is owed to Sidonie Smith and Julia Watson, foremost scholars on autobiography and life writing, for their encyclopedic work on critical autobiographical studies. Their research and exegesis on auto-biographical theory and method supersedes the generational buildup of partial and narrow definitions of autobiography that have kept us unaware of the vast historical and social propositions that emerge from the study of past and contemporary life writing. Their postulations suggest that there is a species-wide autobiographical impulse in human oral and written expression and that the term "autobiography" is of relatively recent coinage in the West. They make clear that cultures in-side and outside of Western civilization have utilized life-narratives to express their personal knowledge since the dawn of time. Indeed, speaking one's life experience is perhaps the most universally practiced application of the "I-narrative" in human societies. Smith and Watson list such traditions as the naming songs of American Indian cultures, Af-rican oral narratives of genealogy and descent, communal "song lines" of indigenous Australians, written modes of self inscription in China and Japan, Islamic-Arabic literature, *bhakti* poetry of India and North Africa as examples of the life-narration among myriad groups and cultures.

Recent scholarship has made it possible and critical for scholars of ethnic life-writing to refocus their attention on their respective traditions and reconsider the particulars that constitute the life-narrative trajecto-ries of these communities. This is an especially urgent task in the case of Chicana autobiography, most especially, when one considers that Chi-cana life-narratives are largely unknown and understudied. It is as if Chicanas themselves did not exist, so absent from theoretical and practi-cal discussions is their disclosure on either personal or public events.

In 1993, Genaro M. Padilla published, *My History, Not Yours: The Formation of Mexican American Autobiography,* a book that accounts for the formation of a distinctly Chicano/a subjectivity by proffering a collective history intimately linked to the U.S.-Mexico borderlands. Padilla's massive unearthing of the previously silenced voices of his *antepasados* proceeds as an archival recovery project that brings to light the lives of Mexican Americans that until recently had been consigned to old diaries, family histories, personal poetry and collections of self-disclosing correspondence. For Padilla, Chicano/a autobiographical disclosure appears after Mexico lost its northern territories and as a direct response to the expansionist war of 1846. Padilla means for his work "to initiate a recovery of that autobiographical formation which emerged after 1848, the year that a vast part of northern Mexico was annexed by the United States in a war of conquest"(4). Padilla found that nineteenth-century forms of Chicano autobiography are nearly always descriptive of the political and social condition of a people conquered by force of arms. These narratives emerge over an extended period of time in which Mexican Americans were required to accommodate themselves to the political and legal regime imposed upon them by the *americanos.*

Padilla also brings forth a gendered reading of the Chicana as a historical subject. Indeed, his most brilliant findings are those that argue for a nuanced understanding of the agency and voice of Mexican women in a dozen or so California narratives. Here women themselves speak of the active role they had in their society prior to and after the Americanization of the U.S. West. In speaking of the narratives of María Inocente Pico de Ávila, Caterina Ávila de Ríos, Apolinaria Lorenzana, María de las Angustias de la Guerra Ord, Eulalia Pérez, and other Californianas, Padilla declares, "In each of the narratives I have read, women push beyond testimonial expectations to discover or invent the narrative space required for reconsidering their lives within a male-controlled domain, for reassessing social transformation that affect them as much as their male counterparts, and, ultimately for celebrating their own lives" (151).

Padilla's work draws a line from the Californiana narratives to the work of another group of writings produced by a group of women in New Mexico who, "wrote books in which cultural traditions, family and community customs, and social history are combined with personal narrative" (19). Beginning in the 1920s and for the next 30 years, a small number of personal life narratives about New Mexico were published by a group of Hispana writers who were interested in correcting the erroneous ideas outsiders had about the culture and society of the nue-vomexicanos. Among the most important of these personal narratives are Nina Otero Warren's *Old Spain in Our Southwest* (1936), Cleofas Jaramillo's *Sombras del Pasado/Shadows of the Past* (1941) and *Romance of a Little Village Girl* (1955), Aurora Lucero-White's *Literary Folklore of the Hispanic Southwest* (1953) and Fabiola Cabeza de Baca's *We Fed Them Cactus* (1954). Padilla concludes "in many respects Jaramillo and other New Mexican writers of this period mimicked an Anglo-American discourse that romanticized the Spanish Southwest, their writing never-theless also operated as a vital form of resistance to Anglo-American ethnocentrism" (21).

Here, I wish to take up Padilla's call regarding the importance of "prior discursive formations," for indeed there is a vast array of life narratives with which to "widen" our understanding of Chicana autobiographical formation.

II. La Malinche and Sor Juana Inés de la Cruz: Precursors

As Smith and Watson remind us, Europe's encounter with the Americas brought forth what Mary Louise Pratt calls a moment of "planetary consciousness" out of which emerged new and complicate inter and intra-cultural subjectivities and when "contact with indigenous people calls "civilizing" practices into question and suggests that "an indige-nous" collectivized subjectivity may be superior to that of the Western "new man" (91). Moving back past 1848 and considering as Smith and Watson do that "in settling the continent, life narrative took on added importance as people had to invent both the landscape and themselves" (97), it is relevant to ask where and when we can begin to speak of Chicana autobiographical impulse?

Feminist scholars, particularly the Mexican novelist and poet, Rosario Castellanos, and, more recently, Chicana critics such as Adeleida del Castillo and Cherrié Moraga have shown us that the life of Malinali Tenepal or La Malinche is about a distinctly post-encounter subject formation: one the begins to reflect the emergence of a mestizo/a consciousness, the bedrock of Mexicano/a identity. As the symbolic "mother of all mestizos," La Malinche assumes archetypal and mythic proportions in the global narrative of conquest, colonization that began in 1492. Her life story signals the re-subjectivization of indigenous peoples in the chronological narrative we now call the post-colonial. Bringing up La Malinche as an antecedent life or as an ancestor to Chicanas has its snares and snags. One could rightly ask: but where is La Malinche's autobiography, where does her autobiographical agency and impulse begin, as she left no documents penned in her own hand that attest to her "narrative 'I'"? That we know anything at all about her is due entirely to the handful of passages in Bernal Díaz del Castillo's *The Conquest of Mexico/La conquista de México* of 1558. Julie Greer Johnson asserts "Bernal Díaz is the only colonial writer to make a woman a major historical figure in the historical events unfolding in Spain's American possessions" (qtd. in Messinger Cypress 28). As Díaz tells the story, Hernán Cortez's success in Mexico was in great measure owed to the intelligence, resourcefulness and strength of La Malinche who he describes as, "this most excellent woman." Díaz, it appears, sensed the exceptional nature of La Malinche or so Sandra Messigner Cypress observes, "doña Marina was first in his thoughts" (36). Díaz consigns the Spanish victory over the Indians to La Malinche saying that once she came among the Spanish, "was the great beginning of our conquests" (qtd. in Messinger Cypress 31).

Díaz is the only colonial writer to paraphrase the indirect monologues she spoke at decisive moments of the Spanish campaign in Mexico. Thus, we can infer that a collaborative speech act suffuses Díaz's biographical sketch of La Malinche, making it possible to think of Bernal Díaz and La Malinche as co-generators of the text. It is reasonable to suppose that Díaz's background information on La Malinche's birth and early life could only have come through conversations with individuals who knew her well or from La Malinche herself. Thus, acting as Malinche's biographer Díaz provides the world with La Malinche's *bios* and gives it its original form. Díaz tells us how La Malinche was born into Aztec nobility and received an education corresponding to her status in that society. While quite young her father died and after the remarriage of her mother to another cacique, Malinche was banished and sold into slavery. Mayan traders then sold or exchanged her to a group of Tabascans from where she, in a group of twenty women, was gifted to the Spaniards. At the point that La Malinche begins the work of translating among the Indians, her actions make her an agent of change, one at the confluence of global history and mythology of the European conquest of the Americas.

I contend that a precise and identifiable set of socio-historical and political conditions birth Chicana/Mexicana subjectivity at this exact historical moment. This subjectivity manifests itself in autobiographical terms as a vast set of individual and collective "I-narrative' stories that arise from the imperatives of a post-contact and postcolonial moment. Said in another way, in choosing La Malinche's life narrative as the starting point, I, in effect propose to make 1519 (not 1848 as Padilla would have it) the historical divide. I do not subscribe to the idea that Mexicana/o, Chicana/o and, importantly, mestiza/o autobiographical subjectivity can be located in a time before this very precise historical date, as it neither continues back into the indigenous world, nor can it be located in Iberia. The Malinche story leaves to posterity what Messinger Cypress calls the "Malinche paradigm," "a thought system in which the negative traits of Malinche as traitor prevail over the quite positive attributes that Bernal Díaz provides her in his originating biographical text" (27). And, since history itself, and in particular a history shaped by criollo and mestizo intelligensia (in Mexico proper) has not been kind to mother Malinche, a discussion of her autobiographical agency is extremely relevant to Chicanas. Accordingly, Cherrié Moraga writes, "As a Chicana and a feminist, I must, like other Chicanas before me, examine the effects this myth has on my/our racial/sexual/identity and my relationship with other Chicanas. There is hardly a Chicana growing up today who does not suffer under her name even if she never hears directly of the one-time Aztec princess" (qtd. in Messinger Cypress, 142).

Starting with the *Confessions* of St. Augustine in 397 A.D. and for "a thousand years thereafter most autobiographical writing in occidental societies was done by religious men as a form of devotion in the service of spiritual examination" (Smith and Watson 85). In Mexico, Sor Juana Inés de la Cruz's famous autobiographical manifesto, "Respuesta a Sor Filotea," could be seen simply as one more medieval spiritual testimonio, pasted onto the millennial rise of Christianity in the West. But, such a reading does not do justice to the remarkable example of woman's intellectual autonomy that is "La Respuesta."

Sor Juana was born in 1651 near the famous volcanoes of Popocateptl and Ixtacihuatl in San Miguel Nepantla not far from Mexico City. We are fortunate in that we know a great deal about the historical person, Juana Ramírez de Asbaje, as her life story is told in her own writings and in a brief biographical essay published eight years after her death, by Padre Diego Callejas. Far more conclusive, is the way in which Sor Juana's famous essay, "Respuesta a Sor Filotea," provides a remarkable and fascinating means to assess Sor Juana's ideological formation and personal subjectivity. "La Respuesta" is an extraordinary, bold, remarkable and audacious assertion of the "ideological self." A wholly, unabashed declaration of intellectual autonomy, "La Respuesta" reveals Sor Juana's deepest longing, her strongest beliefs, and her core determinations.

It is important to keep in mind that even as it left her hand, "La Respuesta" was dialogical and intertextual discourse. It was threaded messaging (*discurso enhebrado*), one in a suite of four interrelated texts that in a sense "speak across space and time," centuries ahead of our strings of email messages in the present age. The hierarchy of the Church in Mexico reprimanded Sor Juana because she dared to speak and think independently. Margaret Sayers Peden clearly lays out the line of argumentation in her introduction to *A Woman of Genius: The Intellectual Autobiography of Sor Juana Inés de la Cruz*. The threaded message begins forty-one years earlier when a famed Portuguese Jesuit, Antonio de Vieryra delivered a sermon on Holy Thursday, 1650 that he titled "Sermon on the Mandate." Vierya sought to give doctrinal evidence for what had been the greatest kindness Christ had wrought upon mankind. Forty years later Vierya's continued to be referenced to the degree that Sor Juana would take it as a challenge and proceeded to issue an equally rich theologically-bound treatise she called "Critique of the Sermon" in which she begged to differ with Vierya's conclusions. By this time Sor Juana was a celebrated poet and a respected member of the religious community in Mexico City and thus her "Critique" came to the attention of Manuel Fernández de Santa Cruz y Sahagún, the Bishop of Puebla.

Sahagún's response to Sor Juana came wrapped in a goodly amount of friendly, even 'fatherly" advice, but laid down a strongly worded remonstrance to the young nun had committed for having strayed from contemplation and moved into what the Bishop denounced as the vain pursuit of human letters. To justify his authority the Bishop alluded to the teaching of St. Paul, specifically the admonition, "let women keep silence in the churches," hoping to halt Sor Juana's forays into theological pronouncements. The rebuke could have daunted a weaker spirit, but for Sor Juana it provided a rare opportunity to speak her mind and to demonstrate the power of her intellect.

In judging the audacity of "La Respuesta," it must be remembered that Sor Juana herself, the historical "I" of her narration, reflects a complete, though quite exceptional form of the intellectual, spiritual and religious training of her time. The particularities of the age demanded that she be versed in scholasticism, the only sanctioned intellectual discourse available to her in colonial Mexico and in the intricacies of baroque metaphor and stylistics, the reigning literary, artistic and cultural fashion of her time. In "La Respuesta" she proceeds to demonstrate her total control of these requisite stylistic and epistemological skills. So seeped was she in the intellectual discourse of her age that she managed to play with, to think in and around her adversaries: those jealous courtiers and complacent clergy who vested their authority to speak, not on the power of the mind, but on the privilege that accrued to them as males. Skilled in rhetoric, Sor Juana was accomplished in her use of double entendre, the play of mistaken identities, chiasmus, allusions to the classical world, indeed, all the preferred tropes of Baroque rhetoricians. She adroitly wields them, managing to level her adversary, the Bishop of Puebla from his lofty social standing. Her exchanges turned the table on the Bishop, ribbing him by calling him a woman and feigning disbelief at being the object of the Bishop's favors and attention:

> And thus say I, most honorable lady. Why do I receive such favor? By chance, am I other than a humble nun, the lowliest of creatures of the world, the most unworthy to occupy your attention? Wherefore then speakest thou so to me? "And whence is this to me?" Nor to the first obstruction do I have any response other than I am little worthy of your eyes; nor to the second, other than

wonder, in the stead of thanks, saying that I am not capable of
thanking you for the smallest part of that which I own you. (16)

Two elements make Sor Juana's interventions remarkable. One is her
boldness in challenging scholasticism and theology, the regime of
knowledge that dominated her world and matters considered the exclusive domain of the clergy. Second, she employs a thoroughly modern
way of dismantling and disarming the Bishop of Puebla's invocation,
"let women keep silence in the churches." Sor Juana at once deconstructs
and contextualizes this scriptural precept in a way that is thoroughly
and unquestionably modern in its argumentation. In this way there is no
question that she predates modernism in its critical and robust analyses
of language. In sum, she produces a number of brilliant reasons to
rethink the postulation on women studying and teaching in the church.
She asks that the "intended meaning" of the Apostle be first examined in
order to understand his message. She bases her own desire to study on
theology itself, noting such desire can only come from "the natural
impulse that God placed in me". She questions whether St. Paul's
admonition was meant to be a prequalifier for both men and women in
writing: "This view is indeed just, so much so that not only women, who
are held to be so inept, but also men, who merely for being men believe
they are wise, should be prohibited from interpreting the Sacred Word if
they are not learned and virtuous and of gentle and well-inclined
natures" (68).

As I write, Sor Juana speaks to me across time and inspired by her
notion of "ejemplos metafóricos," I am moved to ask what other writing
gives form to the autobiographical voice of Chicanas that reaches into
our present century. Padilla's work on the life narratives of Californianas announces the need to delve further into Chicana border
subjectivity since, as Padilla reminds us, the remapping of the Southwest
and the imposition of new political border prefigures the split-voiced
articulations of Mexicanos and Mexicanas that are to follow.

The imposition of the border between the United States and Mexico
established in 1848 is a determinate site of narrative, especially of life
narrative. In this way, personal narrative at the border conforms to what
has been called the "geographics of narrative subjectivity," a major truss
upon which Chicana autobiography rests. Thus, any look at a continuation of the Chicana experience must *de riguer* take a careful and studied

look at words of border residents, be they border straddlers or border crossers, and to the life narratives of those Mexicanas whose lives and work are defined by a proximity to the border and to a transnational understanding of the border. Smith and Watson note the importance of occasional (event-driven) and locational (topos-driven) sites in the production of autobiography. They write, "Site, then, more actively than notions of "place" or "setting," speaks to the situatedness of autobiographical narration" (58).

III. Leonor Villegas de Magnón:
Agency and Revolution on the Border

First, attention must go to *La Rebelde/The Rebel* by Leonor Villegas de Magnón (1876-1955). Recovered by Clara Lomas in 1994, *The Rebel* is a powerful testimonio/testimony of the participation of women in the Mexican Revolution of 1910. The memoir discloses Leonor's involvement in the anti-porfiriato movement and tells of her founding of the La Cruz Blanca, a civilian nursing and hospital corps. Villegas de Magnón provides one of the fullest accounts of women from various class backgrounds, bound up in first deposing of Porfirio Díaz and then giving themselves to activism and public service to rebuild Mexico.

For Clara Lomas the Revolution is the catalyst of these memoirs: "Villegas de Magnón's *The Rebel* provides a stage on which the deeds of the Mexican historical revolutionary figures such as Francisco I. Madero, Venustiano Carranza, and Francisco (Pancho) Villa are dramatized along with those of a cast of border area political activists" (ix). While the Mexican Revolution is indeed the springboard for Villegas de Magnón, the completed text reveals a wider and variegated field of personal identity and border subjectivity behind the author's discourse.

Villegas de Magnón's ethnic and social make-up is complicated. She is daughter of a Spanish merchant whose business ventures take him to live in the border community of Nuevo Laredo on the Mexican side of the U.S. Mexico border. Once situated, Joaquín Villegas marries a local woman, Valerianna Rubio (as was so often the case). Leonor will loose her mother at a young age and she and her brother, Leopold, will come under the tutelage of their father's second wife, Eloise Monsalvatge. Eloise is the daughter of a Presbyterian minister and a Swiss mother, and her class and ethnic background cannot but influence Leonor. Eloise is presumably fully Americanized and she is both cultured and caring of her husband's family. Leonor recalls:

> So wise and practical was her idea that her husband was immediately in accord. She had his children in mind; their future was important. Leopold would go to St. Mary's on the very outskirts of San Antonio and Leonor to the Ursuline Convent in town. (45)

In addition to having access to quality education, the new family enjoys the privilege of visiting desirable destinations in Europe and the U.S. and, as they do, they acquire a refined taste for novelty and fashion. Leonor will eventually graduate from Mount St. Ursula Academy in Bedford Park, New York in 1895 complying with the new standard in the family that "no one was to return home without a diploma" (51). Her father, don Joaquin, will, at the encouragement of his young bride, transfer his business interests to San Antonio, thus in some way he too embraces the Americanization that is already transforming his children.

Villegas de Magnón writes in a detached the third person voice. The first third of her memoirs, told in the stand-in voice of "La Rebelde," provides the details of her early formation. La Rebelde expresses powerful sentiments for her biological mother, the woman who most represents Mexico and her people, as well as an earnest respect for Eloise, the emblem of life in the United States. These tributes to the women in her life resonate as the symbolic references to "unrelenting movement between borders, countries, cultures and languages" (Padilla 45). Similarly, La Rebelde is beset early on by the question of who and what she and her siblings are destined to become. Leonor's mother looking upon her children asks:

> My son born on American soil. My daughter in Mexican territory, and I a Spanish subject. Who will be the more powerful, he or she? In bed, Doña Valerianna held her child in a warm embrace, whispering a benediction. "A Mexican flag shall be yours. I will wrap it together with our brother's. His shall be an American flag, but they shall be like one to me." (7)

Villegas de Magnón's destiny is partially decided by her marriage to Adolfo Magnón in January 1901. Aldolfo's work as an agent for a steamship company takes the couple to live in Mexico City where they will spend the next nine years and where Leonor comes to the decision to work in the anti-Díaz movement that is swelling in the Mexican Capital.

In 1910, Leonor must return to Laredo, Texas to be at her father's deathbed. Reaching the border, Leonor is now fully engaged, not with the question of her own destiny, but with the fate of Mexico as it struggles to overturn its colonial legacy and institute constitutional reforms. Even though she continues to reside on the American side for several more years, she has already come to the unflinching decision to aid the Mexican struggle. It was a decision that she reached four days after her father's death: "On the forth day she had a strong reaction. She remembers her days of work for her country, her mother's country. She must resume her fight for Mexico. It was there in that same house where father, opening the door of the room where she had been born, had said, 'This is the only rebel in the house'" (77).

The last two thirds of *The Rebel* provides an exhaustive array of incidents linked to the Revolution and peopled by Mexicans of all social ranks. We learn of a host of teachers, journalists, activists, business owners, telegraph operators, nurses, women from the working class and upper class who broke with there class rank and gave themselves to the cause of improving Mexico as a nation. Villegas de Magnón expands our understanding of the agency of Mexicanas by going beyond the adelita/soldadera figure of myth and legend.

A third autobiographical track focuses on the years after the Revolution, when La Rebelde finds herself back in the United States, working tirelessly to publish her memoirs. What Lomas calls Villegas de Magnón's "post-revolution self," mirrors the experience of other Chicanos and Chicanas who as a consequence of dominant epistemologies in the United States face a kind of social and cultural death from being unable to see their deeds, thoughts and actions reflected in writing, education and the arts. Villegas de Magnón's wealth of knowledge about the border and about Mexico are effectively walled-off by an internal ethno-cultural border built by a society conditioned to shun all things Mexican. Lomas writes that Leonor, like other Mexican expatriates, came to understand that, "as U.S. citizens their national alliance was continually being questioned. Her narrative was to point to their deeds as acts of an international social justice, which knew no national boundaries. For her all border area participants, regardless of gender, were just as important as anyone else" (xxxix). Lomas found the third track of Leonor's life amply documented in the letters and personal papers kept by her daughter, Leonor Grubbs, who continued to promote her mother's legacy after her death. It is as impressive as it is regrettable that Leonor Villegas de Magnón spent a quarter of a century—from the time she drafted her 300-page memoir in Spanish in 1920s and until she wrote a 483-page English version in the late 1940s—struggling to have her voice heard (Lomas ix). Even more troubling is that another five decades would pass before La Rebelde's memoirs would finally be published.[1] I do think it more than symbolic for Chicanas to consider Villlegas de Magnón's story and to weigh the cost that this silence produced, for in real ways her silence also stands as that of all Chicanos and Chicanas who have seen their collective experience excised from the history of the borderlands.

IV. Lydia Mendoza: Performing Chicano Borderlands Culture

Among certain generations of Chicano/as the legend that is Lydia Mendoza is immortalized in such epithets as "la cancionera de los pobres" [the poor people's singer] and "the lark of the border." *Lydia Mendoza, A Family Autobiography,* published in 1993, is not a conventional autobiography, rather, as the subtitle suggests, it aims to be a collective life narrative. The book insists on telling the story of the Mendozas and, importantly, to establish the organic ties that link the Mendozas to everyday Mexican Americans who where both Lydia's listeners and her inspiration. *Lydia Mendoza, A Family Autobiography* came into being as a shared venture between ethnomusicologist and record producer, Chris Strachwitz, translator, James Nicolopulos and several members of the Mendoza family. Like other collaborative life writing projects, it requires the participation of an informant (the raconteur) and a recorder, (the ethnographer or interviewer) (Smith and Watson 191). As in the case of other oral history narratives the collaboration involves the hand of a translator and interpreter. As editor-compiler, Chris Strachwitz followed the documentary technique he had piloted when he worked with Les

---

[1] Clara Lomas has taken care to list and order the count of the submissions and rejections from major publishing houses in the United States that Villegas de Magnón received. On these matters see her introduction to *The Rebel.*

Blanks on the 1970s film, *Chulas Fronteras,* a documentary on the musical forms of South Texas when Strachwitz first met Lydia Medonza.

As "relational autobiography" (Smith and Watson 201) major install-ments of the narrative come from Lydia's close associates or from family members. Strachwitz and Nicolopulos list five extended interviews in Spanish with Lydia Mendoza done over a ten-year period, five other interview sessions with Lydia's siblings, nieces, nephews and in-laws and twelve separate interviews with a number of Tejano promoters, studio owners and musicians. Thus, *Lydia Mendoza, A Family Autobiogra-phy* cuts a goodly sized swath across several generations of participants in vernacular, Tex-Mex, or Tejano music.

Lydia Mendoza's life story is pure Chicano/a and border history. Interesting, the narrative reaches back to the time of the *porfiriato* and includes a history of the Mendozas criss-crossing the Texas-Mexico border. Lydia recalls how her grandmother Teófila Reyna was an edu-cated woman in the Díaz era, attended a teacher training school and taught music at the high school level in Villa de Arriaga. Lydia's parents Leonor Zamarripa Reyna and Francisco Mendoza Espinosa, both wid-owed and with children from previous marriages, met while working at a brewery in Monterrey at the height of the hostilities in Mexico in 1914 and shortly thereafter moved to the United States. Lydia's older sister, Beatriz, the first child born to the Mendozas, and Lydia herself were born in Houston in 1916. The family stayed in Texas for the next several years but returned to Monterrey where two other children, Francisco and Panchita, were born between 1918 and 1920. Soon after the family would migrate to Texas and it is upon this return trip that Lydia experiences the first in a continuing set of dehumanizing events that she and other Mexicans would be subjected to in the United States. The memory is a painful and one Lydia recalls it in detail and with precision:

> They told us we were infected with lice or some such things. Right away they took us back behind the immigration station where they had a bath, one of those big ones, full of gasoline. It wasn't just me, there were several other children, all Mexicans. And they doused us with gasoline, they threw on plenty. The gasoline got in my eyes and I became very ill. I came out with red eyes. This was the last and only time they did that to me, because afterwards they stopped doing it, this was precisely in 1920. (11)

For the next several years the Mendozas lived an erratic, hand-to-mouth existence, moving between various Texas towns and returning to Monterrey often following the caprices of an alcoholic father whose incapacity to work and hold a job prevented the family from settling down in any one place. The Mendozas' first public performances began around 1927 when the able members of the family, (mother and children) formed *El Cuarteto Carta Blanca.* Lydia recalls: "We stared signing in restaurants, barbershops, on street corners and little places like that. We would arrive at a place and ask permission to sing and, sometimes, they would give it to us,... We sang songs like "Rancho Grande," "Las cuatro milpas" and "La Cucaracha" (28). The group traveled constantly, following the stream of Mexican track workers and farm laborers across the Southwest and to Midwest industrial towns like Pontiac and Detroit. The Mendozas never shunned identification with their working class Mexican American beginnings. Consequently, the Spanish language press accorded them a revered place in the Mexican American community.

In 1934 Lydia recorded "Mal Hombre," a haunting tango she first heard sung at a variety show in Monterrey some years before. Lydia's rendition of the song became an overnight hit in the Spanish-speaking world and talk of Lydia and the Mendoza family quickly extended to all the U.S. Southwest, to Mexico, Latin America, and Spain. In December 1937, San Antonio's *La Opinión* noted Lydia's overwhelming popularity and celebrated the fact that "her name is revered in the households of 'Mexico de Afuera' [Mexico Abroad] and her songs are known by the whole family" (136).

All told, the Mendozas recorded over 1,200 commercial songs, a remarkable cultural treasure. One can easily imagine that these 1,200 songs are the source of a similar number of stories in the life of Lydia Mendoza and the autobiography does capture a number of the anecdotes connected to Lydia's discography, but Lydia's story is also important for the way it illustrates how her musical career and fame parallels the general experience of Chicanos in the United States, particularly that of the immigrant generation of Mexicans that arrived in the United States between 1900 and 1920. The text's collective "I" is ever present in the narrative and so as Lydia tells of perilous border crossings, meager and marginal financial success, poverty, the effects of the Great Depression, the onslaught of World War II and the Bracero Program of the 1950s and 1960s, and in so doing, gives form to the collective experience of Chicanos. Chris Strachwitz sees a close parallel between the musical career of the Carter family of Virginia and that of the Mendoza family, but working to tell the Mendoza story, he argues, has other implications: "The experience of European immigrants have been well documented in books, films and songs, but few who have come from south of our border have ever told their stories on paper" (vii).

Lydia Mendoza, A Family Autobiography's oral narratives unfold from the everyday reality of inhabiting the borderlands, a feature that gives the narrative its authority as testimonio. Then too, the ark of the Mendoza story is impressive, since, as Strachwitz notes, it brings us from the "booming 'jazz age' of the 1920s" and into the 1980s when after some six decades the contributions of the Mendozas to the cultural and musical history of Mexican Americans was finally recognized. In 1982, Lydia Mendoza was among the first recipients of a National Heritage Fellowship Award given by the National Endowment for the Arts and in 1984 she was inducted into the Tejano Music Hall of Fame (Strachwitz ix). In this way, her autobiography narrativizes the history of the masses of Chicano working class families and so it becomes history without the pretense of assuming to write or construct history. It is a classic piece of the Chicana experience, one that conveys the sense of the every day and the consequences of social history.

V. Denise Chávez's Meditative and Culinary Auto-ethnography

> — "Ay, food brings to mind family."
> — "My meditations are just that, ruminations on a life lived among tacos." Denise Chávez, 2006

In noting the desire of ethnic American working women to speak autobiographically about their labor and their lives, Anne E. Goldman argues that the personal disclosure of ethnic women is to be found in what she terms, "unfamiliar scripts," such as cookbooks, labor histories and letters, forms that transgress the canonical definitions of auto-biography (4). Goldman finds that culinary autobiography, a genre located in texts concerned with "the transient and material pleasure of eating" (4), has long been practiced by women of Mexican descent in the

United States. Calling to mind M.F.K Fisher's *Gastronomical Me*, Goldman asserts that to write about food is to write about self (4) and indeed, this is precisely the metaphor at work in the Chávez epigraphs above. Though Chávez's *A Taco Testimony: Meditations on Family, Food and Culture* does not fit the "unfamiliar script" category, given the enormous popularity of the culinary memoir at present, much of what Goldman finds to be true of the culinary-based disclosures of Hispana writers who published in New Mexico in the 1920s and 1930s is also present in Chávez's 2006 memoir.

Denise Chávez writes, "I know borders, real and imagined. I know what it is to have the rabia/anger, the unmitigated rage well up an then subside, wondering how I will enunciate my rights yet another time" and she adds,

> My borderland is a merciless and harsh desert with achingly blue skies. It can be a place and is a place of peaceful, star-filled nights, wondrous nights that make you want to cry, they are so beautiful. And like so many other things you come to love about a place or its people, they can break your heart. (172)

All of Chávez's major works to date are concerned with life in her hometown, Las Cruces, New Mexico, a city some forty miles from the U.S.-Mexico border and, to one degree or another, all of Chávez's writing is autobiographical. Still, *A Taco Testimony* that gives her the largest stage to explore the contradictory and at times vexed realities of place, identity and culture. She evokes a constant sense of awe and surprise about everyday situations as when she writes, "I live very close to the U.S./Mexico border, but you would think I lived on the moon. Many people here are afraid of Culture, afraid of what it means: having to meet other nationalities, most especially Mexicans and Native people, as equals" (179).

A Taco Testimony encapsulates steely meditations and reflections on family, food, and culture. The text nicely fits Louis Lohr Martz's description: "the 'meditation' is a rigorous exercise in self-contemplation whose aim 'is a state of devotion'" (qtd. in Smith and Watson 197). Chávez affirms "this is not a sweet little book about tacos" (10), but tacos are important as they serve as Chávez's touchstone to a personal and collective past. As a rich cultural symbol, the "lowly" taco floods the narrative with meaning-laden memories, becoming the linchpin of collective memory. Chávez perceptively asks, "Does one create memory from food or does food create memory? Both are the case for me. I am indistinguishable from food, family and culture" (158). As Goldman reminds us, culinary autobiography can have the effect of remaining decidedly non-political while "making ethnicity concrete, by representing it as it is experienced by the individual rather than invoking Culture as an abstraction, such auto-ethnographic texts discourage cultural appropriation, whether it be in the domain of economics or of criticism" (31).

A Taco Testimony holds answers to long-held questions about self, community, borderlands, race, ethnicity and multiculturalism. Chávez explores the nature and personality of her mother and father during the years they were married. Second, she invests much thought into describing what is unique and universal about her borderlands home and culture. Third, she wishes to educate the uninitiated by sharing her culture with them and fourth, she offers a recipe—not for tacos but for social interaction—that comes from her appreciation of "Culture" and her core belief that Culture is a way to salve communities from ignorance, intolerance, offensive behavior, hatred, ingratitude and anxiety.

Chávez remembers her mother, Delfina Rede Faver Chávez as someone who "moved effortlessly through a multiplicity of life experiences with all sorts of people" (126). Her memories of her father, Epifanio Ernesto "Chano" Chávez are painful, but honestly expressed: "It's hard to ascertain the depth of my father's devotion or love for any human, being, especially a woman. He was bound heart and soul to the drink. Anyone or anything, almost anything, came second" (106-107). When Delfina, a widow with a young daughter, met Chano in the late 1940 he was "a handsome and talented attorney, just returned from Georgetown University Law School in Washington, D.C. The world awaited him, his life was all promise" (20). Indeed, as a member of the celebrated "Mexican American Generation" and a friend of the powerful U.S. Senator from New Mexico, Dennis Chávez (after whom Denise was named), Chano's fate seemed secure. So it is after the pair marries, after Denise and her sister Margo are born, that years of struggles with Chano's alcholism begin and Delfina is left to fend for the family.

Chávez's quandary about her parents is not about material success, but about the near opposite views that Chano and Delfina held about their identity and about their social relationship to the people that surround them. Chávez writes:

> We were all Mexicans on my Mother's side of my family. My father had illusions of grandeur like many people from that time and place. They were this way because they had been beaten and worn down by poverty and racism, by tremendous lack and its opposite, grasping. They wanted more and got less, and never had enough money to hold on to the land they once owned, out in the hills of Doña Ana. They were a people whose shame shamed them, but they couldn't articulate their anger. As a result they felt inferior. And as a result of their sense of inferiority, they became deracinated. It isn't easy for me to speak about this.
>
> *****
>
> This, then, was the great tragedy of my parents' lives, the fact that they were divorced not only in spirit, but in culture and core ethnicity. My father would never admit being a Mexican married to a Mexican (78).

A Taco Testimony is also Chávez's intervention into the world through cultural work and writing. Like her understanding of food ways, Chávez pronouncements on "Culture" are both personal and collective. Her recipe for respectful relationships among people moves from the idea that, "True Culture does not divide us—instead it brings us together to explore the great mysteries life presents us. The sometimes difficult mysteries reveal to us our great and always present interconnection. We are one, if only we can see this fact through the veil of perceived difference" (181).

VI. Conclusion

I am not suggesting that texts herein be considered the canon of Chicana life-writing. The study of life narrative is by its very nature an open-ended proposition. Personal narratives are of most interest when we avoid treating them like fictional literary texts or as the culminating works of a culture or a people.

While I must confess that my list of border narratives is incomplete, had space and time allowed I would have added Mary Helen Ponce's *Hoyt Street* (1993) to the border narratives examined here. *Hoyt Street*, a project Ponce began in a folklore seminar evolves as a collection of 36 vignettes about life in the predominantly Chicano barrio of Pacoima, California. Thus, the book is at once personal disclosure and a social history of the Chicano/a community in southern California during and after World War II. Like other border narratives, Ponce's stories are intersected by the vestiges of the "geographies of subjectivity" that operate other Chicana border narratives.

Scholars of Chicana literature will rightly note that I purposefully omit the writings of Gloria Anzaldúa and Cherríe Moraga. I have done this since the scholarship on these writers is copious, but more importantly, because I consider these works to be a distinct form of life-writing, one that tends to draw inferences from a wide field of symbolic, conceptual, and figurative associations. And while, I cognizant that the line between what is lived and what is felt is narrow and imprecise, I am also not inclined to consider Norma Cantú's *Canícula* here, since I consider this work to be a highly experimental form of "fictitional autobiography" and not a text singularly driven by the course of life events and occurrences as is the case of the works I include.

Still, the sequence of the works in this paper is impressive in the way they mark the continuity, presence and agency of an autobiographical impulse for Chicanas. They show that across time and generations Mexicanas and Chicanas have actively sought out the means to share their understanding of themselves and the times that shaped their lives and their social world. Here then, is not the canon, but the legacy of Chicana autobiographical speaking and writing. This is legacy that will remain vibrant only by adding other voices, other works and by bring-ing other readers to this rich source of knowledge. As Denise Chávez bravely puts it "As cultural warriors, our greatest task is to allow others to explore their creativity without fear or reproach. The greatest give we can give each other is our lack of fear" (181). ¡Adelante!

Works Cited

Anzaldúa, Gloria. *Borderlands: The New Mestiza*. 1987. San Francisco: Aunt Lute Press, 1999.

Cantú, Norma. *Canícula: Snapshots of a Girlhood en la Frontera*. Albuquerque: University of New Mexico Press, 1995.

Chávez, Denise. *A Taco Testimony: Meditations on Family, Food and Culture*. Tuc-son, AZ: Río Nuevo Publishers, 2006.

De Gómara, Francisco. *Cortes: The Life of the Conqueror By His Secretary*. Trans. and ed. by Lesley Byrd Simpson. Berkeley, CA: University of California Press, 1964.

De la Cruz, Sor Juana Inés. *A Woman of Genius: The Intellectual Autobiography of Sor Juana Inés de la Cruz*. Translated and with an introduction by Margaret Sayers Peden. Salisbury, CT: Lime Rock Press, 1982.

Díaz del Castillo, Bernal. 1558. *The Conquest of New Spain*. Trans. J. M. Cohen. Middlesex: Penguin Books, 1978.

Eakin, Paul, John. *How our Lives Become Stories: Making Selves*. Ithaca and London: Cornell University Press, 1999.

Goldman, Anne, E. *Take My Word: Autobiographical Innovations of Ethnic American Working Women*. Berkeley, CA: University of California Press, 1996.

Jaramillo, Cleofas. *Romance of a Little Village Girl*. San Antonio: Naylor, Co. 1955.

Lomas, Clara. "Introduction." *The Rebel* by Leonor Villegas de Magnón. Houston: Arte Público Press, 1994. vii-lvi.

Mendoza, Lydia. *Lydia Mendoza: A Family Autobiography*. Edited and with an introduction by Chris Strachwich and James Nicolopulos. Houston: Arte Público Press, 1993.

Messinger Cypress, Sandra. *La Malinche in Mexican Literature: From History to Myth*. Austin: University of Texas Press, 1991.

Moraga, Cherrié. *Loving in the War Years: Lo que nunca pasó por sus labios*. 1983. Cambridge, MA: South End Press, 2000.

Otero Warren, Nina. *Old Spain in Our Southwest*. 1936. Chicago: Río Grande Press, 1962.

Padilla, Genaro, M. *My History, Not Yours: The Formation of Mexican American Autobiography*. Madison: University of Wisconsin Press, 1993.

Ponce, Mary Helen. *Hoyt Street: An Autobiography*. Albuquerque: University of New Mexico Press, 1993.

Smith, Sidonie and Julia Watson. *Reading Autobiography: A Guide for Interpreting Life Narratives*. Minneapolis: University of Minnesota Press, 2001.

Strachwitz, Chris and James Nicolopulos. "Introduction." *Lydia Mendoza: A Family Autobiography* by Lydia Mendoza. Houston: Arte Público Press, 1993. vii-xiv.

Sturken, Marita. *Tangled Memories: The Vietnam War, the AIDS Epidemic, and the Politics of Remembering*. Berkeley, CA: University of California Press, 1997.

Villegas de Magnón, Leonor. *The Rebel*. Ed. Clara Lomas. Houston: Arte Público Press, 1994.

A. Gabriel Meléndez is Professor and Chair of American Studies at the University of New Mexico. His books include *Recovering the U.S. Hispanic Literary Recovery Heritage, Volume VI* (2006), and *The Biography of Casimiro Barela* (2003).

Writing the Fragmented Self in
Oscar Zeta Acosta's *Autobiography of a Brown Buffalo*

Philip Bracher

I. Introduction

The opening pages of *Autobiography of a Brown Buffalo* by Oscar Zeta Acosta feature the narrator Oscar standing in the bathroom, and scrutinizing his huge belly: "I stand naked before the mirror. Every morning of my life I have seen that brown belly from every angle. It has not changed that I can remember. I was always a fat kid. I suck it in and expand an enormous chest... I tighten, suck at the air and recall that Charles Atlas was a ninety-pound weakling when the beach bully kicked sand in his girlfriend's pretty face" (11).[1] Watching his self in the mirror, Oscar reflects upon the bodily self-perfection of the 1920s bodybuilder Charles Atlas, an Italian immigrant originally named Angelo Siciliano. After having migrated to the U.S. in 1910, Siciliano radically changed both his ethnic identity and his own body: he renamed himself Charles Atlas and transformed himself from a "ninety-pound weakling" into a world-famous bodybuilder. On the very first page, Acosta thus presents the reader with the core image of the American Dream—the possibility of self-transformation—and one of the fundamental building blocks of autobiographic writing—the idea of the betterment of the self. At the same time, he deconstructs these very notions on the pages that follow by telling the reader about Oscar's chronic ulcers, his deteriorating mental health, his constipation, and his hallucinations. Oscar curses, vomits, defecates, and devours huge quantities of food. In short, he is

---

[1] In this paper, the book is referred to as *Autobiography*. It is regarded as one of the key texts of Chicano literature and has inspired numerous critical and artistic responses. One example of its continuing influence on contemporary Chicano literature is Manuel Ramos' novel *Blues for the Buffalo* (1997), in which Chicano detective Luis Montez searches for a missing writer and also investigates the whereabouts of Acosta. One of the characters advises him: "Young man, Mr. Investigator, you have to read the *Autobiography of a Brown Buffalo* and *The Revolt of the Cockroach People*. How can any Chicano go through life, and have even a tiny clue, without reading the books of Oscar Acosta?" (30).

the antithesis of the American Dream: he is an unreliable, irate wreck of a man with serious alcohol problems and a severe drug addiction, bent not on self-perfection but on self-destruction.

Using this problematic depiction of the self, this essay will concern itself with what historian Carlos Muñoz has called "the politics of identity or the identity problematic" (8). I will trace the orchestration of autobiographical elements in the text of one of the most emblematic figures of the civil rights era: the iconic Chicano activist-writer Oscar Zeta Acosta (1935-1974), also known as the Brown Buffalo, who mysteriously disappeared in Mazatlán, Mexico in 1974. An author of two books, Acosta has been regarded as the *enfant terrible* of *el movimiento*. He prominently appeared in Hunter S. Thompson's well-known narrative *Fear and Loathing in Las Vegas* as the Samoan attorney Doctor Gonzo and presumably played a considerable role in Thompson's invention of the writing technique of Gonzo journalism. In the *Autobiography*, his first book published in 1972, Acosta uses a first-person narrator to collapse the chasm between the real and the unreal. Even though the title of the book and the name of its protagonist suggest an isomorphic relationship between author and narrator, Acosta subtly undermines the reader's assumptions and reflects upon the complex act of Chicano identity formation.[2]

In general, Mexican American literature has produced a substantial body of autobiographical writing, including specifically autobiographical works such as Ernesto Galarza's *Barrio Boy* (1971) and Richard Rodriguez's *Hunger of Memory* (1982), or the veiled autobiographies of José Antonio Villarreal's *Pocho* (1959) and Sandra Cisneros's *The House on Mango Street* (1983). According to James Clifford, "prose autobiography has set out many of the thematic preoccupations of Chicano writing" (219). Chicano autobiography has often been linked to an emerging ethnic consciousness, but also to the creation of an essentialist Chicano identity. This line of interpretation sees Acosta's *Autobiography* as a "Chicano odyssey of self-discovery" which transforms him from "an alienated lawyer of Mexican ancestry" with "no sense of purpose or identity" into "a Chicano activist" and "someone who affirms his Mexi-

---

[2] To clarify the important distinction between Acosta the *narrator* and Acosta the *author*, I will use the first name of the narrator "Oscar" when referring to the narrator and "Acosta" when referring to the author of the *Autobiography*.

can roots" (J. Rodriguez 5). However, this interpretation largely ignores the complexity and ambiguity of Acosta's work.

In contrast, I will argue that Oscar Zeta Acosta's text can be placed in the tradition of carnivalesque writing, and that his work is inherently dialogic and polyphonic—it is an orchestration of diverse discourses inspired by written and oral speech. Bakhtin's concept of dialogic polyphony helps to explain that in writing his *Autobiography*, Acosta has in mind the paradoxical fusion of heterogeneous and fragmented identity concepts while keeping their potential difference. Acosta essays to construct a new model for a Chicano identity not built on coherence, but on dialogic interaction. Bakhtin's concept of the dialogic therefore allows for a structure of fragmentary existence and a unity in diversity. For Acosta, national identity is not a matter of race or place, but the ability to dialogically imagine oneself as a community. In order to illustrate these points, I will trace the elements of Bakhtin's dialogic principle in the *Autobiography* on four levels: First, I will deal with the level of national identity and autobiography; then, I will discuss the question of authorship at the crossroads of fiction and reality; third, I will scrutinize dialogic elements on the plot level and demonstrate in how far the border plays a pivotal role in the emergence of a polyphonic consciousness. Finally, the analysis will explore how Bakhtin's notion of grotesque realism is realized in Acosta's text.

II. National Identity and the Autobiography

In this first section, I want to put three key concepts into conversation: monologism, polyphony, and the nation. Without question, strong ties have always existed between nationality and autobiography. Autobiographical writing is where, as Richard Ruland and Malcolm Bradbury have put it, "the history of America begins" (17), and there have been numerous examples to support their claim: From Cabeza de Vaca's *Relación*, the biographical writings of William Bradford and Benjamin Franklin's *Autobiography* to an emerging racial, ethnic, and gender consciousness in the autobiographical writings of Frederick Douglass, Malcolm X, and Maxine Hong Kingston, nation has been narration.

The underlying assumption is, of course, that the much disputed term "nation" is constructed along the lines of Benedict Anderson's concept of the nation imagined as a limited, sovereign community. From this vantage point, national identity becomes an act of imagination that is a construct rather than an essence. Using Anderson's concept, autobiographical narratives can be and have been posited as one of the fundamental building blocks of the nation. This is hardly surprising, as nations and selves share a similar interest: They are both occupied with establishing themselves in their own imaginary space by differentiating themselves from others, thus claiming their sovereignty and independence from their surroundings. The birth of a new self within the boundaries of autobiographical writing has therefore often been linked to the birth of a nation (204-209).[3] A prominent point in case is Benjamin Franklin's *Autobiography* (1791), which follows the plot of a *Bildungsroman* in that Franklin's self progresses from "Poverty and Obscurity... to a state of Affluence" (538). This linear and steady development from rags to riches and his transformation into a disciplined and rational *zoon politikon* mirrors the unfolding of the American nation after the revolution. Through his individual, subjective and sovereign expression, Franklin's self paradoxically becomes the representative American self. Published after the War of Independence, this autobiography chronicles the birth of a national American identity while simultaneously depicting Franklin's personal growth toward fullness and coherence.

How does Franklin go about defining the American self, and why has his strategy been this successful? One reason is that Franklin presents a unified and coherent picture of self and nation instead of portraying its fragmented and incoherent parts. This effect of unity is achieved through the monologic nature of Franklin's depiction. Going back to Mikhail Bakhtin's fundamental distinction between monologic discourse on the one hand and the dialogic (or alternatively polyphonic) nature of narratives on the other, the monologic discourse employs a single style and expresses a single world-view. Conversely, the dialogic represents an orchestration of diverse discourses entailing different and oftentimes conflicting ideological positions which are put into play with each other.

---

[3] Anderson calls the autobiography the "biography of the nation" and remarks: "[I]dentity..., because it cannot be 'remembered,' must be narrated ... As with modern persons, so it is with nations. Awareness of being imbedded in secular, serial time, with all its implications of continuity, yet of 'forgetting' the experience of this continuity—product of the ruptures of the late eighteenth century—engenders the need for a narrative of 'identity'" (204).

The monologic system is what ties together Franklin's *Autobiography*: The construction of a unifying self and a coherent national identity presupposes that the "I" of Franklin's writing is alone within its own discourse. As soon as "another's voice, another's accent, the possibility of another's point of view breaks through this play," all claims to unity are necessarily destroyed (Bakhtin, *The Dialogic Imagination* 39).

In this sense, Acosta's *Autobiography of a Brown Buffalo* is an utter failure. While Franklin's work charts the teleological development of a representative American self in a unifying way, Acosta pictures the ups and downs of a *vato loco*—literally, a "crazy guy"—whose aimless roaming along the dark underbelly of the American Dream reveals anything but coherence.[4] Acosta aims at rupturing the epic view of the autobiography as a closed unity and at unveiling the process of identity formation as impossible to finalize. Consequently, he posits a new model for a Chicano identity that is based not on a unified and coherent narrative, but on the dialogic principle of identity formation.

Acosta's writing can also be seen as an attempt to present a revisionist perspective on U.S. history, which places him in tradition of what Juan Bruce-Novoa has called the Chicano "obsession with history" (30). Just like Franklin's *Autobiography* contributes to and participates in the symbolizing act of writing history, Acosta's *Autobiography* demands recognition of a distinct Chicano identity within the framework of U.S. cultural production. It is this position that Acosta holds when he remarks: "I speak as a historian, a recorder of events with a sour stomach. I have no love for memories of the past" (18). The argument that Acosta reflects upon the processes of identity formation in the context of a national discourse is supported by the time frame of the book. His *Autobiography* begins on July 1, 1967 and reaches its climax on Independence Day. His character thus comments on racial inequality in the U.S. and demands participation not only on a personal but a national level. However, Acosta does not simply denounce dominant history as partial or false, as his persona realizes that the creation of another monolithic historical account would possibly lead to a mere opposition between two different versions of history. Rather, he seeks to break up the

---

[4] For a discussion of the figure of the *vato loco* in Acosta's works, see Smethurst, 119-132.

monological unity of traditional history by dialogically engaging different voices and perspectives in his *Autobiography*.

III. The Author and the Autobiography

The plot of *Autobiography of a Brown Buffalo* begins on the first day of July
1967: Oscar, an antipoverty-lawyer at the East Oakland Legal Aid
society, drives to his office in downtown San Francisco only to discover
that his secretary—who usually does most of the work for him—has
died over the weekend. Confronted with several women who want to
get temporary restraining orders against their husbands, Oscar flees and
decides to start a new life. He throws away his lawyer's license, fires his
therapist, and spends the rest of the day drinking and doing drugs in a
local bar. The next morning, he sets out on a road trip that seemingly
turns into a quest for his identity. His travels zigzag from San Francisco
to Los Angeles, the Nevada side of Lake Tahoe, Ketchum, Idaho, the ski
resort Alpine in Colorado and finally to the twin border cities of El Paso
and Juárez; at the end of the text he boards a bus to Los Angeles, where
he wants to join the Brown Berets, a radical Chicano activist group. The
episodic journey is interspersed with memory fragments of his childhood in rural California and his time in the U.S. Navy and in Panama.

The question arises: in how far is the *Autobiography of a Brown Buffalo*
an autobiography in the usual sense? Scholars have quibbled extensively
over this problem. Dieter Herms considers Acosta's text an autobiographical novel (166); Ramón Saldívar has called it "semi-autobiographical" (25); Héctor Calderón stresses that this is "an empirical
narrative, a self-portrait" (98), while Frederick Luis Aldama insists that
Acosta's work is "a fictional construct" that calls "attention to the
fictionality of his facts" and wants to "reform conventions of autobiography" (67, 65).

In a Bakhtinian sense, the very structure of Acosta's *Autobiography* is
of a dialogic nature, as fictional elements enter into a dialogue with the
factual ones; while the text is not fully fictional, it is not fully "true,"
either. The author collapses the dichotomy between the real and the
unreal by inventing a persona that is fueled both by imagination and
real life, fiction and history. The result is a narrative form that postulates
a fluid sense of the self that can reinvent itself and throw off the yoke of
historical circumstances. As a result, it is nearly impossible to unravel

the history of the "real" Acosta: This becomes clear at the moment one tries to define the usual starting point for an autobiography—the author's date and place of birth.[5] Acosta's birth is recorded in El Paso, Texas, on April 8, 1935—he himself put down his birthday as April 6, 1935 on his application for the California bar. This imprecision of details is mirrored in the *Autobiography*. His fictional self announces: "I am fourteen today… It was April the eighth, 1949 and I was to complete my first year of high school" (105-106). The reader can thus calculate his date of birth: April 8, 1935. At another point in the text, however, he informs the reader on July 1, 1967: "I am thirty-three, the same age as Jesus when he died" (18). This would place his birth in the year 1934. Yet another passage offers the year 1936 as the date of birth. By suggesting three different possibilities, the narrator willfully distances himself from the author of the autobiography, while also maintaining ties with him.

Numerous other historical persons appear in the text under pseudonyms: Hunter S. Thompson becomes the character Karl King, while Robert Henry, a good friend of Acosta, becomes the fat Irish seaman Ted Casey, the Owl; Robert's wife Ann Henry is featured as Alice. The name of the narrator's grade school teacher Joan Andersson is actually the name of a lawyer who worked with Acosta on a case during his time in San Francisco. Others, like the 60s drug icon Timothy Leary or the author Mark Harris appear under their own names. Harris is yet another example of how Acosta intentionally plays with reality until it is undistinguishable from fiction: in the acknowledgements on the opening pages of the text, Acosta thanks Mark Harris as his "instructor," only to deride him in a later part of the book as belonging to the "intellectuals at S.F. State," those "guys with the tweed coats and fancy pipes" (100). Oscar takes one of Harris's writing courses only to discover the ineptness of his mentor: "[Harris] asked me if I wanted to read his first draft of *Wake Up, Stupid!* I kept it for a week and returned it to him at the next short story seminar. I only read the first paragraph. After that, I was no

---

[5] Acosta's text begins *in medias res*; his background is revealed slowly in a series of disconnected episodic flashbacks. Acosta thus blurs the lines between past and present and disrupts the tradition of chronological order in autobiographies. In contrast, Franklin's *Autobiography*, which follows a chronological structure, begins with Franklin's ancestors and then continues with the birth of the author.

longer afraid of intellectuals. I knew I could tell a better story" (100). Acosta also alters the names of places. In 1967, the author worked as a cook in a Mexican restaurant in Aspen, Colorado. The town appears again in the *Autobiography*, but is called Alpine. Furthermore, important details of Acosta's personal are completely left out, like his family, his wife Betty and his son, Marco. Acosta chose to remodel his persona into an alienated drifter with no family ties. Therefore, the lens that the author Oscar Zeta Acosta uses to portray the life of the narrator Oscar Zeta Acosta distorts and alters biographical realities while simultaneously playing off against them.

Why did Acosta then choose the narrative form of the autobiography to draw up this mostly fictitious life story? The answer lies in the *function* that autobiographies are usually associated with. Writing on Chicano autobiographies, Teresa McKenna has summed it up in this way:

> When we speak of autobiographies, we tend to hold certain notions to be self-evident: (1) that we are given the sum total of a person's life and (2) that the account we are given is true. The first idea presupposes continuity, connectedness, coherence, and closure, while the second underscores the nature of the account as history, narration of events, and, therefore, truth. These commonly held aspects of autobiography are not necessarily so, however, because, as writing, autobiography is nothing other than story or narrative. (51)

Acosta, however, does more than simply draw attention to the fictionality of facts. He interweaves his own life story with that of his narrator, so that fact and fiction become an inextricable web of meaning. From a Bakhtinian point of view, he dialogically engages the real and the imagined and turns the narration into a polyphonic discourse.

IV. The Plot

The same effect can be observed on the plot level. It is remarkable how Oscar shifts through various masks and disguises. Instead of assuming one identity, Oscar stares at his mirror image and begins to imagine himself anew:

> I stare into the mirror for an answer. See that man with the insignificant eyes drawn back, lips thinned down tight? That suave motherfucker is Mister Joe Cool himself. Yes, old Bogey... And now with the upper lips tightly curled under and baring his top

row of white teeth, can't you tell? See how he nods his head, shaking it from side to side as in a tremble of uncontrollable anger? Right! James Cagney, you rotten scabs! And if you loosen up a bit, puff those fat cheeks out slightly and talk deep in my throat... My name is Edward G. Robinson and I don't want any troubles from you guys. See? (12)

This passage is a prime example of what Bakhtin has termed double-voiced or double-oriented discourse. Oscar gives the reader an insight into his own self by borrowing words and phrases, the syntax and the rhythm from movie characters of the 1940s and 1950s that accompany his imitations. He mimics Bogey's coolness, Cagney's uncontrollable rage and the aloofness of Robinson by appropriating their discourse and using it as part of the narrator's voice. When Oscar says "Yes, old Bogey...", the pause behind the monosyllabic utterance lends it weight and self-assuredness. He then uses short exclamatory sentences intermingled with the slang expression "scabs" to represent Cagney's anger, while the long, drawn-out utterance representing Robinson's dangerous quietness can be read as a reference to his part as a gangster boss in the 1948 movie *Key Largo*. The narrator does not present the three characters through the use of direct speech—instead, he utilizes his own voice, but communicates in their manner of speech. This creates a double consciousness, because the voice of Bogart is heard *through* the narrator's voice which consequently "not only refers to something in the world but also refers to another speech act by another addresser" (Lodge 59).[6]

There are numerous other instances in the text when the reader becomes aware of the fact that the author is not addressing him directly, but rather through the discourse of some other persona. This fluctuating and shifting through identities is continued throughout the narrative. Oscar cannot be contained, as he imagines himself as Ernest Hemingway, García Lorca, Dylan Thomas, and Rocky. In a drug frenzy Oscar takes a look at himself in the mirror and believes himself to be transformed into the Wolfman, a character in a 1941 movie, who is half man,

---

[6] In his metalinguistic approach, Bakhtin broadly differentiates between three principal types of discourse: The direct speech of the author, the represented speech of the characters, and the double-voiced speech. The third category is the most important for the dialogic principle and can be divided into several subcategories (stylization, *skaz*, parody, hidden polemic).

half wolf: "I was surprised to see that the drug had made the hair on my otherwise smooth arms grow long and green... My face was now completely covered with hair. Not just the beard, God damn it; I mean my entire body was that of the green Wolfman, good ol' Lon Chaney" (39).

During the course of the text, the narrator's identity is more and more dissolved as he takes on a plethora of jobs: Oscar is an athlete in his high school football team, a binge drinker, a clarinet player in the Air Force Band, writer of the book *My Cart for My Casket*, lawyer, a physical therapist, dishwasher, plumber, and construction worker. As a Southern Baptist missionary in the jungles of Panama, he converts natives to Christianity. In Juárez, he eventually becomes a pimp.

In accordance with these various employments, he freely shifts through ethnic identities. He is identified by himself and others as Samoan, Mexican, Blackfoot Indian, Aztec, "nigger" and "jigaboo." In one instance, Oscar tells the reader: "I grew up a fat, dark Mexican—a Brown Buffalo—and my enemies called me a nigger" (86). In another passage, he writes: "I've been mistaken for American Indian, Spanish, Filipino, Hawaian, Samoan, and Arabian," but concedes: "No one has ever asked me if I'm a spic or greaser" (68). Oftentimes, these identities conflict with each and contradict the authorial voice. For instance, he tells one listener: "My family is the last of the Aztecs" (140). Here, Oscar invokes the mythic past of the indigenous forebears of the Mexicans only to destroy this past in another instance: "I hate for people to assume that I'm an authority on Mexicans. Just because I'm a brown buffalo doesn't mean I'm the son of Moctezuma, does it? Anyway, I told her I was a Samoan by the name of Henry Hawk" (101). Finally, the satire on a stable ethnic identity reaches its climax when he swallows two aspirins and becomes "a gorilla. No, I didn't *look* like one, I *was* one" (164).

Thus, like other elements in the *Autobiography*, ethnic identity is an equally indeterminable and dialogic process. Ethnic identity is rather something akin to Bakhtin's notion of the "idea" that does not reside in one person's isolated consciousness:

> The idea... is not a subjective individual-psychological formation with 'permanent resident's rights' in a person's head; no, the idea is inter-individual and inter-subjective—the realm of its existence is not individual consciousness but dialogic communion between

consciousnesses. The idea is a *live event*, played out at the point of
dialogic meeting between two or more consciousnesses... Like the
word, the idea wants to be heard, understood, and 'answered' by
other voices from other positions. (*Problems of Dostoevsky's Poetics*
98)

Oscar's narrative is not, as some critics have remarked, a search for a
unified and monologic identity or the creation of a unified one out of
many selves, but rather the depiction of the many selves in a dialogic
interaction.[7] All the different personae, voices and opinions are not
leveled, but rather kept and put next to one another. These ideas and
concepts of Oscar's self all undergo an intense struggle of several individual consciousnesses, which are paradoxically all held together in
Oscar's imagination. The contradictory potential of ethnic identity is not
glossed over but fully realized, which leads to an ambiguous—and
oftentimes confusing—narrative complexity.

V. The Border

The ultimate expression of this complexity is Acosta's description of
Oscar's journey down south into Mexico and the literal and
metaphorical act of crossing the border between the two countries. Here,
Oscar undergoes what Bakhtin has termed a *Schwellendialog* ("dialogue
of the threshold") (*Problems of Dostoevsky's Poetics* 111). Oscar's crossing
is strategically placed at the very end of the book. This stands in stark
contrast to the traditional depiction of border crossings in Chicano
writing: Beginning with Daniel Venegas' *The Adventures of Don Chipote*
(1928) and continuing with José Antonio Villareal's *Pocho* (1959), Aristeo
Brito's *The Devil in Texas* (1976), and Genaro González' *Rainbow's End*
(1988), the border crossing as an essential part in the formation of a Chicano consciousness is placed at the opening of the text, not at the very
end. For Oscar, the border marks the end of his journey, but paradoxically also the very beginning. His consciousness opens to accept his

---

[7] See Joe Rodríguez's essay on Acosta. Aldama reads the *Autobiography* as
the "easily recognizable Christian narrative of guilt, confession and redemption" and presupposes a stable final identity because "Acosta will symbolically
die in San Francisco to be reborn, resurrected in El Paso as a Chicano and as a
leader of his people" (98).

fragmented and polyphonic self not as one, but as the interaction of many consciousnesses.

Before traveling down south, Oscar works odd jobs in the ski resort of Vail, Colorado. Eventually, he tires of "those senseless drugs, those lifeless hippies and those tourist funhogs who clearly didn't have the answer" (184) and experiences depressions: "I roamed the mountains, soaking up the snow, and cried at the silent, white death" (184). He knows it is time to move on and makes up his mind to "hit the road once more" in the direction of his home town: "I decided to go to El Paso, the place of my birth, to see if I could find the object of my quest. I still wanted to find out who the hell I was" (184). He confronts the border, or rather, the border confronts him on his way to the checkpoint on the Mexican side:

> When the thick guard in uniform approached me I felt a tingle in my neck. I had no passport, no identification of any kind whatso-ever. I had lost my wallet in Taos several months prior to my entry into Juarez [sic] ... I was certain he would interrogate me... Where have you been? Just who are you anyway, *muchacho*? And just how *would* I explain to him about Mr. Wilkie if I couldn't speak Spanish? And would they provide an interpreter? *Por favor*? No, I knew it wouldn't do. I knew I'd be arrested... Impersonating a *mexicano*? Is there such a charge? (187)

As in the passage quoted earlier, the double-oriented discourse in Oscar speech becomes apparent as he appropriates the discourse of the Mexican border guard. The difference, however, is that this time the narrator has a meta-awareness of the two consciousnesses that collide in his speech act. While impersonating the other's discourse, he is asking himself if "impersonating a *mexicano*" is a charge and therefore expresses his awareness of the act while committing it.

Moreover, Oscar has lost all legal documents that could establish his identity. This proves problematic when he returns from his stay in Mexico and tries to enter the U.S. again. A "tall blond with a .357 Magnum" asks him to prove who he is ("You don't *look* like an American, you know?"). The question triggers a self-reflexion on the part of Oscar: "Jesus Christ, I think, what *do* I have to prove who I am?... There's nothing in my pockets but eight *centavos*. I've got a clarinet and a camera with a few rags in my traveling bag." Then, he realizes that his quest for identity has been futile and admits: "Nothing. I've got nothing on me to prove who I am... just my word" (195).

Oscar's realization that his "word" is the only proof of his identity is more than phrasal expression. The act of crossing the border and confronting an unknown—yet intimately close—culture epitomizes the dialogic nature of self. In *Problems of Dostoevsky's Poetics*, Bakhtin stresses the importance of boundaries and the need for their transgression to reach a full understanding of the self not as an enclosed and finalized entity, but as an open-ended dialogue: "A person has no internal sovereign territory, he is wholly and always on the boundary; looking inside himself, he looks into the eyes of another or with the eyes of another." Oscar's confrontation with an external and fortified border leads to a growing awareness of the importance of "not that which takes place within, but that which takes place on the boundary between one's own and someone else's consciousness, on the threshold" (*Problems of Dostoevsky's Poetics* 287).

This describes what has been called Bakhtin's "principle of permeable boundaries," which he has put into the following words: "[E]verything internal gravitates not toward itself but is turned to the outside and dialogized, every internal experience ends up on the boundary, encounters another, and in this tension-filled encounter lies its entire essence." Essentially, dialogue represents nothing more than a boundary that has to be crossed and re-crossed.[8]

From this perspective, the border is elevated from its marginal status to represent the very essence of the dialogic principle. Oscar's encounter with the boundary of the national territory leads him to accept the impossibility of his quest for a stable and essentialist identity. In the end,

---

[8] In "The Problem of Content, Material, and Form in Verbal Art," Bakhtin underscores that what holds true for the individual self holds also true for entire cultures: "One must not, however, imagine the realm of culture as some sort of spatial whole, having boundaries but also having internal territory. The realm of culture has no internal territory: it is entirely distributed along the boundaries, boundaries pass everywhere, through its very aspect, the systematic unity of culture extends into the very atoms of cultural life, it reflects like the sun in each drop of that life. Every cultural act lives essentially on boundaries: in this is its seriousness and its significance; abstracted from boundaries, it loses its soil, it becomes empty, arrogant, it degenerates and dies" (317).

he pawns his final belongings and rents a room at the Grand Hotel in downtown El Paso. Alone in his room, he finds himself back at the beginning of his journey: "I stand naked before the mirror. I cry in sobs. My massive chest quivers and my broad shoulders sag. I am a brown buffalo lonely and afraid in a world I never made" (195). He then calls his brother and tells him: "I've checked it all out and have failed to find the answer to my search. One sonofabitch tells me I'm not Mexican and the other says I'm not American. I got no roots anywhere" (196). However, the *Autobiography* does not end on a note of despair, but rather of hope. Oscar has realized the polyphonic nature of his self and wants to communicate this experience of identity formation by becoming a writer. On the last page, he soliloquizes:

> My single mistake has been to seek an identity with any one person or nation or with any part of history… What I see now on this rainy day in January, 1968, what is clear to me after this sojourn is that I am neither a Mexican nor an American. I am neither a Catholic nor a Protestant. I am a Chicano by ancestry and a Brown Buffalo by choice. Is that so hard for you to understand? (199)

VI. Grotesque Realism

For Bakhtin, the dialogic type of literary discourse has its roots in the serio-comic genres of classical literature, in Menippean satire, Socratic dialogue, and satyr plays. While the Middle Ages channeled the energies of the parodic polyphonic discourse in the unofficial culture of carnival, the Renaissance began to express the carnivalistic through literature; according to Bakhtin, this "boundless world of humorous forms" served to "oppos[e] the official and serious tone of medieval ecclesiastical and feudal culture" (*The Bakhtin Reader* 196). The rise of the novel through the nineteenth and twentieth centuries further augmented the expression of the dialogic through literature. At the very beginning of the evolution of the dialogic discourse thus lies the folk carnival humor with its parodies, its code-switching between Latin and the vernacular, and the popular curses and oaths. These elements find their representation in a mode that Bakhtin calls "grotesque realism," the expression of the satirical impulse of that folk culture. Since the essential principle of grotesque realism is degradation, the "lowering of all that is high" (*The Bakhtin Reader* 205), the body becomes the central image within this mode of representation. It is exaggerated through the minute depiction of its organs, the act of eating, belching, vomiting, urinating, defecating and copulating.

All these features can be found in Acosta's *Autobiography*, too, as the material body and its degradation play a highly important role. Oscar is perpetually in the process of eating or drinking, he is belching, vomiting and digesting—all the images of his body are offered in an extremely exaggerated form. Like Rabelais, who was proclaimed by Victor Hugo as the poet of the "flesh" and of the "belly" (Bakhtin, *Problems of Dostoevsky's Poetics* 204), Acosta employs the aesthetic concept of grotesque realism to heighten the sense of the communal:

> In grotesque realism... the bodily element is deeply positive. It is presented not in a private, egotistic form, severed from the other spheres of life, but as something universal, representing all the people... The material bodily principle is contained not in the biological individual, ... but in the people, a people who are continually growing and renewed. This is why all that is bodily becomes grandiose, exaggerated, immeasurable. (*The Bakhtin Reader* 205)

Therefore, when Oscar is reduced to his base materiality and transformed into a "gargantuan antihero" (Aldama 73), this strategy only underscores the communal plight of all Chicanos. He consumes large quantities of "Snicker bars, liverwurst sandwiches with gobs of mayonnaise and Goddamned caramel sundaes" (11), so that eventually he is turned into a degenerate mass of brown body: "For twelve months now all I have done is stuffed myself, puked wretched collages in a toilet bowl, swallowed 1000 tranquilizers without water, stared at the idiot-box, coddled myself and watched the snakes grow larger inside my head while waiting for the clockhand to turn" (24). The positive bodily image of the carnivalesque is transformed into its absolute negative and expresses a deep uneasiness about and displacement of Chicano ethnicity in U.S. society. Moreover, this image of the body underscores on yet another level the unfinished, unstable nature of Bakhtin's dialogic principle: Oscar's body is not complete in itself, but is steadily growing and transgressing the boundaries of its own self. By stressing the body parts that are open to the outside world (nose, mouth, ears, breasts, and genitals), the body is in a state of becoming rather than being. The apertures enable a communication with the outside world and show a body that is ever creating and changing through eating, drinking and copulation. Therefore, the body and the world form an inseparable connection and dialogically engage each other.

VII. Conclusion

Summing up, this paper has attempted to show that Bakhtin's principle of the dialogic runs through Acosta's *Autobiography* on various levels: on the macroscopic level, the text lends itself to the observation that contrary to the tradition of a unified, coherent and nationalistically tinged writing of autobiographies, *Autobiography of a Brown Buffalo* engages the factual and the real in a dialogue and posits a model of Chicano identity that is anti-essentialist. The dialogic principle can be traced all the way down to the microscopic level of the plot, where various voices and identities are placed on a horizontal plane and exist in an ongoing contest with one another; they are never put in a hierarchical order. While authors like Franklin pursue the goal of gathering all discourses in a single unified center, Acosta seeks plurality and fragmentation.

This, however, does not mean that Acosta's text is an unmediated cacophony of discourses. The voices remain part of the authorial orchestration, but are allowed to differ and to alter the outcome of events. The literary figure of Oscar as the poetic expression of Acosta is one voice among the many but is not given ultimate authority. All utterances and the various personae that Oscar assumes and the various views expressed by the different characters are kept in a dialogical balance. Dialogization as a basic distinctive feature of the stylistics of the novel is also applicable to the genre of fictional autobiography.

What Bakhtin has remarked about the ending of Dostoevsky's novels also holds true for the *Autobiography of a Brown Buffalo*: "[N]othing conclusive has yet taken place in the world, the ultimate word of the world and about the world has not yet been spoken, the world is open and free, everything is still in the future and always will be in the future" (*Problems of Dostoevsky's Poetics* 165).

Works Cited

Acosta, Oscar Zeta. *Autobiography of a Brown Buffalo*. New York: Vintage, 1989.

Aldama, Frederick Luis. *Postethnic Narrative Criticism: Magicorealism in Oscar 'Zeta' Acosta, Ana Castillo, Julie Dash, Hanif Kureishi, and Salman Rushdie*. Austin: University of Texas Press, 2003.

Anderson, Benedict. *Imagined Communities: Reflections on the Origin and Spread of Nationalism*. London: Verso, 1991.

Bakhtin, Mikhail. *The Dialogic Imagination. Four Essays by M. M. Bakhtin*. Austin: University of Texas Press, 1981.

—. "The Problem of Content, Material, and Form in Verbal Art." *Art and Answerability: Early Philosophical Essays by M. M. Bakhtin*. Eds. Michael Holquist and Vadim Liapunov. Austin: University of Texas Press, 1990. 257-325.

—. *The Bakhtin Reader. Selected Writings of Bakhtin, Medvedev, Voloshinov*. Ed. Pam Morris. London: Edward Arnold, 1994.

—. *Problems of Dostoevsky's Poetics*. Edited and translated by Caryl Emerson. Minneapolis: University of Minnesota Press, 1994.

Brito, Aristeo. *El diablo en Texas/The Devil in Texas*. Tempe, AZ: Bilingual Press/ Editorial Bilingüe, 1990.

Bruce-Novoa, Juan. "History as Content, History as Act: The Chicano Novel." *Atzlán* 18.1 (1989): 29-44.

Cabeza de Vaca, Alvar Núñez. *Adventures in the Unknown Interior of America*. Albuquerque: University of New Mexico Press, 1983.

Calderón, Héctor. *Narratives of Greater Mexico: Essays on Chicano Literary History, Genre, and Borders*. Austin: University of Texas Press, 2004.

Cisneros, Sandra. *The House on Mango Street*. New York: Vintage Books, 1991.

Clifford, James and Marcus, George E., eds. *Writing Culture: The Poetics and Politics of Ethnography*. Berkeley, CA: University of California Press, 1986.

Douglass, Frederick. *Narrative of the Life of Frederick Douglass, An American Slave: Written by Himself*. 1845. New Haven: Yale University Press, 2001.

Franklin, Benjamin. *The Autobiography [Part One]. The Norton Anthology of American Literature. Volume A. Literature to 1820*. Ed. Nina Baym, et al. New York & London: Norton, 2003. 538-583.

Galarza, Ernesto. *Barrio Boy*. Notre Dame: University of Notre Dame Press, 1971.

González, Genaro. *Rainbow's End*. Houston: Arte Público Press, 1988.

Herms, Dieter. *Die zeitgenössische Literatur der Chicanos (1959-1988)*. Frankfurt: Vervuert, 1990.

Kingston, Maxine Hong. *The Woman Warrior: Memoir of a Girlhood Among Ghosts.* New York: Vintage, 1976.

Lodge, David. "Lawrence, Dostoevsky, Bakhtin." *After Bakhtin: Essays on Fiction and Criticism.* Ed. David Lodge. London & New York: Routledge, 1990. 57-74.

Malcolm X. *The Autobiography of Malcolm X.* 1966. New York: Ballantine, 1999.

McKenna, Teresa. *Migrant Song: Politics and Process in Contemporary Chicano Literature.* Austin: University of Texas Press, 1997.

Muñoz, Carlos. *Youth, Identity, Power: The Chicano Movement.* London: Verso, 1989.

Ramos, Manuel. *Blues for the Buffalo.* Evanston, IL: Northwestern University Press, 2004.

Rodríguez, Joe D. "Oscar Zeta Acosta." *Dictionary of Literary Biography. Volume 82.* Detroit: Gale Research, 1989. 3-10.

Rodriguez, Richard. *Hunger of Memory: The Education of Richard Rodríguez.* New York: Bantam, 1982.

Ruland, Richard and Malcolm Bradbury. *From Puritanism to Postmodernism: A History of American Literature.* New York: Viking Penguin, 1991.

Saldívar, Ramón. "Ideologies of the Self: Chicano Autobiography." *Diacritics* 15.3 (1985): 23-34.

Smethurst, James. "The Figure of the Vato Loco and the Representation of Ethnicity in the Narratives of Oscar Z. Acosta." *MELUS* 20.2 (1995): 119-132.

Thompson, Hunter S. *Fear and Loathing in Las Vegas: A Savage Journey to the Heart of the American Dream.* New York: Vintage, 1971.

Venegas, Daniel. *The Adventures of Don Chipote.* Houston: Arte Público Press, 2000.

Philip Bracher is a doctoral candidate and assistant at the American Studies Department of the University of Heidelberg, Germany. His areas of research include the politics of migration, Chicano studies, and border theory.

Referential Ambiguities or Ambiguous Referentialities: The Interactions of History, Language, and Image in Victor Villaseñor's and Sheila and Sandra Ortiz Taylor's Family Autobiographies

Angelika Köhler

I. Contemporary Chicano/a Life Writing

Autobiographical texts are marked by an interesting interaction of the public and the private, of history and fiction that creates infinite spaces for diverse perspectives and ambivalent readings. As Paul de Man has pointed out, autobiography needs to be reconceptualized as a most flexible "figure of reading or of understanding" (70), capable of the discursive management of the inconsistencies and instabilities of present-day life. Claiming an important role in the contemporary postmodern and postcolonial discourses, the autobiographical genre in general and Mexican American personal narratives in particular have produced an astonishing multiplicity of forms. Recent studies of autobiographical texts therefore prefer the term *life writing* to underline the genre's rich potential for revisionist techniques and its capacity to explore the complex interdependencies between historical conditions and changes and the individual's cultural self-understanding.

This essay will discuss two examples of Mexican American life writing, Victor Villaseñor's 1991 family saga *Rain of Gold* and Sheila and Sandra Ortiz Taylor's 1996 family autobiography *Imaginary Parents*. The writers of the two books apply highly diverse narrative techniques of life writing; still, they share the significant characteristic of trespassing the borders between reconstructing their parents' life stories and writing themselves into existence, thus challenging genre definitions by blending autobiography and biography. Searching through photographs and recollecting the stories told by family members and friends, Villaseñor and the Ortiz Taylor sisters reassemble an image of their parents that questions Roland Barthes's narrator's rhetoric of "know[ing] that, *in the field of the subject, there is no referent*" (*Roland Barthes by Roland Barthes* 56). *Rain of Gold* and *Imaginary Parents* negotiate the construction of the autobiographical self in terms of its referentialities to the past as a way to outline prospects for the future. Transforming the individual episodes available to the artists in the form of photographs or remembered incidents into a narrative structure able to revitalize their family's history, the ancestors turn into fictive contemporaries of the writers. Though they are not willing to control the next generation's patterns of life, they evoke an awareness of their cultural roots that can function as a referential framework for their own processes of self-positioning within the contexts of their family histories in particular, but also within those of American cultural history in general.

Victor Villaseñor and Sheila and Sandra Ortiz Taylor redefine the autobiographical individual self in terms of a collective identity whose multiple referentialities support individual readings. Thus, a new reality of subjectivity emerges, in which this self finally manages its sense of personal fragmentation and cultural alienation. Both texts function as testimonies of their authors' belief in the American Dream, but rewriting this myth against the experiences of their families' Mexican American history, they actually create an American *Borderland* Dream. Their recollections "require physical displacement from and return to" the *fronterizo* cultural space in order to reconceptualize it as a free creative realm in which border life is "encod[ed] as a constant movement either realized or potential" (Castillo and Córdoba 30). Appropriating border experiences on the metaphorical level through memory and secondary texts, as suggested in Gloria Anzaldúa's concept of a discursively constructed *la frontera* image, as well as on the level of literally crossing the physical line between cultures, border theory functions as a practical source of empowerment in the work of the three artists (see Castillo and Córdoba 18).

II. A Blend of Autobiography and Biography:
Victor Villaseñor's *Rain of Gold*

Against this background of the borderland we gain a deeper understanding of the serious controversy which Victor Villaseñor fought with G. P. Putnam's Sons, the renowned publisher who had scheduled *Rain of Gold* for publication in the spring of 1989. At face value a promising prospect, the author could not agree to Putnam's conditions which would have meant, apart from some minor revisions, a change of the original title from *Rain of Gold* to *Rio Grande*, in Villaseñor's eyes a most indecent request because, as he argues, "they wanted a Mexican title for a Mexican book, but *Rio Grande* is a John Wayne movie" ("Rain Maker" 1). When the text was finally published in 1991 by Arte Público Press of Houston, the writer concluded his "Foreword" with a strong emphasis on the non-fictional character of his book, thus unintentionally blurring the distinguishing accomplishment of his family history which grows from its being located in-between the binary oppositions of fiction versus non-fiction, a pattern that has traditionally been applied to support the organization of Western cultural thinking.

Genevieve Fabre and Juan Bruce-Novoa argue that history—in general—can never be objective, since the data gathered must be contextualized and presented in a narrative form whose language and rhetoric are significantly shaped by the subjectivity of the authorial voice (1). With regard to Latino culture they even specify that the exploration of these contexts "within the United States [is] often a matter of historical presence, as well as of rereading the standard versions of the national history from a different perspective" (4). As Norma Elia Cantú explains in the introduction to her autobiographical narrative *Canícula: Snapshots of a Girlhood en la Frontera*, "life in *la frontera* is raw truth, and stories of such life, ficticious as they may be, are even truer than true" (xi). In *Imaginary Parents*, Sheila Ortiz Taylor challenges genre geography in similar ways by saying: "Call this book autobiography. Or memoir. Call it poetry. Call it nonfiction. Call it the purest fiction. Call it a codex. Give it a call number" (xiii). If Avrom Fleishman asserts that "life—indeed the idea of a life—is already structured as a narrative," and Oliver Sacks goes as far as to say that "each of us constructs and lives a 'narrative,' and that this narrative *is* us" (qtd. in Adams xii), then *Rain of Gold* needs to be read as another most interesting example of Chicano life writing that inserts itself into the ongoing discussion of contemporary theorizing forms of autobiographical writing. Referring to his text as "a tribal history" of his people (xiii), Villaseñor trespasses the defining borders of Western literary history, since conceptualizing himself as a part of this story, it shares characteristics of autobiographical writing, whereas the broad epic reconstruction of his parents' lives necessarily takes the form of a fictive structure.

Villaseñor's family history establishes an ambiguous claim on the essential truth of his work. For the writer, "history is less something to be explained than a mode of being in the world, less a way of deciphering reality than an inter-pretation, a 'carrying over' of meaning from one discursive community to another" (Fabre and Bruce-Novoa 3). The traditions of oral story telling provide his ancestors with the power to tell narratives that are filtered through the eyes of personal experience, yet recalled against the background of their people's history, they document more than just individual experience, a process in the course of which they become representative and gain authenticity. In Villaseñor's project, these stories function as the "bones"[1] which need to be rearranged in time and place, by means of a variety of narrative techniques thus "writ[ing] history as a symbolizing act [, in which] the principal facets of the signifying system [are constantly] work[ed] and rework[ed]" (Bruce-Novoa, "History as Content" 30).

The author reassembles his family's history as a "great novel of broad vision and sweeping drama" (*Rain of Gold*) in order to create "a tribal heritage" beginning at a time when "we were all indigenous people" and finally finishing at a moment of "circl[ing] back to when the Mother Earth was young, the heaven spoke, and people listened" (Villaseñor, *Thirteen Senses* xvi). In its vivid and passionate language the book gains spiritual depth and power from the techniques of Magical Realism, which—as Wendy Smith argues in her review of Villaseñor's continuation of the family saga, *Thirteen Senses*—the writer would not refer to as such, but rather as "*corazón* realism" (2) thus focusing precisely on that specific quality that distinguishes *Rain of Gold* as an exemplar of Mexican American life writing. The author reconstructs his two fictionalized parents' family histories of migration from war-torn northern Mexico during the Revolution to California in the 1920s as narratives "of survival and wonder" (Miller 1). Linear advancement symbolized by the image of the journey into modernity as a Western cultural concept overlaps with the circularity of archetypal patterns of expulsion, diaspora, and reconciliation as suggested by Espirito's mythic story which opens *Rain of Gold*, thus repositioning the book in indigenous oral

---

[1] This image is developed by Sheila Ortiz Taylor (*Imaginary Parents* xiii). Still, it establishes an interesting parallel to Villaseñor's technique.

traditions, and most strongly supported by the final picture of the text, Lupe's and Juan Salvador's wedding signaling a new "Beginning" (552).

The narratives do not follow a single plot line but, composed of many individual life stories, they read like an oral history that "dissects" the life stories of Guadalupe, 'Lupe,' and Juan Salvador, the author's parents, in a variety of ways, forming what Hélène Cixous has called "one story in place of another story" (178). The polyvocality of the narrative "redefines history as a communal and dialogic act in which the characters create an understanding of their context, and endow themselves with identity, through the words with which they interpret their experience" (Kelsey 80). Exploring the interactions of Mexican American borderland history and the individual developments of his parents, Villaseñor views the autobiographical significance of life writing as a collective experiment that reveals "the spiritual roots of all humanity" (Filips 1). He "cho[oses] from the past the patterns of behavior [he] believe[s] would be worthy of imitation in the present, patterns of survival behavior which had allowed our ancestors to live through difficult times" (Bruce-Novoa, "History as Content" 33). Radiating the central idea of his grandmother's philosophy of survival that "there are no stranger's once we get to know each other's story" (Villaseñor, *Thirteen Senses* xvi), *Rain of Gold* carries on a tradition which Bruce-Novoa has described as the "attempt to recover from the communal past the wisdom of history" ("History as Content" 33).

Victor Villaseñor grew up on his parents' 166-acre ranch in Oceanside, California, but, despite the securities of material comfort, he suffered from the experiences of racial prejudice that made him want to erase this non-white American past from his life. Personal encounters with Mexican people of highly diverse social backgrounds while traveling through his parents' homeland gradually led him to appreciate his Mexican roots and to reevaluate his heritage as something that, if further neglected or abandoned, would create a painful emptiness in his life. The writer felt the urge to "tell my own children about our ancestral roots" (*Rain of Gold* xi), thus not just remembering the stories he had listened to in his youth, but re-positioning himself and his family in the rich traditions of Mexican American history.

For Villaseñor, Lupe's and Juan's stories become 20th century metaphors of the American Dream. Their immigrant experiences of "aspiration, movement, struggle, rejection, prejudice, work [and] acceptance" (*Rain of Gold* 1) rewrite the 19th-century myth of the American self-made man. Juan Bruce-Novoa has criticized the author's repetition of "many clichés of U.S. immigration writing" ("World Literature in Review"), yet Villaseñor revises these clichés as vehicles of a multicultural communal American experience against the background of which he is able to position his specific Mexican American borderland identity. The writer creates larger-then-life images of his parents, celebrating Lupe and Salvador as his visions of a New Chicana and a New Chicano, constructing both a semi-documentary and a semi-fictive panoramic picture of Chicano history that reconnects the healing powers of spirituality in an everyday life filled with violence and oppression with the quest for realizing the human dream of a life of dignity and happiness.

Juan Salvador Villaseñor's story takes him from Texas through the Southwest up north to Montana and finally to California and includes a series of adventures in mining camps, jails, brothels, gambling halls until he finally settles into bootlegging. The writer reconstructs his father's story in the tradition of a literary form deeply rooted in Mexican (border) history, the *corrido*[2] which features a hero who manages "significant events, such as social conflicts, natural disasters, political issues, or individual crises" (Saldívar 27) and finally transforms himself into a representative figure for the community. Still, Villaseñor rewrites the traditional pattern by constructing Juan Salvador's narrative growth as a Mexican American role model and the myth of his rebellion against dominant Anglo-American culture in complementary interaction with images of heroic women, in particular that of his mother Maria de Guadalupe Gomez and those of Doña Margarita and Doña Guadalupe, his paternal and maternal grandmothers.

Lupe's story is shaped by the clash between the harsh realities of California migrant farm life in which her family struggles for survival, and her desire to gain education in order to work in an office job. She finally develops into the "stable center of her family, and a practical counterbalance to the more passionate Juan Salvador" (Kelsey 81). Both

---

[2] Villaseñor was very familiar with this literary form, in particular with the *corridos* of border conflict, since he wrote the screenplay for *The Ballad of Gregorio Cortéz* (see "Víctor Villaseñor Biography").

young people's strong quest for self-fulfillment makes them encounter animosities and friendships with many Americans of diverse ethnic and social backgrounds. Guided by a 20th-century American pioneer spirit, Lupe and Juan Salvador experience themselves as part of a microcosm of U.S.-American cultural pluralism during the 1920s in which they learn to cope with intra- and interracial forms of injustice and prejudice, preparing themselves to redefine difference as a powerful unifying concept. *Rain of Gold* negotiates basic American notions of novelty and identity in terms of rather complex—Mexican American borderland— concepts of the postmodern/postcolonial self.

The writer affirms his protagonists' insistence on becoming some-body new by simultaneously appreciating and preserving the wealth of one's past, a concept insisted on by the grandmothers. Referring to them as the "two old she-boars" (550), Villaseñor has found a telling image for these *gran mujeres* whose experiences have taught them to challenge dualisms. Both are God-fearing mothers and women who possess the power to heal spiritual and physical wounds. Convinced that "the greatest gift of all by the Almighty Himself is the gift of love" (525), they are at the same time practicing *curanderas* who have to question the word of God from time to time. Throughout their lives they celebrated their femininity in their maternal role as the "heart" of the family yet, to keep this institution alive, they must exercise power and control in the pursuit of their families' survival and happiness. Doña Guadalupe's ex-periences as a mother "who raised [her] children alone half of the time" makes her doubt "that men alone were made superior by God" assum-ing the Church to "mak[e] our tradition sound as if it came straight from God" (381). And Doña Margarita frequently faces situations and conflicts in her family life which leads her to a secret contract with the Virgin Mary. With "the Bible on her lap, a cigarette hanging from her lips, and a glass of whiskey in her left hand" (434) she talks to her "woman-to-woman" signaling that she is her "most humble servant, but not a docile one, … You do Your part up in heaven or I'll do more than my part here on earth, and there'll be trouble!" (*Rain of Gold* 427).

Juan's mother tells Lupe that "God didn't just give love to us… No, in His infinite wisdom, He gave love to us only in half and then left it up to us to go out into the world and find our other half" (525). Her strength is based on the premise that "life only has the value that we place on it"

(491) and she expects in particular her son Juan Salvador to "place... a value of the highest order... by remaining faithful to our customs, no matter how far we've come from home" (491). Doña Margarita's wisdom is deeply rooted in the indigenous traditions of Mexican culture, still, at the same time she is aware of the individual's responsibility for the course of his or her life which builds up an ambiguous allusion to the American notion of the self-made man.

Conceptualizing the sun as "the right eye of God" (25, see also 137), the two grandmothers ground their powerful belief in survival on a religious practice in which God and nature are worshipped as one. Negotiating visions of Christianity and indigenous spirituality both women manage to always reunite their families by simultaneously not openly interfering with the individual quests of their members. Their permanent effort to establish a balanced relationship between the wealths of the past and the promises of the future distinguishes them as the outstanding characters of this piece of life writing in which historical biography and autobiographical self-positioning blend into the story of *Victor Villaseñor's* Mexican American identity formation.

III. A Dialogue Between Text and Image:
Sheila and Sandra Ortiz Taylor's Imaginary Parents

Sheila and Sandra Ortiz Taylor's approach to creating the story of their family adds other, highly complex and not less challenging, aspects to the debate about the future of autobiographical writing. Their way of fusing textual and visual interpretations of the past explicitly echoes Eakin's assertion that "autobiography is nothing if not a referential art" (3). *Imaginary Parents* opens with some brief prefatory remarks about the sisters' specific technique of producing this collaborative autobiography, in which "we did not try to make art and text replicate each other but rather to refract, casting new shadows, throwing new angles of light" (xiv).

For Adams, this description "sounds as much like a photograph as prose" (69), a suggestion supported by Sheila's statement that "much of my writing was inspired by our conversations and mutual re-collections as we... dreamed our way through boxes of family photographs" (xiv) and is further enhanced by a glance at the table of contents. Besides the *La Vía* section, a collection of black-and-white photographs showing the closed boxes, and the *La Galería* section, a series of colored photographs giving insight into the opened boxes of Sandra Ortiz Taylor's collages, it lists nine subchapters entitled *"Photograph,"* also formally marked by italics.[3] The photographs apparently act as the historical basis for the individual narratives that compose the image of their family and the story of their own selves, when they begin to connect themselves to the pictures by interpreting them in interaction with personal experiences.

The creative energy and experimental power of the project develops from the code which photography and autobiography share: Both are ways of reading the past as a network of ambiguous referentialities, created by a unique pattern of selecting and reconstructing memories. In this process, Sheila Ortiz Taylor casts herself in the role of *"La Huesera,* Bone Woman, crouching over the bones of my parents, remembering and transforming" (xiii), thus trying to "heal" the family history. The writer puts extraordinarily strong emphasis on physical objects which intensifies the photographic component of her work; yet at the same time she claims the results of her rearranging the bones as her own creations, products of her own imagination: "All the ghosts that rise up are mine" (xiii). This enables the protagonists of the book to move between history and fiction.

As the title of their *Family Autobiography* signals, *Imaginary Parents* reconstructs the stories of Juanita Loretta Ortiz Taylor, by her own definition an early Southern Californian, and John (Jack) Santray Taylor, a lawyer and Jazz musician from Texas. Recollecting their parents' ability to imagine themselves "as liv[ing] out the American Dream, Southern California style" (xv), thus believing in their capacity to re-invent themselves, each daughter uses a specific artistic genre to medi-ate selected memories and interpretations. This technique ultimately results in each one's own self-positioning not just in relation to her parents but in relation to the concept of American culture they repre-

---

[3] The image of the *boxes* indicates a significant concept that both artists share. Sandra Ortiz Taylor has created *art boxes,* which can be opened and closed, showing differently arranged "found objects" that "keep her rethink her family history in plastic form" (Castillo and Córdoba 98). Sheila Ortiz Taylor recon-structs the memories of her childhood and adolescence in the form of a series of rather short episodes, loosely arranged like movie clips which directly associ-ates to the impression of *text boxes.*

sent, thus in relation to history. Filtering their personal ideas through the lenses of their parents at the same time that their parents' views shape their own perspectives, their rearrangements seems to echo the image produced by a two-fold broken prism, in which the concept of referentiality requires redefinition. The Taylor sisters create a story of their family along the borderline of the *imaginary* as that "which exists only in one's mind and not in real life" (*Merriam Webster's Collegiate Dictionary* 578) and the *image* as the mental picture of the events and the objects of the past. They rewrite the story of their parents as an "imaginative autobiography," an autobiography based on history turned into a myth (xv), according to Barthes a second-order semiological system ("Myth Today" 114-15) in which referentiality is newly defined.

The two artists approach history not as authentic fact but as a moment in life that can never re-appear—a moment in stasis comparable to a photograph which William Mitchell refers to as "fossilized light" that transforms a "fugitive reality" into a "permanent image" thus producing a direct physical imprint (qtd. in Adams 62). In order to understand the "evidential efficacy" (Mitchell, qtd. in Adams 62) of the image, it needs to be reconnected to life by exploring its referential potential. For Sheila and Sandra Ortiz Taylor a photograph functions as "a prop, a prompt, a pre-text [which] sets the scene for recollection." They agree with Annette Kuhn that "[f]amily photographs are supposed to show not so much that we were once there, as how we once were: to evoke memories which might have little or nothing to do with what is actually in the picture" (qtd. in Adams 62). Although both sisters acknowledge the crucial role of photographs for their project, neither of them makes direct use of these "physical traces of actual objects" (Adams xv). Instead, Sheila Ortiz Taylor prefers to "deliberately work... from recollection because I was more interested in what I selected to remember" (qtd. in Adams 61).

On the one hand, reproducing the photographs in their book would have limited their perspectives to a single point of view identical to that of the image. Still, the Taylor daughters want to perform what Adams refers to as "a transformation from still image to home movie" (73). Adding movement to the image by converting it into a textual and visual narrative, which, as already said, means revitalizing it by establishing interactions between this moment and the people participating in this moment, Sheila and Sandra Ortiz Taylor overcome the limitations of a fixed point of view (Adams 73). They open up the photographed states to change, inviting for diverse readings and suggesting ambivalent referentialities. Transcending the power of photographs to "bear witness" (Goldberg, qtd. in Adams 61), on the other hand, allows them to transform themselves from observers into participants in the history of their parents and to create their own stories of life. Their *Family Autobiography* rebuilds their parents' belief in a Gatsby-like self-invention set against the backdrop of the Hollywood-inspired atmosphere of Los Angeles during the 1940s and 50s; but creating the myth of their family, the daughters perform their own "self-invention" by liberating themselves from the myths of the past and writing themselves into self-reliant female personalities whose individuality rises from the referential ambiguities of the myths they simultaneously construct and deconstruct.

The Taylor sisters remember their parents less as living individuals than as constructions of themselves which are supposed to play certain roles. They negotiate the problematic conflict between how they want to appear and how they actually are in a multiplicity of loosely arranged kaleidoscopic episodes realized in the form of text and collage, which remind the reader of randomly selected snapshots that read like movie shots. There is the beautiful castle-like home on the Horseshoe, the father's pride, designed by himself, who, as "a great projector" (8), feels exposed to a somehow problematic tension with reality. He is a multi-talent man incapable of coping with his multiple personality: a professionally trained lawyer, he is also a passionate jazz musician. He possesses a strong sense of family and home, still, he puts a "For Sale by Owner" sign in front of his house signaling his constant wish for change.[4] Born in Texas he feels a spirit of restlessness and adventure in himself and dreams of going to Mexico (significantly, he is the only family member who, a self-proclaimed atheist of Anglo descent, speaks

---

[4] What, at face value, seems to set up a moment of difference between the couple, on a deeper level turns out to be a uniting element. Juanita Ortiz was a yo-yo artist before marrying Jack Taylor. As Castillo and Córdoba point out, "the father's 'For Sale' sign also has a yo-yo quality to it: it goes up and down upon being taken out irregularly" (113).

Spanish fluently and loves talking about God) or sailing around the world.

In "*Photograph 6,*" Sheila tells her version of the family's sailboat history. Her memories are inspired by a picture that shows the two sisters "[r]educed, but somehow not into insignificance" in front of a "skeleton of a boat" (137). She begins her description with the boat by paying primary attention to the background, but referring to it as a "skeleton" immediately relativizes its dominance by associating it with the opening image of the bones Sheila rearranges in order to gain a deeper understanding of her family history. The term evokes unpleasant associations ranging from its implications as a symbol of death to its suggestions of incompleteness (in fact the boat requires a lot of rework carried out by all family members [see 138]) and to feelings of discomfort.

The father's sailboat plays an ambivalent role in the family history. It separates and reconnects the daughters at the same time. Sandra, the darker-skinned girl, shows resistance to her father's plans since they threaten the family harmony of their Los Angeles home in general and her mother's (at least at face value) state of content in particular. Sheila seems more ready to participate in her father's adventure; the three-fold repetition of the passage "at an angle" (137) suggests the narrator-protagonist's condition of being in-between, of an undecidedness rather similar to the one frequently acted out by her father. Still, what Jack Taylor is not prepared to handle "when his life seems to be splitting in two: music or law, left or right ventricle" (144), since he perceives options as elements of binary oppositions which demand a decision for the one or the other, Sheila has learned to redefine as an arbitrarily established social pattern of mutually exclusive choices. As Adams has observed, the writer opens "her description of "*Photograph 6*" in the first person, [but] shifts her point of view so that by the end she refers to herself as 'this other,' Sandra as 'this girl'" (72). Sheila Ortiz Taylor is apparently able to negotiate two sides against each other, focusing primarily on their moments of interaction instead of separation. For this reason, the two girls in the picture will always "remain… in relationship" (138) despite a variety of differences: "While our individual memories always differed, we learned to value this difference and to use it as a way of layering our work" (xiv).

Sandra Ortiz Taylor has reconstructed her memories of the event captured in the photograph in the form of the collage "Catch the Wave" (173). Its lower part is formed by what seems to be the reproduction of the actual black-and white photograph of the sailboat. But the boat is magnified and the part showing the two sisters is rearranged in triplicate form, becoming larger from left to right. In her "Descriptive annotations," she refers to her composition as "my father's dream in process" and explains: "At the base of this piece, the hull of his boat dwarfs his young daughters. His musical instruments are evoked, as well as something of the fearsomeness of the experience of sailing on the open sea as a family" (xi).

Adams argues that "Sandra uses the photograph to create a darker version of the scene than Sheila" (72) and supports his observation with the writer's reference to sisterly difference in contrast to the visual artist's triple emphasis on sisterly unity. Yet a careful rereading of text and collage reveals both women's intention to uncover the constructed artificiality of their father's concept of life. Dissatisfied with his inability to establish a balance between his responsibilities as an attorney and his ambitions as a jazz musician (which has serious effects on his physical condition), Jack Taylor tries to escape into his dream of sailing around the world, an adventure that would seriously interfere with the "family harmony." His two daughters struggle against the danger of being neglected due to their father's self-deceptive activities, Sheila by experimenting with her narrative point of view, and Sandra by manipulating dimensions to relativize proportions. Photography does not simply reinforce "autobiography's referential dimension," but operating in a multidimensional system of interaction, their combination "intensif[ies] rather than reduce[s] the complexity and ambiguity of each taken separately" (Adams xxi). The stories told by the sisters complement each other in their effort to challenge established patterns of power and authority. They speak about the incongruencies that mark the daily life of the Ortiz Taylors: understatements, discrepancies between external facades and internal substances, between signifying terms and signified objects.

Sheila and Sandra Ortiz Taylor focus their critical recollections of their father's self-construction as a man in full control of his life, as the traditional provider and protector of his family—as the man in power—

and on the subordinate role his wife is supposed to play. Juanita apparently performs the part of a movie star-like accessory to his possessions comparable to his dream-like Los Angeles home. Only a short remark in Sheila's *"Photograph 6"* offers a brief glimpse of the uneasiness Juanita feels about her role in the family and in her home, which has turned out as a trap that she, as her husband must realize, "is always laying plans to leave" (59).

Being raised as *Mymama's* daughter, Juanita Loretta Ortiz wants to realize her American Dream in the form of the perfect U.S.-American family, but it does not completely work out for her: reality leaves her with the images of an impeccably beautiful mother and two tomboy daughters. Yet she neither articulates her disappointment in public nor acts out in her own right, thus supporting the superficial impression of a functioning traditional gender role pattern of male domination and female subordination. Only after her husband's heart attacks and subsequent death, Juanita does claim her own right to realize her quest for happiness and freedom and turns into a powerful personality. She speaks English and Spanish, drives her car, sells their Los Angeles home, manages the family's public affairs, and travels to Mexico together with her daughters. The images Sheila and Sandra create of their mother materialize her dual personality by operating on the levels of the exterior versus the interior. Apparently, photographic and textual narratives "conceal as much as they reveal, through their built-in ambiguity, their natural relationship to the worlds they depict which always seems more direct than it really is" (Adams xxi).

In *"Ofrenda for a Maya"* (177), Sandra Ortiz Taylor tells her mother's story, a narrative deeply rooted in Mexican maternal power and, at the same time, significantly shaped by the social concepts and material achievements of her life as the wife of a Los Angeles attorney. This story finds its completion in the liberating experience of a female community in Mexico. As the collage suggests, Juanita Loretta Ortiz started her "solo voyage of discovery" (xi) as an "Early Californian" and finished it as a self-determined American woman of Mexican descent. Even though Sandra argues that "only with the death of my father does she begin to emerge as a self-defining individual" (xi), the photographs framing the central part of the triptych give evidence of Juanita's decision to realize her quest for happiness. Marriage and motherhood transformed her into a responsible woman who, although invisible at the surface of her life, always appreciated her cultural past, symbolized by the artificial red hibiscus flower which controls the entire composition. She therefore negotiates her experiences in terms of options and restrictions, as her watchful eyes suggest. In her philosophy of existence, she envisions life as an infinite space like the ocean which she cruises in a large liner in order to share her adventure as a collective experience. This version contrasts with that of her husband, who always dreamed of sailing around the world accompanied only by his family.

The double presence of the photograph of Juanita Ortiz Taylor's eyes in *"Ofrenda for a Maya"* is echoed by Sheila's rereading of *"Photograph 9,"* a picture taken in a Mexican night club, in which the mother is the "only one looking directly into the camera" (249). It marks the moment when both sisters begin to recognize the past as "a storage room" not just "containing little items that trigger of memory," but radiating signals for their future (Fellner 158). The writer-protagonist articulates this new awareness in a further change of the narrative perspective. Sheila Ortiz Taylor opened her recollections in the first person singular and continued to reconstruct selected moments from the family's life, regardless of whether she experienced them herself or heard about them in stories told by other family members, in the voice of a more distanced third person. She apparently tried to decipher the ambivalences of the images of the past in order to find parameters for her and her sister's place within the multiple roots of their history which made her trespass the threshold from individual to collective experience. Significantly, only in the final chapter, the female family members' reunion in Mexico, the narrative voice re-emerges in the first person plural: "In this house under the stars we will fall asleep, dreaming the past into tropes and signs and symbols, beginning the dangerous art of fitting it all back inside the heart of a child" (257).

Like parts of a puzzle the fragmented memories are discursively assembled until they come full circle in the image of the straw puppet of Pancho Villa which the two sisters acquire as part of their collection (252). Being able to reclaim their grandmother's Mexican heritage, Sheila and Sandra feel prepared to carry on her tradition on the level of discourse. Similar to *Mymama* who collected her *pocadillas* in glass shelves in order to keep the past alive by remembering the stories they all have to tell (48), the granddaughters reconstruct "the small objects with big meaning" from the altar of their family life by telling *their* stories of their parents and by presenting *their* collages of family scenes. Reestablishing their connections to the past they are able to bring "together different parts of their selves [to] fill gaps [and to] name absences" in order to position their multiple identities (Fellner 158).

IV. *Rain of Gold* and *Imaginary Parents* as Sites of Genre Mediation

Investigating the various ways in which text and image interact and reflect on each other opens up a completely experimental approach to reading autobiography within the contexts of history and imagination. When Timothy Adams maintains that the two media "complement, rather than supplement each other, since reference is not secure in either, neither can compensate for lack of stability in the other" (xxi), he establishes striking parallels between the two texts discussed in this essay. Villaseñor pushes genre boundaries by reconstructing his family history as a blend of historically documented facts, orally transmitted folk wisdom, faith and humor, and stories of personal experience thus forming a narrative based on "both data about, and the subjective experience of, events" (Kelsay 80), in which referentiality constantly requires redefinition. The three artists imagine their families' past as a way to negotiate the interactions between self and history, in general, and self and place, in particular, in order to develop a racial, ethnic and gender consciousness (Saldívar 154).

Rain of Gold and *Imaginary Parents* create dialogical responses to the traditional autobiography as a male Eurocentric genre. As much as the image of the borderland, which provides the Mexican American writer with a theoretical frame for identity construction, functions as a site of cultural mediation, life writing, the process in the course of which he or she succeeds in self-positioning by reconstructing cultural experiences, either directly or indirectly through stories and photographs, redefines autobiographical writing as a site of genre mediation. The contestatory forms of autobiography claim innovative ways of creating meaning and alternative narrative structures. Their authors are border crossers in a variety of contexts. The texts suggest concepts of autobiographical writing that grow from discourses of flexibility and ingenuity in which "language shapes behavior" (Rodriguez 272). *Rain of Gold* and *Imaginary Parents* demonstrate their writers' creative power to alter the mainstream patterns of a classical Western genre in order to transform it into a means of articulating hybrid Mexican American cultural and national awareness. Reconstructing their family histories Victor Villaseñor and Sheila and Sandra Ortiz Taylor have produced two *fronterizo* autoethnographies that "reframe the genre of autobiography [by] exploring alternative genealogies of life-story telling that do not privilege the individual 'I' as the epistemological ground of narration, but rather evoke a multiplicity of times, places, memories and countermemories, resonant metaphors, and internationally embedded networks of relationships" (Castillo and Córdoba 115). They support a concept of life writing as a revisionist autobiographical design capable of establishing ambivalent referentialities and referential ambiguities, respectively.

Works Cited

Adams, Timothy Dow. *Light Writing & Life Writing: Photography in Autobiography*. Chapel Hill, NC: University of North Carolina Press, 2002.

Anzaldúa, Gloria. *Borderland/La Frontera: The New Mestiza*. San Francisco: Aunt Lute, 1987.

Barthes, Roland. "Myth Today." *Mythologies*. New York: Noonday, 1972. 109-159.

—. *Roland Barthes by Roland Barthes*. New York: Hill and Wang, 1977.

Bruce-Novoa, Juan. "History as Content, History as Act: The Chicano Novel." *Aztlan* 18.1 (Spring 1987): 29-44.

—. "World Literature in Review: English: *Rain of Gold*." *World Literature Today* 66.2 (Spring 1992): 346.

Cantú, Norma Elia. *Canícula: Snapshots of a Girlhood en la Frontera*. Albuquerque: University of New Mexico Press, 1995.

Castillo, Debra A. and María Socorro Tabuenca Córdoba. *Border Women: Writing from La Frontera*. Minneapolis: University of Minnesota Press, 2002.

Cixous, Hélène. *Rootprints: Memory and Life Writing*. London: Routledge, 1997.

De Man, Paul. "Autobiography as De-Facement." *The Rhetoric of Romanticism*. New York: Columbia University Press, 1984. 67-81.

Eakin, Paul John. *Touching the World: Reference in Autobiography*. Princeton: Princeton University Press, 1992.

Fabre, Genevieve and Juan Bruce-Novoa. "History and Chicano Cultural Production: Introduction." *Aztlan* 18.1 (Spring 1987): 1-5.

Fellner, Astrid M. "'Lyrics Alone Soothe Restless Serpents': The Fiction of Sheila Ortiz Taylor." *Daughters of Restlessness: Women's Literature at the End of the Millennium.* Eds. Sabine Coelsch-Foisner, Gerlind Reisner, and Hanna Wallinger. Heidelberg: Universitätsverlag C. Winter, 1998. 153-163.

Filips, Janet. "Happiness: Secret of Paradise." *The Oregonian.* October 1991. http://www.victorvillasenor.com/oreg8_91.html; (Viewed on June 27, 2005).

Kelsey, Verlene. "Mining for a Usable Past: Acts of Recovery, Resistance and Continuity in Villaseñor's *Rain of Gold.*" *Bilingual Review* 18.1 (1993): 79-85.

Merriam Webster's Collegiate Dictionary. 10th ed. Springfield, MA: Merriam Webster, Inc., 1994.

Miller, Tom. "Children of Another Revolution." *New York Times Book Review.* September 1991. http://www.victorvillasenor.com/nytr9_91.html; (Viewed on June 27, 2005).

"'Rain of Gold': A family's history is America's." *USA Today.* January 1992. http://www.victorvillasenor.com/usat1_92.html; (Viewed on June 27, 2005).

"Rain Maker: Victor Villaseñor strikes Gold with the story of his Mexican immigrant family." *People Magazine.* September 1992. http://www.victorvillasenor.com/pmag9_92.html (Viewed on June 27, 2005).

Rodriguez, Joe. "United States Hispanic Autobiography and Biography: Legend for the Future." *Handbook of Hispanic Cultures in the United States: Literature and Art.* Ed. Francisco Lomelí. Houston: Arte Público Press, 1993. 268-290.

Saldívar, Ramón. *Chicano Narrative: The Dialectics of Difference.* Madison: University of Wisconsin Press, 1990.

Smith, Wendy L. "In the Realm of the Senses." *The San Diego Union-Tribune.* September 9, 2001. http://www.victorvillasenor.com/sdu9_01.htm; (Viewed on June 27, 2005).

Sheila and Sandra Ortiz Taylor. *Imaginary Parents: A Family Autobiography.* Albuquerque: University of New Mexico Press, 1996.

"Victor Villaseñor Biography." http://victorvillasenor.com/bio.html (Viewed on June 27, 2005).

Villaseñor, Victor. *Rain of Gold.* New York: Dell Publishing, 1991.

—. *Thirteen Senses.* New York: HarperCollins, 2002.

Angelika Köhler teaches American Literature at the University of Technology in Dresden, Germany. Her research focus is on ethnic literature and women's writing.

Asian American Narratives of Return: Nisei Representations of Prewar and Wartime Japan

Patricia P. Chu

I. The Myth of Return

In *The Woman Warrior*, Maxine Hong Kingston articulates her mother's expectation that she will one day "return" to the ancestral village and recognize it as a site of her family's origins, though she has been born and bred in the United States. Numerous Asian American texts also register this expectation, instilled both by family members and by other Americans who perceive Asian Americans as foreigners or guests. While the second-generation return visit may be a familiar ritual for some, the experience of "return" to an ancestral homeland has been less accessible for other Asian Americans due to financial limitations, political estrangement, wars, or the homeland's hostile relations with the U.S. For example, the opening of the People's Republic of China to Westerners coincided with the coming of age of a generation of Chinese American writers. In this context we may situate the "return" myth so memorably constructed in Amy Tan's bestseller *The Joy Luck Club*, in which the myth of return unites a number of conventions that recur in Asian American "return" narratives. One, Asian Americans are born lacking a fundamental sense of their parents' home culture. Two, the homeland and the narrator's parent or parents are symbolically intertwined. *Joy Luck,* for instance, is pervaded by the feeling that the Chinese American daughter cannot know her mother, and hence her own essence, without visiting China. To understand the country is to understand the parent, and to understand the parent is to understand oneself. And finally, when second-generation offspring come to terms with their parents by visiting an Asian homeland, this enables them to establish a new balance between their Asian heritage and their identification with America. In Tan's novel, the American-born daughter June is prepared for return to China through a series of narratives establishing it as a site of suffering and patriarchal oppression. In that text, June's "return," actually her first visit, represents her personal reconciliation with long-lost relatives, her reclaiming of a Chinese heritage presumed to be "in her bones," and her restoration of a deep bond with her recently deceased mother.

Offering this version of "return" as a starting point, I acknowledge its specificity: second-generation, baby-boom Chinese Americans may have romanticized their homeland more than some other groups due to China's isolation from the West throughout the Cold War. A broader look at "return" narratives must also address those works in which emigrants and expatriates—"first generation" Asian Americans—return to homelands where they were born or where they have lived. As a first step in extending this basic model, this essay will explore how the basic model of return as an uncanny homecoming shifts when one examines the writings of a different ethnic group, Japanese Americans.

II. From Quietism to Questioning: Japanese American Writers

Like Chinese Americans, Japanese Americans have been subject to exclusionary immigration laws and exclusion from citizenship during the late nineteenth and early twentieth centuries, and perennially perceived at outsiders or enemy aliens. Yet the Japanese also have a unique history in the United States, due to Japan's rise as an imperial power in the East at the end of the nineteenth century, a history that has shaped their literary output in ways specific to their ethnic group. Readers of Sui Sin Far's 1909 essay, "Leaves from the Mental Portfolio of an Eurasian," may recall her contemporaries' association of the Chinese with lowly, sinister workmen, and the Japanese with civilization and culture (218-230). In keeping with such perceptions, most Chinese immigration was cut off in 1882, whereas some Japanese immigration continued until the passage of a stricter immigration law in 1924 (Chan 54-55). With the rise of Japan's imperial ambitions, culminating in its disastrous decision to attack Pearl Harbor in December of 1941, Japanese Americans found themselves demonized, associated with the enemy nation, and in the case of the great majority of Japanese Americans on the west coast, exiled to internment camps in desolate inland areas.[1] Because of Japan's enmity towards the U.S., Japanese Americans did not gain the right to naturalized citizenship until 1952, more than 80 years after they had be-

---

[1] See Ian Buruma's *Inventing Japan 1853-1964* for a concise summary of modern Japanese history.

gun coming to Hawaii and the U.S. (to Hawaii in 1968 and the mainland in 1869) and nine years after Chinese immigrants won the right of naturalization (Chan 11, 122). While Japan rebuilt itself as a competitive, modern state and U.S. ally under U.S. tutelage in the years following 1945, Japanese Americans as a group responded to the shock of the internment by internalizing the "Puritan" work ethnic (which some would call "Confucian") and remaking themselves into a "model minority" known more for middle-class achievement and assimilation than political activism.[2] In addition to narratives of Japanese American resistance and critique of racist government policies, one also finds in Japanese American literature many representations of the "quietist" approach to political life and the "camouflage" approach to social life and culture, and its implications for the Japanese American self, such as the many representations of creative stifling, self-sacrifice, self-erasure, and literal suicide noted by such critics as Traise Yamamoto. Women nisei authors such as Hisaye Yamamoto, Wakako Yamauchi, Jeanne Wakatsuki Houston, and Velina Hasu Houston have documented the sacrifice of individual aspirations for the sake of the family by women of the *issei* (first) and *nisei* (second) generations. Meanwhile, male authors such as John Okada, Milton Murayama, Philip Kan Gotanda, and David Mura have highlighted Japanese American male resistance, both to the ethos of individual sacrifice for the family and community and to the ethos of political quietism associated most strongly with the JACL's pro-government stance in the years following Pearl Harbor. Paradoxically, the most politically important Japanese North American text by far, Joy Kogawa's 1981 novel about the internment of Japanese Canadians, *Obasan*, helped energize the Japanese Canadian redress movement by portraying political silence as part of a larger pattern of uprooting and spiritually starving the Japanese American community.

What we gain from literary sources that may not be as evident in the record of Japanese Americans in the political sphere is a body of ob-

---

[2] Numerous observers have questioned why Japanese Americans complied with the government during and after the internments, while others have noted that a minority did challenge the government directly, albeit with little public support. See Chan 122-139. For the original "model minority" article, which focuses on Chinese Americans, see "Success Story of One Minority Group in U.S.," *U.S. News and World Report, 1966,* in Wu and Song, 158-163.

servations about the particular horror of internalizing the demand for "camouflage," the demand that Japanese Americans attempt to claim citizenship by denying their ethnic heritage, culture, and physiques. Not until the 1980s, with Japan's rise as an economic power, the claiming of civil rights by more Asian Americans, and the success of the Japanese American redress movements in the U.S. and Canada, do Japanese American literary texts emerge that address the touchy issue of Japanese imperialism in the 1920s, 30s, and 40s. In the eighties, "returns," or exploratory visits to Japan, were made by *sansei* (third generation) authors David Mura, Lydia Minatoya, and Dorinne Kondo, resulting in a spate of provocative texts reflecting on Japanese culture and Japanese American identity. More recently, Lydia Minatoya's novel, *The Strangeness of Beauty* (2001), uses a return plot to raise questions about Japanese American political agency in wartime Japan; and the newly published letters of Mary K. Tomita (1995), a nisei stranded in Japan throughout and after the war, raise provocative and urgent questions, not only about Japanese motives, but about the duties of citizens who disagree with their governments in wartime. By focusing on these texts' questions about Japanese American identity and political agency, we may observe how Minatoya, Tomita, and Tomita's editor Robert G. Lee appear to bring a politically questioning sensibility to their scrutiny of this crucial period in Japanese and Japanese American history.

III. *Nisei Daughter*: Inventing Japanese American Identity

The best known nisei narrative of return occurs in Monica Sone's 1953 memoir, *Nisei Daughter*, one of the first Japanese American books to break the public silence about the Japanese American internments.[3] Sone's groundbreaking book is most commonly read in one of two ways. For Shirley Geok-lin Lim and Traise Yamamoto, this is a book that claims American citizenship for the author by disavowing her affinity to Japanese culture and avowing her deep identification with American culture, masking the author's rage at the internment and other instances of discrimination. For Stephen H. Sumida, *Nisei Daughter* is a pluralist trickster text that subtly redefines Americanness to include Japanese

---

[3] Cf. Okubo. On the vexed question of "silence" about the internments, see Simpson.

food, customs, and values, a text that, having disarmed non-Japanese American readers with good-humored anecdotes, slyly documents the internment of Japanese Americans and leads the reader to see the outrageous injustice of such events. Sumida's view seems readily supported by the "return" chapter, "We Meet Real Japanese," in which the author's parents take their American-born children to visit relatives in Japan for the first time. In it, Sone depicts Japan as an exotic place to her and her brothers, who associate it with earthquakes and odd customs, such as bowing instead of hugging relatives, but the strangeness of the country to the American children is softened by their older relatives' kindness and warmth—thus reaffirming the family's belonging in Japan. After the narrator describes such Japanese phenomena as the silkworm season, Japanese baths, and earthquakes, Sone reaffirms the family's Japaneseness in the farewell scene. Parting reluctantly with their beloved grandfather, the author's brother Henry invites "Ojih-chan" to come to live with them in Seattle. The grandfather's gentle refusal, on grounds of old age, is expressly refuted by Sone, who artfully folds her explanation of a racist law into a reassertion of this clearly Japanese family's claiming of America:

> Many years later I learned why he could not come with us. In 1924 my country had passed an Immigration Law which kept all Orientals from migrating to America since that year. Those who had come in before that time could stay, but there would be no more new ones. That was why Father had taken us to Japan, so Grandfather could see us and say farewell to his son who had decided to make his home across the sea. The children who had been born in America belonged there, and there he and Mother would stay. (107)

In the end, *Nisei Daughter* uses the nisei's return to an ancestral home to balance, but not to supplant, her fundamental allegiance with America.

IV. Most Unskillful: Sansei Adaptations

If Sone's memoir finds a graceful balance between her affiliations with Japan and America, narratives of lengthier, adult sojourns by sansei authors such as Dorinne Kondo, Lydia Minatoya, and David Mura record a clash between their desire to fit in and their consciousness of being viewed as cultural curiosities by the Japanese of the 1980s, who must work hard to reconcile the authors' Japanese faces with their lame Japanese language and cultural skills, their fluent English, and their American manners and lifestyles. In her memoir *Talking to High Monks in the Snow*, Lydia Minatoya recalls the disbelief and puzzlement of three Japanese to whom she appeals for help, explaining that, as she is American, her Japanese is "most unskillful." After crying, "But you are Japanese. You are speaking Japanese. You have a Japanese face!" they argue "as to whether such a thing, an American with a Japanese face, really could exist" (90).

As Traise Yamamoto has noted, Minatoya's experience resonates with anthropologist Dorinne Kondo's observation in *Crafting Selves*, an ethnography of an artisan community in Tokyo, that most Japanese found her, a Japanese American with limited cultural skills, a "conceptual anomaly" who provoked responses of "bewilderment, incredulity, embarrassment, even anger"; these in turn drove Kondo to adapt by renouncing her American persona and striving to reduce others' dissonance by "'fitting in,' even if it meant suppression of and violence against a self I had known in another context," which was "preferable to meaninglessness" (qtd. in Yamamoto 87-92). While it seems that Japanese Americans are no longer so unheard-of in Japan, the difficulty of negotiating a position as an outsider with a Japanese face must still remain for long-term visitors.

Central to Kondo's study of Japanese selfhood is her landlady's observation that the Japanese "don't treat themselves as important," but spend time "doing things for the sake of maintaining good relationships, regardless of their 'inner' feelings" (22). Kondo argues that Japanese define their subjectivities in fluid, relational, contextual modes rather than as self-contained, continuous entities, which she argues is a typically Western set of assumptions. Citing Japanese grammar, in which personal pronouns, verbs, and proper nouns are continuously adapted to signal the relationship between the speaker and the addressee, she argues, "Awareness of complex social positioning is an *inescapable* element of any utterance in Japanese, for it is *utterly impossible* to form a sentence without *also* commenting on the relationship between oneself and one's interlocutor" (31). By contrast, she argues, the English language encourages an assumption that "the self" is a whole, bounded subject who marches through untouched and unchanged from one situation to the next" (32). In addition, she cites Takie Lebra's study of women's autobiographies. Lebra finds that, even for women writers, American autobiographies focus on the authors as central, relegating others to the background and obscuring questions of relationships, whereas Japanese autobiographies emphasize "a woman's life as a single thread in a richly textured fabric of relationships," and Japanese women writers portray themselves as accommodating duty and others' needs rather than asserting themselves as "independent decision makers" (qtd. in Kondo 32-33). Such interpersonal self-definition and social integration appears to be held up as an ideal, a sign of maturity in Japanese culture; to be individualistic or self-directed can, according to Kondo, be interpreted as being selfish and immature.

V. Conceptual Anomalies:
A Double Return in Minatoya's *Strangeness of Beauty*

Like other second-generation narratives of return, Lydia Minatoya's novel *The Strangeness of Beauty* (2001) combines a sentimental mother-daughter plot with running comparisons of American and Japanese culture, including the Japanese genres of haiku and the "I-novel," and speculation about the influence of East-West cultural interactions on the transnational Japanese American self. However, Minatoya's novel is the first Japanese American novel to focus on Japan in the 1920s and 30s, a time when Japan sought to secure its position as a world power by occupying Korea, colonizing Manchuria, and invading China.[4] If Minatoya's version of events verges on revisionist (though well-researched and fictional), her particular slant may illustrate the author's wish to create a more nuanced representation of Japan that includes modern Japanese subjects who are neither geisha nor warriors, who are educated and hold liberal democratic values, and who seek to challenge their government in a time of war. In *Strangeness*, an immigrant (issei) narrator, Etsuko, helps her issei brother-in-law raise her motherless niece, Hanae, born in Seattle in 1922. When Hanae's father sends her home to be raised in her samurai grandmother's household in Kobe, Japan, Etsuko (widowed,

---

[4] For recent fictional treatments of this period from Japanese perspectives, see Golden, Ishiguro, and Hasu Houston. Cf. also Tan's scenes of Japanese invasion and Ronyoung's Korean "return" episode, both set in the 1920s.

childless, and in her thirties) accompanies her. Minatoya, a sansei author whose own mother was born in America and raised in Japan, draws upon her mother's experience as a *kibei* (a nisei raised in Japan) to imagine what life in Kobe might have been like in the years from 1928 to 1939.

Like Tan, Minatoya weaves a mother-daughter reconciliation plot into her narrative of return, but Minatoya's Etsuko is both Japanese and Americanized, surrogate mother and estranged daughter. Etsuko seeks to overcome her prior estrangement from Chie Fuji, the widowed head of the samurai household who had sent her away in infancy, and whose only living offspring are Etsuko and Hanae. In her memoir, *Talking to High Monks in the Snow*, Minatoya revealed that her maternal grandmother, a picture bride, fell in love with another man after arriving and marrying in America. Lydia's *issei* grandfather first responded by sending his wife back, with their children, to live in their home village in Japan, then divorced her five years later, long after she could have married her lover. Following Japanese tradition, she was also cut off from seeing her children from that time forward. They were brought up by his family in Wakayama prefecture, under an unexplained cloud of disgrace. In her novel, Minatoya invents a history that seems informed by her mother's past: Etsuko, born in the wake of a beloved son's death, is rejected as an infant by her samurai mother Chie and raised by Chie's tenant farmers, who teach her to view Chie as her landlord rather than her mother. Years later, returning to Kobe as a young widow charged with the care of Hanae, Etsuko struggles belatedly to win Chie's acknowledgement, respect, and love. Her need to understand and win over her mother and to find a self-determined identity drives the sentimental plot of the novel.

As a returned issei, Etsuko exemplifies Kondo's observations about Japanese subjects and Japanese American women narrators, but also challenges East-West dichotomies in her representations of Japanese culture and character. By having Etsuko write an "I-novel," Minatoya slows her narrative pace and provides space for her character to emerge gradually, through personal observations and historical details. According to Etsuko, an "I-novel" is an impressionistic autobiographical genre very popular in the 1920s in Japan, a genre that dispenses with Western narrative demands for conflict, linear progress, action, and suspense; if it rambles, that's because its primary purpose is an autobiographical one, that of articulating the impressions of a single mind. Using this genre, Minatoya creates a character who clearly defines her subject relationally, in the terms suggested by Kondo and Lebra. Throughout the novel, Etsuko's identity is defined by familial relations and obligations; in the latter part of the novel, her growing political development is dramatized in terms of her relationships with others and her negotiations with their expectations. Etsuko is characterized indirectly, by her observations and responses to others, rather than by acts or choices that obviously drive the narrative. Her cheerful neutrality and quiet support of others are linked within the novel with her idea that Japanese strengths are "receptivity and the appreciation of human and physical nature" (111), and beyond the novel, with Traise Yamamoto's concept of narrative "masking," in which Japanese American women narrators conceal extreme personal reactions and present a cheerful demeanor to readers with the deliberate aims of retaining their privacy and of attaining greater persuasiveness with readers holding a radically different worldview (116-126). In short, Etsuko nicely exemplifies Kondo's claim that Japanese prefer to spend their time doing things for others; but if this claim is the novel's main point, how will it explain Japanese imperialism in the 1930s?

Surprisingly, Minatoya uses haiku and the aesthetic principle of *myo* to interrogate Japanese militarism. The entire novel is built upon the principle of confounding expectations, or what she identifies as surprise, a crucial element of *myo,* the strangeness of beauty. For instance, a boy's improvised haiku about the beauty of autumn morphs into a celebration of Japanese imperialism—"Fall down, fiery leaves / Your beauty is like the splendor of falling bombs / Advance, imperial glory!" (264). Etsuko's asides about Japanese culture gradually explain the oddly buoyant feeling of this novel. Praising the brevity and structure of haiku, Etsuko describes the form as "Two lines of dreaminess followed by the jolt of awakening... wrapped in mystery and surprise," and explains that human connections, like the last line of haiku, bring one back to life precisely by being jarring and demanding attention (181-182). Defining surprise as "a twist in perspective or mood, something that sets you off balance, that causes you to gasp. A reaction found both in heartbreak and joy," Etsuko concludes that surprise, also known as mystery and anticipation, "is the basis of life" (230). Surprise, for Etsuko, is not only an aesthetic value but also a life stance that stands for liberty of thought, a liberty she sees curtailed in wartime. Thus Minatoya transforms aesthetic values into political ones.

As the novel begins to address Japan's military situation more directly, its historical consciousness shifts to the more serious problem of Etsuko's agency as a Japanese citizen. (As mentioned above, Japanese were ineligible for U.S. citizenship until 1965.) Chie, who embodies samurai rigor and self-scrutiny, suggests that Etsuko as a mother should model not only such peaceful virtues as "patience, devotion, kindness... [a]n eye for beauty, [and] a sense of humor," but also "integrity, commitment, and valor." A good way to do this, Chie suggests, would be to refuse to support the war, even by saving tinfoil. The year is 1933. If this seems too mild, one could claim some agency for Etsuko as narrator of an I-novel that illuminates Japanese history for American readers. For instance, she explains that, in the wake of the 1923 earthquake precipitating widespread financial ruin, not only have foreigners become unwelcome, but ruined army officers have taken to assassinating military leaders perceived as moderates, the press is prevented from reporting on substantive issues by the "Peace Preservation Law of 1925," and the sons of bankrupt families are increasingly moved to join "a glorious war."

As the novel moves into its closing years (1937-39) it again poses the question of agency for Chie, Etsuko, and her friends. Japanese women can't yet vote, but the Fujis find individual ways to contest the prevailing mood of militarism. As a landowner, Chie sells off family heirlooms rather than dispossessing bankrupt tenants, thereby reducing their incentives to join the armed forces. From 1934 through early 1936, Etsuko and two women friends publish a dissident newsletter whose efficacy Etsuko doubts until she receives some feedback from the police. In February 26, 1936, a violent and short-lived military uprising against statesmen and senior officers is marked in the story by a brief summary (274-275). Though the uprising is put down, its militaristic momentum remains unquelled. Along with a crackdown in formal government censorship, the newsletter mimeograph is violently dismantled by police, ironically confirming the publication's importance by shutting it down (275). Under the shroud of increased surveillance Etsuko and her friends attempt to gather and distribute censored news from international women's magazines, but the extreme horror of the Nanjing massacre of 1937 seems to trivialize the usefulness of such efforts, and the group lapses into inactivity.[5]

Etsuko's war resistance in the next chapter takes the form of a supportive visit to Mr. Tanida, an antiwar filmmaker who, having survived imprisonment by the government, has appeared to make a public speech endorsing the war; Etsuko's friend Matsunaga explains that the speech, a form of public humiliation, is the last stage in the filmmaker's forced "reeducation." When Etsuko visits Tanaka, he does not receive her, but sends her a book of "haiku master Basho's life journey poems." Seeing how Basho's haiku and Tanida's banned films are both suffused with *myo*, Etsuko concludes that her friend is secretly reaffirming those values, in spite of government condemnation, offering reassurance that he'll "do just fine" (318).

In a climactic scene, Hanae finishes off her education in March 1939 with a valedictory speech that inflames her audience and brings the ceremonies to a halt by suggesting that her audience question their motives in supporting the war "that we say is to benefit Asia" (366-367). Even Chie gets involved, shouting out a maxim from Abraham Lincoln. Together, these two incidents suggest that Etsuko's political agency is severely restricted, and that it is difficult to mobilize opposition to the war, but that her personal efforts have affected those she meets, such as Tanida, Hanae, and even Chie. More notably, Minatoya creates in American fiction a space in which Japanese and Japanese American women are portrayed as independent political thinkers contesting their country's militaristic values, and seeking the basis for action against their country's leadership, and she collapses certain East-West dichotomies by depicting native Japanese as modern, transnational subjects with liberal democratic values.

VI. Mary Kimoto Tomita: The *Nisei* in Wartime

Mary Kimoto Tomita's book, *Dear Miye: Letters Home from Japan: 1939-1946*, takes up the thread of Japan's past just at the moment when Minatoya's leaves it. As a collection of letters, Tomita's book sheds fur-

---

[5] See Buruma, 102-106.

ther light on the political and material conditions depicted by Minatoya, who in turn shares her perceptions of Japan from a *nisei* woman's perspective. Like other nisei visitors to Japan, Mary Kimoto finds herself a conceptual anomaly, both to Japanese and to Caucasian Americans; her concern with everyday matters and the daily projection of self that emerges from writing is analogous to such elements in the memoir and the I-novel. For Mary, as for other nisei and sansei, the need to conform to Japanese social roles is counterbalanced against her yearning for relationships and social structures that would affirm her sense of self.

Arriving in 1939, Mary is one of many nisei in Japan at that time, including an estimated 50,000 from the U.S. and Hawaii, as well as groups from Brazil, Peru, Korea, Manchuria, the Dutch East Indies, and Indochina. Many study in Japanese universities and colleges or take special courses designed to prepare nisei in Japan for university study, so Mary is not as singular as the sansei writers appear, but she and her fellow nisei visitors are nonetheless curiosities to the native Japanese (Lee 11-12). Like Monica Sone, Mary avoids conforming to traditional Japanese standards for femininity, which she disparages, by attending a nisei school where the majority of her class were male; by being the only female to take lessons in *kendo* (Japanese stick fighting); by being outspoken; and by exploring Tokyo, with her Christian host family's son, beyond the ten o'clock curfew expected of Japanese women her age. When Mary's return to America is aborted due to the bombing of Pearl Harbor, and Mary is returned to Japan without savings, jobs, or support from home, she faces discrimination from all sides. Among Japanese, nisei are considered "materialistic, ignorant, and ill-mannered" (Yamashita Soen, qtd. in Lee, 11-12); Mary in particular is subjected to harsh working conditions in her first domestic job after her involuntary return to Japan, until someone kindly arranges other housing and funding for her. As the war drags on, she is persuaded to accept an arranged match into a "well-to-do and presumably enlightened" Japanese family. First ignored and then abandoned to her in-laws by her husband, Mary is first treated like a servant, then finally dismissed by the family with a payment of 500 yen in March 1945, leaving her with an anomalous sexual status: emotionally, abandoned and divorced, but legally, never married. Forced to enter her name into her ancestral family register in order to receive food during the war, Mary finds her citizenship cut off by the U.S. government, which construes this act as one of "recovery" of Japanese nationality in the case of nisei. In 1940, the U.S. passes a law defining such a "recovery" as "naturalization" and eliminating the option of dual citizenship, automatically stripping registered nisei such as Mary of their U.S. citizenship (Lee 19). Stranded in Japan until she is able to reclaim her U.S. citizenship in 1946 (Tomita 351), Mary finds work with the U.S. occupation forces after the war but is constantly irked by being denied basic privileges because the army still considers her a "foreign national". In all these ways, Mary finds herself treated as a conceptual anomaly.

In regard to Kondo's theory of Japanese subjectivity as shifting, fluid, and contextual, Mary's candid letters to trusted but absent friends offer a unique view of her internal sense of self in a time of extreme flux. Moving between roles as a student, housekeeper, bride, daughter-in-law, and worker for the U.S. Occupation forces, Mary finds little structural stability until she is employed by the Occupation. In her letter of April 5, 1946, to her sister Blanche, Mary describes her aborted marriage, a memorable example of a nisei attempting, in Kondo's terms, to "fit in," "even if it means suppression of and violence against a self [she has] known in another context" (217):

> Now I don't see why I stood all that humiliation, that uncertainty, that cruelty… The Jap bride is supposed to… get up the earliest, go to bed the latest, never express her own opinions, always smile— never show anger, bow humbly, lick the dirt,—O it's awful. (216- 217)

Against this radical denial of her subjectivity, Mary retrospectively rebels by writing to her trusted sister. In the same month, she notes the restorative powers of receiving mail from home and writing to her friend, Miye Yamasaki, every day (218, 219). Her letters become the channel for recreating and affirming her sense of herself as a person deserving respect, justice, and affection. Mary's correspondence, filled with accounts of social interactions, the comings and goings of friends, and her private thoughts, combines the attentiveness to context that Kondo and Lebra describe as typically Japanese with the insistence on a constant, even self-contained self that Kondo finds typically Western. Although the central voice and protagonist of this book is "Mary," the author's narrative persona, "Mary" is always created in dialogue with her correspondents; even in solitude this self is created by the social context of writing. The strong balance between Mary's social personae and her powerful drive to write are arguably both particular to nisei in Japan and general to travelers living in exile. It's suggestive, too, that in her recreation of the lost wartime letters, she complains vociferously against the unreasonable woman doctor who employed her, and describes the bombing of her dorm and her near brush with death in vivid detail, but of her divorce, she writes, "I must write, and yet I can't," and her letter, though heartfelt, is brief (144-146, 151-152). The sense of having her validity as a subject denied is, it seems, more devastating to her writing capacity even than being bombed.

Just as Minatoya's novel is memorable in Etsuko's attempts to fight for peace, Mary's correspondence captures the divergence of Japanese perspectives on the war. While ordinary Japanese such as teachers, and Mary's friend, the Reverend Ito Kaoru, disbelieve in the divinity of the emperor, some are jailed for expressing that disbelief.[6] Sobered by the high mortality rates of Japanese servicemen, Mary and her friend Izaya Nagata argue with a Japanese who believes Japan "has a mission and duty to help and teach and lead the Chinese," and that this is not aggression but a holy cause (80). In the same letter, Mary describes the suppression from the press of a political speech against the war by a prominent politician, Saito Takao, and Saito's expulsion from his party (80). Mary feels neither the people nor the government want war, but that no questions are allowed and that even the government doesn't know what to do (80). By December 1940, Mary has begun to internalize Japan's rhetoric of self-preservation, arguing that Japan is both peaceloving and justified by the cruelty of Western powers' imperialism; that the country is fighting for survival; and that it wouldn't be "forced" to be so aggressive if only the U.S. would be "friendly," trade with "her" and quite persecuting "her" (86,110). To her credit, Mary is too inquisitive to accept this kind of argument uncritically for long. By January 1941 she has gotten hold of Freda Utley's *Feet of Clay* (1937), an anti-Japanese critique, and is mulling over Japan's untenable war and the consequences of failure for the Japanese. Most memorably, Mary preserves a

---

[6] No wonder they are skeptical. According to Buruma, the supposedly ancient practice of Emperor worship was a Meiji-era political invention (55-57).

copy of a farewell letter of July 1, 1941, sent her from the front by her friend Izaya Nagata, who shares her deep doubts about the war, but affirms both his love of peace and his deep love of country, citing this love as his reason for joining the war:

> Why must I—who want to live in a world of peace and art—why must I spend thought and energy in constructing fearful armaments—aeroplanes—and improving them to be more dreadful monsters which will butcher people and destroy beautiful cities and ships which took years to build? ...
>
> I love the mountains of Japan... Any Japanese who has spent even one day amid such a lovely environment would never hesitate to sacrifice his life even for the sake of protecting only these picturesque mountains.
>
> ... I shall probably never see you again. Goodbye. (137)

If there is a tradition of patriotic civil disobedience in Japan, neither Mary nor Izaya (who did survive) invokes it. While she admires her friend, Reverend Ito, for going to jail for denying the Emperor's divinity, the general sense is of a population confused by events, led by force and by the suppression of dissent to support the war out of a completely misguided nationalism. Mary's letters support Minatoya's image of Japan as dominated by nationalists who will go to any length to suppress dissent; yet both authors also depict ordinary Japanese as mixed in their views of the war, and both include accounts of prominent men disciplined for criticizing the war in public. This nuanced view of the Japanese is almost completely silenced in nisei literature, which tends to emphasize nisei loyalty to the U.S. and to reject pro-Japanese militarism as alien to nisei.[7]

Given that all Japanese suffered harsh conditions, and that Mary is actually an American cut off from her own country, her agency during her years of nominal Japanese citizenship is even less than that of Minatoya's narrator. While she has the liberty of a foreign student until 1941, during the war itself she is reduced to choosing the least disagreeable means to survive. Though she begins with a strong sense of herself as an American woman, her lack of survival options after 1941 causes her to tolerate conditions destructive to her sense of herself. With the

---

[7] Cf. Sone, Okada, Murayama, and Iko.

arrival of the occupation forces, she reclaims agency on many levels, by fending off "wolves," writing a letter of protest persuading Occupation authorities to permit nisei to use their mail service, rebutting uninformed letters denigrating the war-stranded nisei, helping to found a library, co-authoring a book on Japanese slang for U.S. servicemen and visitors, regaining her citizenship, and, of course, writing to her friend Miye. While Mary is no more able to resist the tide of war than the Japanese people themselves, she becomes as active as possible once conditions improve, and for her the conditions depend largely on her reclaiming affiliation and citizenship with her own country. While no one can deny Mary's firmness of character, it is clear that even the most robust individual cannot claim agency without the recognition of her government, and that Mary's identification with the U.S. is strenuously confirmed by her stay in Japan. Yet her feeling for Japan is also deepened, and upon her return to the U.S., she marries a Japanese man who has been stranded in the U.S. during the war and wishes to return to help rebuild his homeland, though he has to give up this dream for Mary's sake (392-393). As in other cases, Mary's narrative of "return" and wartime exile in Japan sharpens her affiliation with the U.S., yet also strengthens her connection with other Japanese within the American context.

In short, to enter these narratives of "return" is to place the internment stories into dialogue with the tragedy of Japan's rise and fall, and to see the perhaps unique testimony of the nisei as intimate strangers in Japan, neither Japanese nor American, but both. These nisei writers share my questions, as a Chinese American scholar of Asian American literature, about what the Japanese "mainstream," ordinary Japanese, felt about their country's wartime ideology and activities. Through the fictional confrontation between *myo* and militarism in her novel, Minatoya depicts a small pacifist minority silenced by a more militant majority. Tomita, who lived through the war in Japan, bears witness to the population's struggles to understand and come to terms with their country's wars. Her friend's letter, an unprecedented statement within American culture, lends unexpected beauty and thoughtfulness to the images of the Japanese patriot and serviceman, and suggests that even individual Japanese must have felt deeply divided, as servicemen everywhere must. Were mainstream Japanese of that time truly peaceloving and sensitive to *myo*, or deeply flawed in their patriotic commitment to their country? It is difficult to say. However, I would like to suggest that Tomita's editor, Professor Robert G. Lee, and contemporary author Lydia Minatoya may be bringing to their publication of these texts similar questions about the relationships of mainstreams and margins in the U.S. With the so-called mainstream American public deeply divided about matters domestic and international in this era of U.S. imperialism, what is "mainstream" about these texts may be their fundamental agnosticism about the fiction of a singleminded majority.

Works Cited

Buruma, Ian. *Inventing Japan 1853-1964.* New York: Modern Library-Random House, 2004.

Chan, Sucheng. *Asian Americans: An Interpretive History.* Boston: Twayne, 1991.

Far, Sui Sin. *Mrs. Spring Fragrance and Other Writings.* Urbana, IL: University of Illinois Press, 1995.

Golden, Arthur. *Memoirs of a Geisha.* New York: Knopf, 1997.

Gotanda, Philip Kan. "Day Standing on Its Head." *Asian American Drama: 9 Plays from the Multiethnic Landscape.* Ed. Brian Nelson. New York: Applause Theatre Book Publishers and London: A&C Black, 1997. 1-42.

Houston, Velina Hasu. "*Asa Ga Kimashita (Morning Has Broken).*" *The Politics of Life: Four Plays by Asian American Women.* Ed. Velina Hasu Houston. Philadelphia: Temple University Press, 1993.

—. "Tea." *Unbroken Thread: An Anthology of Plays by Asian American Women.* Ed. Roberta Uno. Amherst, Massachusetts: University of Massachusetts Press, 1993. 155-200.

Iko, Momoko. "*The Gold Watch.*" *Unbroken Thread: An Anthology of Plays by Asian American Women.* Ed. Roberta Uno. Amherst, Massachusetts: University of Massachusetts Press, 1993. 105-154.

Ishiguro, Kazuo. *An Artist of the Floating World.* New York: Vintage-Random House, 1989.

Kingston, Maxine Hong. *The Woman Warrior: Memoir of a Girlhood Among Ghosts.* New York: Knopf, 1976.

Kogawa, Joy. *Obasan.* 1981. New York: Anchor, 1994.

Kondo, Dorinne K. *Crafting Selves: Power, Gender, and Discourses of Identity in a Japanese Workplace.* Chicago: University of Chicago Press, 1990.

Lee, Robert G. "Introduction." *Dear Miye: Letters Home from Japan: 1939-1946.* Edited and with an introduction by Robert G. Lee. Stanford: Stanford University Press, 1995. 1-22.

Lebra, Takie. *Japanese Women: Constraint and Fulfillment.* Honolulu: University of Hawaii Press, 1987.

Lim, Shirley Geok-lin. "Japanese American Women's Life Stories: Maternality in Monica Sone's *Nisei Daughter* and Joy Kogawa's *Obasan.*" *Feminist Studies* 16.2 (Summer 1990): 289-314.

Minatoya, Lydia. *The Strangeness of Beauty.* New York and London: W.W. Norton, 2001.

Minatoya, Lydia Yuri. *Talking to High Monks in the Snow: An Asian American Odyssey.* New York: HarperCollins, 1992.

Mura, David. *Turning Japanese: Memoirs of a Sansei.* New York: Anchor-Doubleday, 1991.

Murayama, Milton. *All I Asking for Is My Body.* Honolulu: University of Hawaii Press, 1988.

Okada, John. *No-No Boy.* 1957. Seattle: University of Washington Press, 1979.

Okubo, Miné. *Citizen 13660.* 1946. Seattle: University of Washington Press, 1983.

Simpson, Caroline Chung. *An Absent Presence: Japanese Americans in Postwar American Culture, 1945-1960.* Durham, NC: Duke University Press, 2001.

Sone, Monica. *Nisei Daughter.* 1953. Seattle and London: University of Washington Press, 1979.

Sumida, Stephen H. "Protest and Accommodation, Self-Satire and Self-Effacement, and Monica Sone's *Nisei Daughter.*" *Multicultural Autobiography: American Lives.* Ed. James Robert Payne. Knoxville: University of Tennessee Press, 1992. 207-247.

Ronyoung, Kim. *Clay Walls.* 1986. Seattle: University of Washington Press, 1990.

Tan, Amy. *The Joy Luck Club.* New York: Vintage-Random House, 1989.

Tomita, Mary Kimoto. *Dear Miye: Letters Home from Japan: 1939-1946.* Edited and with an introduction by Robert G. Lee. Stanford: Stanford University Press, 1995.

Wu, Jean Yu-wen Shen and Min Song, eds. *Asian American Studies: A Reader.* New Brunswick: Rutgers University Press, 2000.

Yamamoto, Traise. *Masking Selves, Making Subjects: Japanese American Women, Identity, and the Body.* Berkeley, CA: University of California Press, 1999.

Patricia P. Chu is Associate Professor of English at George Washington University. She is author of *Assimilating Asians: Gendered Strategies of Authorship in Asian America.*

Mediating Autobiography and Criticism: Ihab Hassan and Edward Said

Ioana Luca

The contemporary theoretical scene on autobiography or "life-writing" (a term preferred by many of the newer critics) has been thriving in recent years, providing one with many different or even contradictory perspectives on this literary genre, whose definition and scope have frequently been reformulated.[1] My paper focuses on the life-writing projects of two contemporary critics: Ihab Hassan and the late Edward Said. Leading literary and cultural critics, Hassan and Said have marked a turning point in the critical discourse related to postmodernism and postcolonialism respectively; they have both undergone the experience of displacement from their native country; they have both positioned autobiographical detail in their criticism; finally, they have both written highly challenging and intriguing autobiographies. Focusing on *Out of Egypt* (1986) and *Out of Place* (1999), this essay analyzes how these autobiographies can be best perceived as a continuous game of reflection of and reflexion on their literary criticism, how these two critics perceive displacement and exile in their personal narratives and how the autobiographical detail in their work and their autobiographies enact almost opposite interventions as far as the ontology of the genre is concerned. Starting from their very titles—*Out of Egypt*, a place on the map, versus *Out of Place*, ambivalently pointing both to placelessness as an existential experience and the lack of location for Palestine—and continuing with the interrelation between the autobiographical detail and literary criticism that characterizes both texts, I discuss how Hassan and Said perform significant interventions in the study of autobiographical discourse and its interrelations within the cultural context at large.

I. Background Matters

The challenge post-structuralism posed to critical objectivity led even academics, the group considered initially least likely to appeal to auto-

---

[1] For differing perspectives on this genre, see Couser, Eakin, Lejeune, de Man, Olney, Smith and Watson, and Stone.

biography or the autobiographical detail, to produce personal criticism, hybrid combinations of scholarship and life writing, and memoir proper. We cannot fail to notice that many critics have either turned to autobiography[2] or, even more commonly, to autobiographical criticism, as such collections as *Intimate Critique: Autobiographical Literary Criticism* (1993) or Adam Veeser's *Confessions of the Critics* (1996) illustrate. We may indeed be witnessing an "autobiographical turn" for academics (Gorra 143). The post-structuralist challenge to critical objectivity opened the debate about the function, or the necessity, of the personal or autobiographical *within* criticism. The term "personal criticism" was coined in the 1990s and has been associated with Nancy K. Miller's *Getting Personal* (1991). Numerous other similar categories such as "creative non-fiction," "confessional criticism," "new belletrism," "personal criticism," "autobiographical criticism" indicate the constant presence of the autobiographical 'I' in places that it has not appeared previously (Veeser x). The 1996 *PMLA* Forum acknowledges the "inevitability of the personal," discusses its problems, and elaborates on the "place, nature or limits of the personal" in literary criticism (1146).

Anchoring my analysis in the still "emerging genre" (Freedman, *Autobiographical Writing* 2) of academic life-writing and current debates on it, I probe first into Ihab Hassan and Edward Said's autobiographical representations within their literary and cultural criticism and then discuss their autobiographies, in an attempt to unravel the risks and possibilities, advantages or disadvantages, in taking up life-writing and including autobiographical detail in their academic work. While trying to answer these questions I will point out the similarities and differences in the autobiographical project of these two major American critics, and the significance such an endeavor acquires for their professional and private lives, as well as for their reading public.[3]

---

[2] See, for example: Henry Luis Gates, Clifford Geertz, Sara Suleri, Nancy K. Miller, and Jane Tompkins.

[3] Alfred Hornung offers in "Out of Egypt, Out of Place" an insightful analysis of the two autobiographies with a focus on their similarities and the contribution of these two "exiled intellectuals …. to the advancement of the humanities" (340).

II. Ihab Hassan's *Out of Egypt* or the Metamorphosis of the Postmodern Critical Discourse

Hassan's reputation as a leading American literary scholar was established in the 1960s, but it is for his contribution to framing and defining the concept of postmodernism in the mid-seventies to mid-eighties that he is best known and recognized. A complex critical personality, in the last two decades, Hassan has increasingly shifted his interest toward autobiography and travel writing. His *Out of Egypt: Scenes and Arguments of an Autobiography* was published in 1986 and ten years later, in 1996, he published a memoir travelogue, *Between the Eagle and the Sun: Traces of Japan*. A third volume of this ostensible trilogy, *Coming to the Antipodes: A Late Memoir*, is announced as forthcoming. While academic autobiography now seems an established category, Hassan's memoir *Out of Egypt* is one of the first of its kind, and may even have triggered the wave of autobiographical writing by literary critics holding jobs as distinguished professors at universities.[4] In opposition to his fellow scholar-autobiographers, the practice of postmodern criticism, which Hassan launched, has always involved an element of autobiography. His critical books were from the very beginning characterized by a growing tendency to increase the personal character of critical discourse. This tendency was announced in 1971 in Hassan's introduction to the *Dismemberment of Orpheus*, but *Paracriticisms* takes the proposal a significant step forward. Commenting on the original form of this volume, Hassan writes:

> I am not certain what genre these seven pieces make. I call them paracriticism: essays in language, traces of the times, fictions of the heart... In these essays I write neither as a critic nor scholar... but try to find my voice in the singular forms that speculation sometimes requires. (*Paracriticisms* xi)

Hassan rejects the traditional literary critic's stance and stresses the subjectivity and the personal character of the book. Aspiring thus to go

---

[4] Numerous other literary critics have produced autobiographies in the 1990s. See Alice Kaplan's *French Lessons*, Marianna De Marco Torgovnick's *Crossing Ocean Parkway*, Frank Lentricchia's *The Edge of Night*, Henry Louis Gate Jr.'s *Colored People*, and Jane Tompkins' *A Life in School*.

beyond criticism and find his own voice, he constantly offers flashes of insight into the creative process, his personal queries and speculations. At the same time this inscription of the critic's self into his discourse has been perceived as reflecting the denial of a categorical distinction between the world of fact and fiction and an equation of author and critic, at a time when the "death of the subject" was en vogue (Hornung 339).

The Right Promethean Fire follows the pattern of injecting autobiographical insight into books of criticism and opens with "A Personal Preface" where the critic describes the book as "fragment of an autobiography, meditation on science and imagination" (xxi). Moreover, the presence of a self-reflective and autobiographical element is more conspicuous than in the previous volumes, as the critical chapters are interlaced with entries from his journals. The book is structured in five chapters, separated by four excerpts (edited and revised) from journals Hassan kept while writing the book. The "journal," Hassan notes:

> discloses no intimate facts, events; still it avows a degree of subjectivity, perhaps intersubjectivity, which I hope can modify the incantatory abstractions of the Promethean theme. The journal suffers its own abstractions; indeed, it seems at times less journal than allegory… the journal, after all, was not meant to muse eternity but to slip behind certain scenes of the writing self. (xvii)

The journal entries included here enter into a sophisticated interplay with his critical study, illustrating certain statements and questioning or adding meaning to others. In the journal excerpts we encounter the inception of his later memoir, as well as explanations of some choices and perspectives. Quite different from the critical chapters as such, the "Serbellioni" and "Camargo" journals emphasize the "critic's freedom and responsibility within the changing frames of current theories" (*Right Promethean Fire* 16), they foreshadow and clarify Hassan's new critical attempt and are meant to interrogate "that genre we call academic criticism" (*Right Promethean Fire* xvii).

Hassan's move towards autobiography was gradual but definite: he not only made his criticism increasingly personal and published accomplished memoirs, but he also directly expressed his scholarly interest in the genre of autobiography (especially in the *Postmodern Turn, Selves at Risk, Rumors of Change* and in several interviews). He did so, without leaving his interest in and exploration of postmodernism behind. On the contrary, as both his critical dedication to the genre and innovative practice of it demonstrate, Hassan's concept of postmodernism and the genre of autobiography inform each other in a mutual process of definition and redefinition. Beginning with the first autobiographical disclosure in his criticism, one notices a continuous tension and struggle between the theoretical determinisms of post-structuralist subject theory and a pragmatic conviction (insistently asserted through his recurrent life-writing) about the authenticity of the self and of personal experience. He tries to reconcile the post-structuralist subject theory which denies the existence of a unified self or any real lived experience with his own autobiographical practice which stresses the lived experience of the self.

Having briefly pointed to the evolution and relevance of self-disclosure and autobiographical details in Hassan's criticism, I will focus now on *Out of Egypt*. I consider this 1986 autobiography to be a reference point which previous work anticipates, and to which his later work writes back: most of his later books (including his 1996 memoir travelogue), articles and interviews relate to it and to his life as depicted here.

Brief and concentrated, *Out of Egypt* comes close to a traditional autobiography of childhood and adolescence, but like his earlier volumes, it is a multi-layered and complex work, which becomes "a theoretical speculation on literary and non-literary subjects in its own right" (Durczak, *Selves Between Cultures* 127). The primary layer, the autobiographical narration, covers the first twenty-five years of the author's life which Hassan spent in his native Egypt. As the title suggests, the book is more concerned with the author literally getting out of Egypt. The opening scene–which inaugurates a non-linear, discontinuous narrative, infused with intertextuality, abundant in citation, incorporating mystical and philosophical speculations, reflections on King Kong and *Beauty and the Beast*, and self-reflexive meditations on the autobiographical act that include an imagined interview between "Autobiographer" and "I.H." (91)–establishes Hassan's personal relationship to Egypt:

> On a burning August afternoon in 1946… I boarded the *Abraham Lincoln* at Port Said and sailed from Egypt, never to return… I saw the town, the minarets, the high cupola of the Compagnie de Suez, recede… I could only think: "I did it! I did it! I'm bound for New York!" (1)

Full of echoes of other descriptions of immigrant passage to the Prom-ised Land, this scene emphasizes how the author has never felt particularly attached to the country of his birth. At the same time, by self-consciously drawing upon the generic immigrant autobiography he inscribes himself into the American ethos of a self-made man, the ur-immigrant who has made it in America. Although he shares with Edward Said important aspects of his early life in the Middle East—they spent their childhood and adolescence around the same time in the same geographical area, they both enjoyed the privileges of class and elite background, and were educated in colonial schools which marked them in important ways—Hassan's experience of displacement and reaction to it comes in stark contrast to Said's. His journey "out of Egypt" to the U.S. presents the image of an emigrant's total dissociation from his own cultural and familial heritage: "I was born on 17 October 1925, in Cairo, Egypt, and though I carry papers that solemnly record this date and place, I have never felt these facts decisive in my life. I do not recall the house I was born in… my parents were dead to me perhaps before they entered their grave" (2, 31).

Throughout his autobiography Hassan constantly plays down the importance of his origins, though, paradoxically enough, his autobiogra-phy requires a return to the beginning. The autobiographical discourse, which continues in his later work, constructs Hassan's identity as an American, not an Egyptian-American or Arab-American, but as one whose chosen national and intellectual affiliation abrogates any ties to Egypt and its culture: "Roots, everyone speaks of roots. I have cared for none" (4).[5] The irony of this claim at the beginning of an autobiography set mostly in the Egypt of his childhood is a characteristic contradiction in Hassan's performance and assertion of his self and lived experience. The accomplished autobiographer, however, attempts to nuance it by inserting the remark by his son Geoffrey: "You're writing an autobiogra-phy? But you never spoke of Egypt at home!" (11). With typical self-irony, Hassan poses the question himself: "But why this autobiography now?… [I]s autobiography my own warrant for American self-exile?"

---

[5] He considers himself neither hyphenated, nor an exile, and he rejects and even argues against the "rubric" of "postcolonial intellectual" (Hassan, "Be-yond Exile" 453).

(106). Hassan's perspective on identity comes in contrast with Edward Said's, who always defined himself as a Palestinian first and an American second, and who wrote extensively on his physical and metaphorical condition of exile and who always, irrespective of the risks and dangers, asserted his Palestinian identity and his support for the Palestinian cause.

Once again in contrast to Said, Hassan's Egypt is "feudal," (17) "prodigal and corrupt sometimes" (3), a "place of unspeakable pollution and occlusion" (14). Hassan's depiction of his early life is contextualized in an Egypt that seems to be a fixed essence, suspended in a clear biblical-mythical time, with corruption and dissolution as an endemic feature. In fact, the phrase "out of Egypt," a potent biblical metaphor, recurs throughout the text. He flagrantly rejects the place where he was born and embraces a more desirable location, that of "America".[6] Rather than with sentimentalism and nostalgia, Hassan's "native home" is recollected with either dread, amusement, or intellectual rather than emotional curiosity. Both Egypt and the family house in Cairo are Sphinx-like figures for Hassan; both seem "always closed against [his] gaze, as if holding some riddle" (2). Paradoxically enough for a staunch proponent of post-structuralism, Hassan's blunt articulation of his desire to be severed from his Egyptian past may reinscribe the Orientalist discourse that simultaneously desires and dismisses the non-West (Coleman 70). By representing the Orient, Egypt in this case, as an inferior, exotic "other" to the Occidental self, he collaborates with the Orientalist discourse that separates the "East" from the "West" by negative force.

While the defining moment in Hassan's relation to Egypt is his "escape," as he puts it, aboard the *Abraham Lincoln*, what defines Said's relationship to his native country is a sense of nostalgia and irrecover-

---

[6] From this perspective it is tempting to see Hassan's memoir as an instance of immigrant autobiography and, on one level, *Out of Egypt* does reside comfortably within this literary tradition through an employment of certain topoi and leitmotifs (for instance that of exodus from the native land and arrival at the adopted one, or the dream of self-creation). But on another level, Hassan's vast array of comments on cultural developments and social changes as well as his intense self-consciousness destabilizes the genre and creates a close alliance with the American intellectual autobiographical writing of Henry Adams and William James.

able loss. It is true that the question of Palestine lays a special historical burden on Said, but Said's Palestine is depicted in a more nuanced and contextualized way which undermines the essentialist representations and oppositions present in Hassan's narrative. The highly mythicized Egypt and America appear constructed as polar opposites and sometimes Hassan makes use of biblical and Orientalist stereotypes of Egypt in order to distance himself from his country of birth. This is thus another significant irony and inner tension in the autobiography of one of the main proponents of postmodernism in the U.S. and it testifies to the double edge of the genre even when taken up by one of the most gifted literary critics.[7]

As already mentioned, Hassan firmly rejects nostalgia. No exilic sadness or sentimentality is to be found in his memoir. Neither does he celebrate the modernist understanding of exile. Contrary to Said, who suffers from "many displacements" (*Out of Place* 217) and constant motion, Hassan consciously seeks new places and enjoys mobility, systematically and resolutely countering in, and through his autobiography the conflation of home and self. Thus, the autobiographical move for Hassan does not constitute a backward turn towards home, nor does it intend to anchor the self in nostalgic reconstruction. In many instances, it may appear that Hassan uses his autobiography as a pretext for demonstrating his thoughts and opinions on the subjects that he analyzed in a less personal way in his earlier critical and para-critical works. In this sense his autobiography becomes, to use the critic's view of autobiography, "a quest rather than the record of a quest" (*Selves at Risk* 30). At the same time autobiography for Hassan, gesturing toward the Puritan origins of the life-writing in America, is a way to inquire into and create the self: "Is not autobiography… a labor of self-creation no less than self-cognizance or self-expression? And does not this quest, this labor of self-creation, in turn affect the real, living, dying subject?"

---

[7] However, the overtly celebratory account of his "version of the American Dream" is sometimes laced with images of darkness, gloom, and apprehension as the text resounds with anxiety, doubt, and melancholy. For instance, describing his arrival in America (in New Orleans), Hassan writes: "I… imagined myself, like Marlowe, pushing into the heart of darkness" (102). He continues: "I had entered America, it seemed, from its secret, gloomy underside, not like Columbus or 'stout Cortez'" (*Out* 103).

(*Rumors of Change* 188-189).

Given Hassan's almost obsessive return to the episodes described here and his insistence on his "lived experience" in most of his later interviews and articles, one notices again the tension and contradiction characterizing his autobiographical endeavor: its terms are the post-structuralist framework he helped establish versus the belief in the authenticity of personal experience. Although, as an accomplished critic-autobiographer, he attempts once again to reconcile opposite views, affirming that "we choose autobiography because it expresses all the ambiguities of our postmodern culture" (*Rumors of Change* 188), the postmodern theoretical framework that he championed to define and establish is undermined when put into practice and tested as auto-biography by its very proponent. Or, to put it differently, autobiography becomes for Hassan another battleground, another genre he explores and explodes, relativizing its ontological status. Hassan's innovative use and creative experiments with autobiography demonstrate once again the complexities and elusiveness of the genre, the many purposes auto-biography can lend itself to, and the metamorphosis of his postmodern critical discourse.

III. Edward Said's *Out of Place*: Postcolonial Revisions

Edward Said, the Palestine-born literary and cultural critic and social commentator, was a highly significant, and at times very controversial, figure in America's intellectual life, whose voice and authority were influential far beyond the academia. His more than twenty books, count-less articles on literary criticism or political analysis, and collections of interviews, could be organized around a central axis, namely the rela-tion between history, narrative, and politics. Said's interest in histori-cally and socially-anchored literary criticism, already evident in his first two books, becomes explicit in his ground-breaking *Orientalism* (1978) which examines the development of Western conceptions and repre-sentations of the Orient from the mid-eighteenth century to the present.

We find a constant and acknowledged preoccupation with the role of criticism in the contemporary world, as well as the role of a socially and politically engaged critic (*The World, the Text and the Critic*), the role of the intellectual (*Representations of the Intellectual*), or the condition of exile (*Reflections on Exile*). His identity as a Palestinian American lies at the core of another series of volumes that negotiate the politics of the Middle Eastern conflict, the situation of Palestine in this conflict, as well as questions of Palestinian identity, history, national narrative, its representation in the West. We notice thus that Said's construction of identity, his writing on Palestinian issues, and his literary and cultural theory are inextricably linked. His experience of geographical dislocation and metaphorical exile became a text he elaborated on and rewrote through-out his life, intersecting with and articulated by all his other work. For this reason, I analyze his memoir by placing it in constant dialogue with his central critical concerns and by pointing to the way the autobiography illuminates his earlier work.

Said began writing his memoir after being diagnosed with leukemia in 1991. He found it important, he says, "to leave behind a subjective account of the life I lived in the Arab world, where I was born and spent my formative years" (ix). The story, like Hassan's narrative, starts with the portrait of his family, its genealogy, and complicated web of relatives, maternal and paternal grandparents, uncles, aunts and cousins who are present throughout the book. Further, as with Hassan's, Said's memoir emphasizes his dislocation: it is the story of a boy who felt out of place as a Palestinian in Egypt, as a Christian in a Muslim world, and as an Arab, holding an American passport and citizenship (his father emigrated to the U.S. in 1911 and returned to Palestine after World War I) in a colonial world. The search for understanding of and coming to terms with his identity is inextricably linked to the historical moment he lived in and the changing realities of the world around him. To recreate his story is in some sense to recreate those places, and the book abounds in topologies and description of places; it maps all his departures and travels—Talbiyah, Zamalek, Cairo, Ramallah, Dhour el Shweir. We trace the story of a young self as told retrospectively through the mature eyes of a narrator extremely perceptive of sights and voices of power. Reading the memoir, one examines the historical, geographical, cultural, political, linguistic and personal voices that went into creating Edward Said the literary and cultural critic.

Following Ricoeur's ideas, we may posit that we are born already belonging to meanings that we gradually discover, recognize, modify, and make our own in returning to them.[8] We narrate changes and become the character of our own story, and we do so within a field of others with whom we literally share the plot of history. From a Ricoeurian perspective, then, the condition of Said's own life and the text of his identity are woven into and form the defining context for all his writing. Said illustrates himself this point:

> Much of the personal investment in this study [*Orientalism*] derives from my awareness of being an 'Oriental' as a child growing up in two British colonies... In many ways Orientalism has been an attempt to inventory the traces upon me, the Oriental subject, of the culture whose domination has been so powerful a factor in the life of all Orientals. (*Orientalism* 25)

Starting from Ricoeur's assumption, Said's memoir may be said to map his intellectual development and, consequently, become our guide to mapping his work. Identity itself may be seen as a text that is continually elaborated and re-written, intersecting with and articulated by all the other texts he writes. The trichotomy of the word autobiography — *auto-bios-graphe* — points to the connection and the interplay between the elements: autobiography implies writing the life, writing the self, and writing the writing. While with Said the three elements are in a continuous game of mirrors, reflecting and reinforcing each other, I consider the third component, i.e. *writing the writing*, as essential to understanding the complex web of interrelationships his autobiography involves, and this is the reading I suggest next.

Exploring *Out of Place*, one immediately notices Michel Foucault's influence on Said's work. The way Said describes his early education and discipline bring to mind the final chapters of *Discipline and Punish* in which Foucault studies the various systems invented by a reform school for invading and colonizing a little truant's mind. The following fragment, which is emblematic for the protagonist's early years, echoes with no doubt the Foucauldian idea of "disciplinary power":

> By the age of nine right through my fifteenth birthday I was constantly engaged in private remedial therapies after school and on weekends: piano lessons, gymnastics, Sunday School, riding classes, boxing... This regimentation... produced in me a fear of

---

[8] See Ricoeur's *Time and Narrative*.

falling back into some horrible state of total disorder and being
lost, and I still have it. (25)

Everything in the memoir is placed in the larger context. Said the protagonist can only be understood within his family and his family only
within the systems of society at that time. In this way the reader learns
about the cultural hegemony exercised by the Anglo-Americans in the
Middle East. Writing about his childhood appears at times the pretext
for a genuine understanding and in depth analysis of each and every
institution that he came across in his early life. The narrator revealing
the cultural hegemony of the colonial system is at his best when he tells
about the films he watched:

> It is very odd, but it did not occur to me that the cinematic Alad-
> din, Ali Baba, and Sinbad, whose genies, Baghdad cronies and
> sultans I completely possessed in the fantasies I counterpointed
> with my lessons, all had American accents, spoke no Arabic, and
> ate mysterious food... that I could never quite make out. (34)

The British Victoria College in Cairo, which Said attended, is presented
in his memoir as an imperialist structure. It turned its students into
"natives": "Rule 1 states categorically: 'English is the language of the
school. Anyone caught speaking other languages will be severely pun-
ished'" (184). The differences between British and American school
systems, told in a very nuanced way and with subtle irony, might be
another pretext for the analysis of various types of colonizing powers:

> At CSAC we were all given 'workbooks' in marked contrast to
> GPS's copybooks, which were lined exercise books as anonymous
> as bus tickets; workbooks had charming, chatty questions, illustra-
> tions, pictures to be appreciated, enjoyed, and when relevant, filled
> in. To write in one of our GPS textbooks was a serious misde-
> meanor; in American workbooks, the *idea* was to write in them.
> (84)

A fundamental component of Said's identity and writing, as already
mentioned, is his sense of exile. This genuine feeling is deeply conveyed
in the memoir. Said the narrator shares with Said the protagonist an
experience of exile that transcends the metaphoric to become both an
objective reality (exile from Palestine) and a subjective feeling (permanently out of place). Significantly, Said's sense of exile links in multiple

ways with his definition of the "intellectual as a permanent exile." This crucial thread in his writing, the role of the intellectual, is enriched in the memoir by the dramatic and complex figure of Charles Malik, "who began his public career during the late 1940s as an Arab spokesman for Palestine at the UN, but concluded it as the anti-Palestinian architect of the Christian alliance with Israel during the Lebanese Civil War" (264). Malik's story is the parable story of the Arab intellectual Edward Said did not become. In contrast with Malik, there is another figure, that of Farid, who chose never to betray his cause and was beaten to death in jail. Said concludes that: "Farid's life and death have been an underground motif in my life" (124). The portraits of these intellectuals in his memoir might be seen as a continuation of the image of the Arab intellectual described in "Gods that Always Fail" in his *Representations of the Intellectual*.

A deep sense of loss, the loss of Palestine, combined with a certain understanding and coming to terms with it, permeates the memoir. He unfolds the way the child became aware of the events of 1948: "My mother never mentioned... I had no available vocabulary for the question" (115). Only once did he hear something related to it, when his father said, "We lost everything too." When he queried for an explanation, "'Palestine' was all he said" (115). In this sense, the memoir reiterates, on a more personal note, one of Said's central concerns, Palestine. *Out of Place* may be seen as Said's next step in encountering and responding to questions of Palestinian identity, but this time he turned, to his individual story, to his childhood in Jerusalem, Cairo, and Dhour el Shweir between his year of birth and his departure for the U.S.

Although there is an "autobiographical turn" for academics, memoirs by academics rarely cause angry public stir, as happened with Said's memoir. The personal circumstances of its writing (his leukemia), stated directly, entered as a powerful actor in the debate triggered off by the book. For Said, his book necessarily meant going back and attempting to rescue from oblivion times and places that had all but disappeared. Of course, writing your life story, as therapy, as healing, as an act of remembering (the past) but also of forgetting (the present) might stand as possible interpretations of Said's memoir. However, none of the critics and reviewers of the book focused on the psychological valences of this memoir.[9] Without exception, the book was analyzed either in the context of the Palestinian–Israeli conflict, or in relation to Said's commitment to the Palestinian cause, as its main representative and spokesman in the U.S. Said was accused of embroidering his story and "fabricating" his life (Weiner 23), of having a "light-hearted attitude to facts" (Wheatcroft 32), and of "inconsistency and hypocrisy" (Mo 67). Interestingly enough, while some critics challenged the authenticity and truth value of the book, and accused Said of non-representability for the Palestinian cause, others found it *emblematic* for all those who left Palestine (Benvenisti 218). Said responded by stressing the truth value of his memoir ("Defamation") and, as a result, three different websites, those of *CounterPunch*, *Salon Books* and *The Guardian*, launched a debate on the debate; there has also been a constant outpour of articles related to this point.[10]

Why was Said's memoir more controversial than any of his other books? What are the implications of explicit autobiographical writing in this case? More precisely, what are the implications of autobiographical writing by the most representative spokesman for the Palestinian cause in the U.S., who also happens to be a highly influential and well-established critic in American academia? In the conundrums of Palestine's past, assembling experiential history can function as counter-memory, as a means to re-narrativize the past, break the silences, and fill in the gaps of official history. In the face of no official narrative, or distorted narrative, individual memory can become the source for the representation of history.[11] Criticism of Said's autobiography becomes political in this way: because of its generic claims to truth, the genre of autobiography offered Said the opportunity to promote himself as a representative subject, a subject who stands for others, but it also threatened him with unsympathetic scrutiny. Said embarked on his memoir after having written a great deal and after his authority and voice in the American

---

[9] See Weiner, Wheatcroft, Mo, Benvenisti, Elon, Hitchens, Grossman, and Buruma for these reviews.

[10] See "Commentary 'Scholar' Deliberately Falsified Record in Attack on Said." Also Offman; Borger.

[11] In my "Edward Said's *Lieux de Memoire: Out of Place* and the Politics of Autobiography," I discuss the implications of personal memory and autobiographical writing for Said.

academia and American public sphere at large had long been insti-
tutionalized and respected. In this particular framework, the Palestine of
the title of his book, *The Question of Palestine*, even then indirectly set
under question, is now fully a "place." *Out of Place* turns Palestine from
a trope into a full-fledged *topos*, from a "question" into a "place."

IV. Conclusions

Two major literary critics of our time write their autobiographies. Beginning with their titles and continuing with the interrelation between the
autobiographical detail and literary criticism that characterizes both
texts, these autobiographies are clear reflections of their authors' critical
work and the perfect re-writing of their literary and cultural criticism.
The resemblances in using the autobiographical detail and taking up life
writing are many and striking. We see in both a hyphenated identity,
they are exiled literary critics who early in their life established themselves in the United States; both have a rich Eurocentric background and
similar preoccupations in the field of literary criticism; both concern
themselves with re-conceptualizing the role of the critic and humanist,
redefining the role of criticism and its consequent implication within a
larger context, outside literature, in the contemporary world; finally,
they both describe Egypt, specifically Cairo, at the same historical moment. And yet, the differences are overwhelming. Hassan openly expresses his disagreement with the Foucauldian paradigm over-present
in current literary criticism. He disregards any brand of postcolonial
approach, which he dismisses as "jargon," "shibboleth," politicization of
the curriculum, or an angry and revengeful attitude, and implicitly criti-
cizes Said's taking up and exploring the autobiographical detail within a
postcolonial perspective.

Hassan's autobiography is just another brick in his developing theory
on postmodernism and its contradictions. Paradoxically enough, he
returns to it continuously, inserting fragments from *Out of Egypt* in most
of his later criticism. He does so in an attempt to stress ambiguity,
playfulness, postmodern *topoi*, as well as to reinforce his lived experience, exploring and exploiting, once more, the ambiguities of the genre
of autobiography. For Said, his autobiography has a thoroughly existential and profoundly human dimension. It has an existential dimension
for him as an individual in a moment of personal crisis, as well as for

him as a spokesman for the Palestinian cause, a cause in crisis. His memoir works in two ways like the Derridean *pharmakon*. Given the reactions of the press, it certainly works as poison; given the fact that he fulfills his mission to narrate, it does function as remedy, healing. Healing at the individual level, the writing of the memoir gave him "something to look forward to... a purpose" (*Out of Place* 216); it was a reversal of his illness. Also, it was healing in the sense of enabling him to leave an account of those remote times and places, of facing loss and forgetting.

In my analysis I have focused on the way in which the life-writing projects of two leading academics and literary critics intersect with literary theory, thus generating sprawling and productive boundaries which inform and enrich both literary criticism and the genre of life-writing. The experience of displacement and exile that they share configures their work in opposite ways. The liberating, pleasurable aspect of cultural difference together with the aesthetization of memory and the ludic metamorphosis of the autobiographical representation is the predominant feature with Hassan, while for Said physical and metaphorical exile leads to an increased awareness and resistance to oppressive systems, as well as to a more politically engaged mnemonic representation. I argue that their autobiographies parallel their individual type of displacement and exile because as a genre, autobiography is a succession of translations, displacements and adaptations to various times and selves. Moreover, I take the two texts, which display radically different strategies of negotiating the role of autobiographical detail, to be emblematic for the divergent currents in cultural politics and the ontology of autobiography in the second half of the twentieth century.

Works Cited

Anonymous. "Commentary 'Scholar' Deliberately Falsified Record in Attack on Said." *CounterPunch* 1 Sept. 1999. www.counterpunch.org/said1.html

Benvenisti, Meron. "Blank Spaces: Talbiyah and Rehavia." *SAIS Review* 20.1 (2000): 215-220.

Borger, Julian. "Friends Rally to Repulse Attack on Edward Said." *The Guardian Unlimited Online Version* www.guardian.co.uk/israel/Story/o,2763,203150,00.html (Viewed August 23, 1999).

Buruma, Ian. "Misplaced Person." *New York Times* (3 October 1999): 10.

Coleman, Daniel. "Masculinity's Severed Self: Gender and Orientalism in *Out of*

Egypt and *Running in the Family.*" *Studies in Canadian Literature* 18.2 (1993): 62-80.

Couser, G. Thomas. *Altered Egos: Authority in American Autobiography*. New York: Oxford University Press, 1989.

De Man, Paul. "Autobiography as Defacement." *Modern Language Notes* 94 (1979): 919-930.

Derrida, Jacques. "Plato's Pharmacy." *Dissemination*. Trans. Barbara Johnson. Chicago: University of Chicago Press, 1981. 61-171.

Durczak, Jerzy. *Selves Between Cultures: Contemporary American Bicultural Autobiography*. Lublin: Rozprawy Wydzialu Humanistycznego, 1994.

Eakin, Paul John. *Touching the World: Reference in Autobiography*. Princeton: Princeton University Press, 1992.

Elon, Amos. "Exile's Return." *New York Review of Books* (18 Nov. 1999): 12-15.

Forum *PMLA* 111.5 (1996): 1145-69.

Freedman, Dianne and Olivia Frey, eds. *Autobiographical Writing Across the Disciplines*. Durham, NC: Duke University Press, 2003.

—. *Intimate Critique*. Durham, NC: Duke University Press, 1993

Gates, Henry Luis. *Colored People, A Memoir*. New York: Knopf, 1994.

Geertz, Clifford. *After the Fact: Two Countries, Four Decades, One Anthropologist*. Cambridge: Harvard University Press, 1995.

Gorra, Michael. "The Autobiographical Turn." *Transitions* 68 (1995): 143-153.

Grossman, Edward. "Speaking for Himself." *American Spectator* 33.2 (December 1999-January 2000): 38-43.

Hassan, Ihab. *Between the Eagle and the Sun: Traces of Japan*. Tuscaloosa: University of Alabama Press, 1996.

—. "Beyond Exile: A Postcolonial Intellectual Abroad." *Southern Review* 29.3 (1993): 453-465.

—. *Paracriticisms: Seven Speculations of the Times*. Urbana, IL: University of Illinois Press, 1975.

—. *Out of Egypt: Scenes and Arguments of an Autobiography*. Carbondale, IL: Southern Illinois University Press, 1986.

—. *Rumors of Change: Essays of Five Decades*. Tuscaloosa, TN: University of Alabama Press, 1995.

—. *The Right Promethean Fire: Imagination, Science and Cultural Change*. Urbana, IL: University of Illinois Press, 1980.

Hitchens, Christopher. "Whose Life Is It Anyway?" *Nation* (4 October 1999): 9.

Hornung, Alfred. "Out of Egypt, Out of Place: Humanist Critics at Home in America." *Return to Postmodernism: Theory-Travel-Autobiography*. Ed. Klaus Stierstorfer. Heidelberg: Universitätsverlag Winter, 2005. 339-349.

Kaplan, Alice. *French Lessons: A Memoir*. Chicago: University of Chicago, 1994.

Lejeune, Philippe. *On Autobiography*. Trans. Katherine Leary. Minneapolis: University of Minnesota Press, 1989.

Lentricchia, Frank. *The Edge of Night*. New York: Random House, 1994.

Luca, Ioana. "Edward Said's *Lieux de Memoire: Out of Place* and the Politics of Autobiography." *Social Text* 24.2 (2006): 125-144.

Miller, Nancy K. *Bequest and Betrayal: Memoirs of a Parent's Death*. New York: Oxford University Press, 1996.

—. *Getting Personal: Feminist Occasions and Other Autobiographical Acts*. New York: Routledge, 1991.

Mo, Timothy. "Alpha or Gamma for Behaviour." *The Spectator* 1 (8-25 December 1999): 66-68.

Offman, Craig. "Edward Said to Respond to Claims He's Not a True Palestinian." (August 1999): http://www.salon.com/books/log/1999/08/26/said

Olney, James, ed. *Autobiography: Essays Theoretical and Critical*. Princeton: Princeton University Press, 1980.

Ricoeur, Paul. *Time and Narrative*. Chicago: University of Chicago Press, 1984.

Rose, Jacqueline. "Edward Said Talks to Jacqueline Rose." *Edward Said and the Work of the Critic: Speaking Truth to Power*. Ed. Paul A. Bove. Durham, NC: Duke University Press, 2000. 9-31.

Said, Edward. "Defamation, Zionist-Style." *Al-Ahram Weekly* 26 Aug. 1999. http://weekly.ahram.org.eg/1999/444/op2.htm.

—. *Orientalism*. 1978. New York: Vintage, 1994.

—. *Out of Place: A Memoir*. New York: Vintage Books, 1999.

Smith, Sidonie and Julia Watson. *Reading Autobiography: A Guide for Interpreting Life Narratives*. Minneapolis: University of Minnesota Press, 2001.

Stone, Albert. *Autobiographical Occasions and Original Acts: Versions of American Identity from Henry Adams to Nate Shaw*. Philadelphia: University of Pennsylvania Press, 1982.

Suleri, Sara. *Meatless Days*. Chicago: University of Chicago Press, 1989.

Tompkins, Jane. *A Life in School*. Reading: Addison-Wesley, 1996.

Torgovnick, Marianna De Marco. *Crossing Ocean Parkway*. Chicago: Chicago University Press, 1994.

Veeser, Aram H. ed. *Confessions of the Critics: North American Critics, Autobiographical Moves*. New York: Routledge, 1996.

Weiner, Justus Reid. "'My Beautiful Old House' and Other Fabrications by Edward Said." *Commentary* (September 1999): 23-31.

Wheatcroft, Geoffrey. "Israel v Palestine: Which Side is the Left On?" *New Statesman* 128.4459 (18 October 1999): 32-33.

Ioana Luca is a lecturer in the Dep. of English at the University of Bucharest, where she teaches courses in American studies and literature. She is completing her Ph.D dissertation "The Autobiography of Displacement in Contemporary American Literature".

Ethnic Life Writing in an Era of Postethnicity: "Maxine Hong Kingston" and "Alice Walker" at the Millennium

Pirjo Ahokas

While some scholars claim that ethnic life writing has become a leading form of expression in contemporary postcolonial and minority literature (Eakin 5), the two past decades or so have also witnessed the rise of postethnic ideology in the United States. This latter development is linked to transnational neoliberal capitalism and its advocacy of a global consumer lifestyle. It is claimed that the conservative politics of postethnic ideology represses the formation of diverse identities and neutralizes resistance to inequality and injustice. This is achieved by promoting the idea of free individual choice when assimilating to a dominant "American" identity. The so-called "New Face of America," which appeared on the cover of *Time*'s 1993 special issue on immigration, has been quoted as a good example of assimilationist celebrations of multiraciality. The attractive female image was created by a computer process from a mix of several races (qtd. in Santa Ana 17).[1] Postethnic thinking not only entails racial and ethnic self-erasure, but, by extension, it also promotes the denial of differences in gender and sexuality (Santa Ana 19). This quickly becomes evident if one takes a cursory look at the history of the civil rights movement and other progressive movements of the 1960s and 1970s, where postethnic ideology seeks to frame public discourse on these issues within the bounds of race, ethnicity, gender, and sexuality.

Personal narratives published by minority conservatives express their authors' desire for assimilation in what is conceived as "a postethnic America." Employing the discourse of ethnic and racial assimilation, up-

---

[1] The mix includes "15% Anglo-Saxon, 17.5% Middle Eastern, 17.5% African, 35% Southern European, 7.5% Hispanic, and 7.5% European," (qtd. in Santa Ana 17). The term "postethnic" was proposed by the historian David A. Hollinger in *Postethnic America: Beyond Multiculturalism*. Amritjit Singh and Peter Schmidt claim that there is a split into at least two groups in American studies, which they define as the "postethnicity school" and the "borders school." See Singh and Schmidt, "On Borders" (6-7, 10-12, 49-50n. 11).

wardly socially mobile writers such as Richard Rodriguez and Shelby
Steele—to name only two—have developed a critique of the civil rights
movement in the post-1960 era and promote the possibility of free individual choice in a white-dominated society (Dillard 49, 104, 113). The
idea of individual autonomy in the making of American identity also
looms large in Eric Liu's *The Accidental American: Notes of a Native Speaker*
(1998). While Rodriguez and Steele are respective advocates of Latino
and African American multicultural conservatism, Liu, a second-
generation Chinese American and former speechwriter for President
Clinton, wishes to surmount his Asian American identity. In claiming
that it is an invented identity thrust upon him, Liu underestimates the
persistence of racialization in the United States and asserts a generic
Americanness (Li, "On Ascriptive" 108, 122). Nevertheless, he appears
to project the dissolution of racial difference into the future (Li, "On
Ascriptive" 126-127).

In contrast to personal narratives by assimilationist minded minority
conservatives, texts by ethnic life writers demonstrate the inherently
oppositional nature of this genre. Maxine Hong Kingston and Alice
Walker are not only two of the leading American women authors, but
are also feminist/womanist social activists, whose writings have usefully
challenged sexism and racism in their ethnic communities and in
America's white-dominated society. In their recent books, which show a
deepening engagement with autobiographical writing, each author
utilizes strategies of ethnic life writing. As a genre, this form of writing
focuses on the different ways in which ethnic group identities and ethnic
history shape the discursive construction of self. Moreover, recent life
writing theory regards life writing as a form of ethical inquiry, which
includes both ethical and political dimensions (Howes 256, 257, 259).
Hence, in this essay, I propose to study the extent to which the textual
identities of the autobiographical protagonists which emerge in parts of
Kingston's *The Fifth Book of Peace* (2003) and Walker's *The Way Forward Is
with a Broken Heart* (2000) can still be conceived as sites of resistance
against historically ingrained notions of inequality and injustice.

In their previous landmark books such as *Meridian* (1976) and *The
Woman Warrior* (1976), Walker and Kingston resisted racism and chal-
lenged the dominant masculinist ethos of identity politics in the African
American and Asian American nationalist movements of the late 1960s

and early 1970s, respectively. They did this by depicting their opposi-tional female minority protagonists in terms of performative gendered identity construction. The new textual Walkers and Kingstons, which have appeared in a neo-liberal "era of postethnicity," were created at a time when, informed by the theoretical discourses of feminism and postmodernism, new scholarly explorations of the autobiographical literature by women not only challenge essentialist notions of gender, ethnic and racial identity, but also the existence of the autobiographical self prior to autobiographical expression. Furthermore, Sidonie Smith, who draws on Judith Butler's work on performativity, points out that, unlike earlier strands of autobiography theory, contemporary theorizing understands the autobiographical speaker to be a performative subject (108). "Through tactical dis/identification" this figure "adjusts, rede-ploys, resists, [and] transforms discourses of autobiographical identity" through recitations (Smith 111). The production of autobiographical identity is pertinent to my examination of the texts by Walker and Kingston as they involve an ongoing process of identification and dis-identification with the action of culturally pervasive public discourses. In addition, they generate practices that not only undermine and de-stabilize but can also "be unfixings of imposed systems of identification" (Smith 111).

It has been claimed that vacillations of identification characterize a racial subject's emotional attachments in postmodern consumer culture. In his insightful article on what he refers to as "affect-identity," Jeffrey J. Santa Ana claims that feelings "are intrinsic to the construction of identity formations in an age of economic globalization" (22). However, due to the consumption-based flattening and waning of emotional diversity, "euphoria and indifference are the primary emotions of postethnicity" (Santa Ana 23). In contrast to this argument, the works under consideration display a wide range of profound emotions. Santa Ana further contends that painful emotions, based on historical factors, are concealed in the culture of neoliberalism (22). Yet, the retrospective narratives of the past, in the self-referential sections of Walker and Kingston's books, begin by foregrounding experiences of loss and mourning.

Recent scholarship on African American and Asian American fiction has argued for the centrality of mourning and racial melancholia in the formation of minority subjects.[2] While earlier interpreters of Freud's work tended to draw a clear distinction between these mental states, many contemporary theorists expand upon his revised notion of melancholia, claiming that it is the precondition for subjectivity and the work of mourning. Furthermore, they emphasize that loss, as a creative process, may encompass alternative strategies for reimagining the future (Eng and Kazanjian 2-5). These notions seem to apply to Walker's and Kingston's books. Indeed, the painful emotions of loss and mourning not only generate resistance but also give rise to new subjectivities in their works. Transnational and diasporic subject formations have often been seen as alternatives to the assimilationist models of subjectivity propagated by global consumer culture, owing to their far flung connections. I propose to explore whether these concepts are applicable when delineating the new identities which unfold in the works under discussion.

I. The Past as a Point of Departure

Kingston's *The Fifth Book of Peace* begins with a description of the Berkeley-Oakland fire of 1991 in which the autobiographical protagonist not only loses her middle-class suburban home and possessions but also a finished manuscript for a book entitled *The Fourth Book of Peace*. Her consciousness of enormous loss is compounded by the fact that the disaster began while she and her family were performing fire rites for her recently deceased father, who was a classical scholar and a teacher in China before he immigrated to America and became a laundryman. Moreover, the autobiographical protagonist's sense of personal and local devastation acquires a global dimension when she associates the fires with the bombing of Iraq during the Gulf War. Taken together, this sequence of events seems to signal the passing of a historical phase not

---

[2] Influential examples of work on mourning and racial melancholia include Anne Anlin Cheng's *The Melancholy of Race: Psychoanalysis, Assimilation, and Hidden Grief*, David L. Eng's *Racial Castration: Managing Masculinity in Asian America*, David Eng's and David Kazanjian's *Loss: The Politics of Mourning*, and Anissa Janine Wardi's *Death and the Arc of Mourning in African American Literature*.

only in the author-protagonist's life but also in narratives of Asian American subject formation.

In *China Men* (1980), Kingston wrote about the labor exploitation of male Chinese immigrants, over several generations, who were excluded from American citizenship. While the father figure in *The Fifth Book of Peace* represents Chinese American male immigrants who were "feminized" in relation to white male citizens, the daughter figure belongs to the generation that contested white American racism in the Asian American movement. Literature played an important role in the post-exclusion movement lending credence to Patricia P. Chu's claim that Asian American literature is a form of cultural struggle and "the emergence of authorship a central trope for establishing oneself as an American subject" (10). Indeed, Kingston became the leading Asian American author by challenging the narrative norms of Asian American literature with her feminist revisions of Chinese myths in *The Woman Warrior*. This highly original work attracted the attention of the white mainstream literary establishment and gained a wide readership, thereby helping to secure wider distribution to texts for other Asian American women writers.

Significantly, the emergence of Asian American literature has been tied to the professionalization of Asian American writing, as well as to the rise of an Asian American middle class (Li, *Imagining the Nation* 186, 188). Influenced by the Black movement in the 1960s, Asian American activists demanded an end to racial inequality. However, the varied spectrum of heterogeneous Asian Americans voices also included those who were persuaded to be an assimilated "model minority" by the emergent dominant discourse of upwardly mobile Asian Americans. The term "Asian American" was mobilized as an empowering political category in the 1960s in order to champion panethnic solidarity. In the 1990s, however, Asian Americans have increasingly been identified as "New Jews," thereby linking them to white, middle-class ethnicity (Li, "On Ascriptive" 107). In Kingston's book, the autobiographical protagonist epitomizes the generation of American-born Asian Americans of Chinese descent "who have moved out of downtown Chinatowns and moved up socioeconomically into suburbs" (Chun 130). Indeed, the distance between the house, which her parents own in a run-down neighborhood of Stockton, and her "next smallest" house in a multicultural middle-class area indicates her class divergence from older generations of Chinese immigrants. With her house as a signifier of her move to the center of American life, Kingston's racialized protagonist is seemingly assimilated into a complacent middle-class life, but nevertheless resists identification with the political discourse of the dominant culture.

As discussed earlier, euphoria is one of the primary emotions of postethnicity. During the continuing war the households in the formerly segregated neighborhood respond to the militant president's cries of "Euphoria!" by tying "the trees and poles and gates with yellow ribbons" (*Fifth Book* 13). However, the narrator is one of two women who put up peace signs on their property. A sense of shared oppression united Asian American opposition to the Vietnam War (Chun 103; Kim 222). In *The Fifth Book of Peace*, the sole Asian American protester not only associates the recent war with the fires that consumed her manuscript but also with the fires of the Vietnam War and the war against Japan. Hence, the beginning of the autobiographical narrative clearly focuses on the protagonist's concomitant losses, in order to underscore the meaning they have had for her secure second-generation Chinese American identity.

A paradigm shift took place in Asian American Studies in the 1990s, which has directed an increasing amount of critical attention to globalization and explored diasporic and transnational formations of Asian American identity. In *The Fifth Book of Peace*, Kingston diverges from the older political necessity to claim America in Asian American literature. In the text, she emphasizes the international links involved in negotiating a new Asian American subjectivity, which is no longer solely defined by the nation-state. The autobiographical speaker traces the reiterative processes through which a new political identity comes into existence by placing her displaced, mourning and pacifist self at the center of the book. This identity is suggestive of the new subject constructions produced within a transnational context both inside and outside the United States. Ultimately, the autobiographical protagonist's new subjectivity emerges from her renegotiation of her multiple affective bonds with Asia and Asian culture.

Kingston is famous for her creative manipulations of Chinese texts. While the historical world is the basis of the narrator's lived experience in *The Fifth Book of Peace*, it is also partly comprised of Chinese myths imparted by her parents. Indeed, the impetus for the novel entitled *The Fourth Book of Peace*, which turned into ash, as well as for the subsequent Fifth Book which the autobiographical protagonist begins to create, are the legendary Books of Peace. The narrator recounts how these came into existence "when Chinese civilization began" (*Fifth Book* 38), but they were presumably lost in fires. Instead of attempting to re-inscribe what she may have heard about the lost books, the narrator crosses national boundaries in search of them in Taiwan, Hong Kong and Beijing. Ironically, she is confronted with myriad confusing words for "peace" in China where the ex-minister of culture, who was deposed after the tragic events which occurred in Tiananmen Square in 1989, tells her that she should write the Books of Peace as she has invented them herself.

Autobiographical writing by women of color tends to challenge dominant cultural models of identity and to stage interventions in normative identification. The "model minority" thesis, which emerged in the latter half of the twentieth century, asserts that upwardly mobile Asian Americans have assimilated into a "color-blind" mainstream society. While this white stereotype continues to bolster the image of the United States as a tolerant "postethnic" society, it has also been used as evidence of the fact that, unlike African Americans and Latinos, Asian Americans constitute an exemplary minority group that achieves success "without demanding fundamental changes in American society" (Chu 65). With regard to autobiography, Smith usefully argues that "the fascination of autobiographical storytelling as performativity" lies in the subject's failure to produce a unified, coherent self by taking up normative subject positions (110-111). Moreover, it is this failure that, according to performative theory, signals the possibility of constructing one's self differently. Instead of conforming to the dominant white society's coercive normative models of Asian American selfhood, the autobiographical protagonist of Kingston's book reiterates a process of ongoing reinvention of self, which defies gender and racial boundaries.

II. The Return of the Repressed

Sau-ling Wong points out that even though "[a]utobiographies predomi-nate in Chinese-American writing in English" (261), this tradition was accommodationist until the publication of Kingston's controversial *The*

Woman Warrior in 1976 (267). According to Wong, this was due to a history of exclusion from the dominant group (265). In stark contrast to Chinese American autobiographies, it has been argued that the auto-biographical writings of African American women in the twentieth century extend "the implications of nineteenth-century self-assuredness of black womanhood into a complex recognition of different levels of power in the self, even under the racist and sexist conditions of modern American life" (McKay 100). Furthermore, when Nellie Y. McKay examines three black women's autobiographies published between 1942 and 1991, she sees a tradition in which they write "as a weapon in the continuing search for black freedom" (101). As with the beginning of Kingston's book, the opening of the first autobiographical chapter of Walker's *The Way Forward* is pervaded by a sense of grief. The chapter is entitled "To My Young Husband" and consists of an autobiographical letter to the narrator's former spouse. It is an intricately crafted narrative involving a number of different time periods. The narrator's fragmenta-tion of chronological sequence not only suggests the multiplicity and intersectionality of the autobiographical protagonist's identity process, but as a narrative strategy it also links her to the tradition of resistance outlined by McKay.

The beginning depicts the return of the narrative's "I," with her lesbian partner twenty years later, to the black middle-class neighbour-hood in Mississippi, where she used to live with her Jewish husband. The narration underscores her continuing affirmation of multiply oppressed identities as well as her challenge to the erasure of homo-sexuality in a sexist society, by calling attention to the autobiographical protagonist's sexual preference. The reminiscences of the auto-biographical speaker are awoken by the sight of the old family house, which unites the literal and the symbolic. Needless to say, the interracial union parallels Walker's real-life marriage to Melvyn Leventhal, a Jewish civil rights lawyer. When the couple moved to Mississippi, the pressures of an interracial marriage were compounded by the fact that their mere presence there was deemed "a crime against the state" (White 157). The retrospective contemporary scenes are interspersed with memories, and realizing that identities are marked by time and place, the autobiographical "I" reflects on her present identity: "If I looked into the mirror would I see the serious face I had then?" (*The Way Forward* 7).

The seriousness of the young protagonist stems from the fact that the young couple's life together is jeopardized from two sides. On the one hand, the narrated events of the past take place in a context in which civil rights workers were threatened by white supremacists and, on the other hand, by militant black separatists who wanted to expel white activists from their movement. A much more recent memory underlines the psychological ramifications of the story. This memory depicts the divorced couple's therapy session, which was arranged by their adult daughter, in Manhattan in the mid-1990s. The epilogue of *The Way Forward* dates from 1999. While Walker's text draws the reader's attention to its construction process, the nestling of life stories within life stories from different periods in the narrator's life enhances the self-reflective and self-critical quality of the narrative.

As suggested earlier in this essay, it is claimed that the postethnic 1990s was characterized by emotional emptiness and a consumption-based flattening of human feelings. In the scene in the therapist's office, the husband is depicted as a "successful corporate lawyer and a devoted nuclear family head" and the wife as an equally successful author, whose hotel suite, when she travels, "is nearly as large as our old house" (*The Way Forward* 31-32, 39). However, despite her material wealth, the wife describes the world which they inhabit as a place where "emotions have been battered into a more bearable numbness," and which from the vantage point of the turn of the twenty-first century looks like "we have reached a place of deepest emptiness and sorrow" (*The Way Forward* 15, 244). Yet, the autobiographical journey into the past generates possibilities for the sustenance of a political vision based on what Jodi Dean calls "an affectionate solidarity: 'the kind of solidarity that grows out of intimate relationships of love and friendship'" (qtd. in Ahmed 141).

In ethnic literature, interracial and interethnic romances have traditionally been employed to represent "melting pot love," that is a romantic union which signifies volitional allegiance with America as the country of choice (Sollors 72-74). Interethnic and interracial marriages also figure in the background of neoliberal consumer culture, which celebrates stylized multiraciality as an image of painless assimilation into a homogeneous national culture (Santa Ana 16-19). In fact, Liu's *The Accidental American* provides a good example of a postethnic melting pot of love: the author's euphoria about his interracial marriage invokes his deep emotional attachment to the white majority (Li, "On Ascriptive" 129). In the works presently under discussion, both Walker and Kingston use interracial marriage as a narrative device. Instead of invoking postethnic assimilation into the dominant society, however, the progressive interracial couple—associated with civil rights struggles and the peace movement, respectively—serve as a metaphor for the possibility of racial equality without the erasure of differences.

It is well-known that the civil rights movement generated an alliance between American blacks and Jews, with the latter being subject to anti-Semitism even in the United States. The husband figure in Walker's narrative represents the significant number of young Jewish volunteers who arrived in the deep south during and after the summer 1964 to work for the black cause. Even if the history of the relationship between these two groups has been fraught with conflict, the narrating "I"'s reminiscences about an early stage of her marriage in Walker's story conjures blissful feelings of interethnic and interracial solidarity: "I reveled in the ease with which, urging each other on, sometimes in our own voices, more often in a welter of black and white Southern and Brooklyn and Yiddish accents—which always felt like our grandparents were joking with each other—we'd crumple over our plates, laughing" (*The Way Forward* 4). If the symbolic house brings back many pleasant memories, the autobiographical narrator also stresses her feelings of conflict from the start: "Whenever I remember the house it was vibrant, filled with warmth and light, even though, as you know, a lot of my time there was served in rage, in anger, in hopelessness and despair" (*The Way Forward* 3). The temporal distance from the young self apparently induces the older self to reflect on the ambivalence of her past emotional life. While the dissolution of the integrated civil rights movement is mirrored in the young couple's growing apart, the retrospective moment of telling helps to highlight the younger self's identity process. The possibility of varying the performative reiteration of her black female self is signalled by the haunting of the unconscious and the excluded domain of her psyche.[3] Multiple subject-positions and mobility echo diasporic identity formations, which contemporary black studies associate with the fluid and heterogeneous nature of black identity.

---

[3] See Smith 110-111 for a discussion of this process.

Moreover, scholars perceive subjects produced by diasporan cultures such as the African diaspora as oppositional (Ong 12-13). The emergent black female identity in Walker's text seems to fit this description.

Initially, the lonely narrator's repressed feelings of pain and isolation are projected onto two disowned racial doubles—a female beggar and a black woman who also shares her life with a white activist—who begin to haunt her while she still lives with her husband in Mississippi. For Kathleen Brogan, modern stories about cultural haunting explore "elements of ethnic identity experienced just below rational grasp" and thereby assist in re-creating ethnic identity through an imaginative recuperation of a collective past (19, 4). This applies to Walker's autobiographical protagonist because the process of inner identification with her doubles ultimately helps her to understand her severance from historical memory. Thus the encounters provide a way to access the traumatic legacy of black and white relations in the United States, especially with regard to black women and slavery. Yet, the autobiographical narrator resists the reductive binary thinking which not only pervades the political scene but also the poor rural working-class black community where her parents live. While exacerbating her own situation, it renders her Jewish husband "a white blur wearing clothing" and strikes "an ancient terror" (*The Way Forward* 41) into the hearts of her whole family.

Brogan further claims that while "haunting in women's texts tends to attach to reproductive issues" such as rape, it also implies women's power and liberation (25). Like her real-life counterpart, the aspiring black woman writer in Walker's autobiographical story links black women's liberation from their racial and gender oppression with precursorial black female authors by establishing artistic connections. Indeed, she finds the discourses of black women's literature so empowering that her otherwise literate husband's refusal to read an unnamed slender novel by a black woman leads to the formation of a barrier between them. However devoted the husband figure is depicted to be to the black cause, his failure to understand the meaning of the emerging literary tradition of African American women towards the formation of his wife's diasporic black female identity inadvertently contributes to them drifting apart. By extension, his indifference towards the imbrication of gender and race clearly reflects the general marginalization of the concerns of African American women at this particular historical juncture in the United States. In a different way, literature and autobiographical writing also play a significant role in the making and unmaking of performative identities in Kingston's book.

III. Peace and Interracial Harmony

A central unifying theme in Walker's and Kingston's otherwise rather dissimilar autobiographical texts is the dream of multicultural hybridity and racial harmony. Kingston takes up the interracial theme in her first novel, *Tripmaster Monkey* (1989), which is set in the 1960s and depicts the attempts of Wittman Ah Sing, who is a fifth-generation Chinese American, to define his place in the United States. In general, the playful book has been praised for its inclusive politics, as well as its textual representation of a multiply determined and performative Chinese American identity.[4] Yet, the novel's ending has been rightly criticized for its simplistic narrative solution, in which Wittman marries a Caucasian American woman (*Imagining the Nation* 85-89). In an interview, Kingston stated that this union was envisaged "as a way to integrate the planet" (qtd. in *Imagining the Nation* 85). The third section of *The Fifth Book of Peace*, entitled "Water," is a reworking of Kingston's lost novel. It continues the story of Wittman, who is now a draft dodger, and has moved to Hawaii with his wife and their mixed-race son. At first glance their new home suggests an American idyll and seems to embody a multicultural paradise and a haven for racial peace. However, soon the parents discover that it is not free from racism and homophobia. Ironically, the hiding place also proves to be "the center of operations for staging the Viet Nam War" (*Fifth Book* 117). Wittman joins the local peace movement, which echoes the pacifism of Walt Whitman, to whom his name alludes and who is invoked in the text,[5] and also of Kingston herself. Moreover, calling attention to gender-crossing, the autobiographical narrator explicitly links Wittman's life to her own and to the experiences she shared with her white husband, an actor, during their "real Hawai'i years" (*Fifth Book* 241).

---

[4] Chun injudiciously labels Wittman "postethnic" (130).

[5] For an account of the intertextual references to Whitman in Kingston's novel, see Tanner, "Walt Whitman's Presence."

Although much is not made of the symbolic Gold Mountain trunk, which the fictional interracial family brings with them from California to Hawaii in Kingston's book, it nevertheless serves as a reminder of the history of Chinese exclusion in the United States. In contrast to Walker's narrative, however, both of the interracial and heterosexual couples in Kingston's book are supported by their loyal friends and relatives, which provides them with emotional sustenance for the fostering of their political identities. Moreover, the importance the textual Kingston attaches to her Asian American authorship as a vehicle for agency seems to empower her to launch "strategic interventions in American literary constructions of race, ethnicity and gender" (Chu 11). While grieving, her ethical commitment to pacifism leads her to conduct life writing workshops for American war veterans in a collaborative effort of creating a Book of Peace.

In many regards, the bringing together of ethics and politics by an "I" reflects Judith Butler's ideas about an ethical response to loss and violence in post-September 11 America. In *Precarious Life*, Butler proposes that a prohibition on public displays of grief in regard to foreign casualties of the "war on terror" in America not only leads to a generalized melancholia but also to more violence and a hierarchy of grief (32, 37). Looking for a way out of the vicious cycle of violence, Butler insists that we need to perform a recognition of a "common," globally distributed vulnerability. This presupposes that we are already involved in a reciprocal exchange, which dislocates us from our fixed subject-positions and allows new kinds of interdependent international ties to emerge (Butler 44). A similar ethos animates the writing workshops, which Kingston's protagonist runs on Buddhist principles for her male and female students from various ethnic backgrounds. Perhaps ironically, the Buddhist reiteration of new pacifist identities, which are supposed to transcend dominant gender and racial hierarchies, is also reminiscent of the influence of eastern religions on the traditional canon of American letters. The purpose of the workshops is to establish a multiracial "sangha," or a community that lives in peace and harmony and some of them involve personal encounters with Vietnamese veterans.

While Kingston's text abounds in multicultural and multiracial mixing, Walker's autobiographical narration specifically foregrounds the mixed nature of the "I"'s African American background. Looking back upon the formation of what she calls her "tri-racial self," the narrator explains: "Everything that was historically repressed in me has hungered to be expressed, to be recognized, to be known... That the Native American and European, no less than the African, desired liberation. Exposure to light" (*The Way Forward* 45). Significantly, Walker's *The Way Forward* is dedicated "To the American race." This intertextual reference to Jean Toomer, who served as one of Walker's literary models and about whom she writes in her essay "The Divided Life of Jean Toomer," provides a key to the conflictual nature of the auto-biographical "I"'s identity process. Toomer's lifelong quest for racial transcendence was linked to his wish to challenge both the essentialism of 19th century scientific assumptions about race and the unnatural basis of anti-miscegenenation laws (Hawkins 167, 170). Toomer came to regard interracial subjects as prototypes for the "New American" race, which he envisioned would signal the end of racism and racialist discourse (Hawkins 152, 157). In one way or another, all the components of the multiracial identity of Walker's autobiographical protagonist have been implicated in slavery and racial oppression. Notably, diasporic subjects are perceived to be struggling "against adversity and violation by affirming their cultural hybridity and shifting positions in society" (Ong 13). This provides a new diasporic identity related to historical factors, which consequently becomes a means of resistance. Finally capable of not only mourning her personal loss but also the assassinations of black leaders, the transformed narrator returns to Toomer's utopian idea of a new transracial American at the end of the chapter. At the same time, she affirms her empathic bond to her former husband, whose figure is endowed with symbolic significance. The epilogue is dedicated "To the Husband of My Youth." Told through a flash-forward it also contains a reference to Toomer, which underscores the continued relevance of anti-racism and cultural hybridity.

Although scholars like Homi K. Bhabha and Stuart Hall claim that cultural hybridity and heterogeneity can be enabling, several other theorists, including Santa Ana, argue against the celebration of hybridity and multiraciality, which they link to a conservative notion of postethnic multiculturalism (Santa Ana 31). The commodification of human feeling is typical of consumer capitalism, but Santa Ana suggests that feelings that express affective bonds with one's own ethnic and historical backgrounds are still central to racial and ethnic identity formations (22, 32). While this is true about Walker's and Kingston's autobiographical protagonists, they also seek to create an empathic connection with other groups and their histories when challenging racism and other forms of oppression. Indeed, the various retreats described in Kingston's book, such as the Buddhist community of Plum Village in France, leave the reader with the impression that they can help many individual participants to come to terms with their racism and war trauma. However, even though the "I" enacts an identity reminiscent of transnational subject formations, which resists the decision-making of the dominant white power structure, it is imbued with an unreal degree of utopianism. A case in point is that, by and large, Kingston's autobiographical speaker manages to ignore her privileged elite social position and the prevailing globalized political-economic conditions characterized by the uneven flow of goods, products and capital, which contribute to international warfare.

IV. Conclusion

In both Walker's and Kingston's autobiographical texts, the performative reworkings of identity in the discourses of self-representation clearly resist the homogenizing and normalizing tendencies of the supposedly apolitical culture of neoliberalism. In their different ways, the protagonists' ongoing diasporic and transnational identity formations highlight the legacy of racism in the United States and in a global context. Moreover, the two books critique unthinking consumer multiculturalism by means of historicized narratives of exclusion and displacement. In contrast to emotional poverty, which characterizes postethnicity, both narratives move from grief and melancholia to expressions of joy, empathy and interracial harmony. Instead of the reified hybridity of postethnic ideology, they embrace cultural hybridity as a means of empowerment. The unabashed utopianism of Walker's and Kingston's autobiographical protagonists can be criticized on several grounds. One must bear in mind, however, that this utopianism arises from their own racial and historical backgrounds, and expresses a need for real social change that responds to the current political climate.[6]

---

[6] Research for this paper was funded by the Academy of Finland (p. 204616).

Works Cited

Ahmed, Sara. *The Cultural Politics of Emotion*. Edinburgh: Edinburgh University Press, 2004.

Brogan, Kathleen. *Cultural Haunting: Ghosts and Ethnicity in Recent American Literature*. Charlottesville: University Press of Virginia, 1998.

Butler, Judith. *Precarious Life: The Powers of Mourning and Violence*. London: Verso, 2004.

Cheng, Anne Anlin. *The Melancholy of Race: Psychoanalysis, Assimilation, and Hidden Grief*. New York: Oxford University Press, 2001.

Chu, Patricia P. *Assimilating Asians: Gendered Strategies of Authorship in Asian America*. Durham, NC: Duke University Press, 2000.

Chun, Gloria Heyung. *Of Orphans & Warriors: Inventing Chinese American Culture & Identity*. New Brunswick: Rutgers University Press, 2000.

Dillard, Angela D. *Guess Who's Coming to Dinner Now? Multicultural Conservatism in America*. New York: New York University Press, 2001.

Eakin. Paul John. "Introduction: Mapping the Ethics of Life Writing." *The Ethics of Life Writing*. Ed. P. J. Eakin. Ithaca: Cornell University Press, 2004. 1-16.

Eng, David and David Kazanjian, eds. *Loss: The Politics of Mourning*, Berkeley: University of California Press, 2003.

Eng, David L. and David Kazanjian. "Introduction: Mourning Remains." *Loss: The Politics of Mourning*. Eds. David Eng and David Kazanjian. Ewing, NJ: University of California Press, 2002. 1-25.

Eng, David L. *Racial Castration: Managing Masculinity in Asian America*, Durham, NC: Duke University Press, 2001.

Hawkins, Stephanie. "Building the 'Blue' Race: Miscegenation, Mysticism, and the Language of Cognitive Evolution in Jean Toomer's 'The Blue Meridian.'" *Texas Studies in Literature and Language* 46.2 (Summer 2004): 150-189.

Hollinger, David A. *Postethnic America: Beyond Multiculturalism*. New York: BasicBooks, 1995.

Howes, Craig. "Afterword." *The Ethics of Life Writing*. Ed. P. J. Eakin. Ithaca: Cornell University, 2004. 244-264.

Kim, Elaine H. *Asian American Literature: An Introduction to the Writings and Their Social Contexts*. Philadelphia: Temple University Press, 1982.

Kingston, Maxine Hong. *China Men*. New York: Knopf, 1980.

—. *The Fifth Book of Peace*. London: Secker & Warburg, 2003.

—. *The Woman Warrior: Memoir of a Girlhood Among Ghosts*. NY: Knopf, 1976.

—. *Tripmaster Monkey*. New York: Vintage, 1987.

Lauret, Maria. *Alice Walker*. Houndsmills: Macmillan, 2000.

Li, David Leiwei. "On Ascriptive and Acquisitional Americanness: *The Acciden-tal Asian* and the Illogic of Assimilation." *Contemporary Literature* XLV.1 (2004): 106-134.

—. *Imagining the Nation: Asian American Literature and Cultural Consent*. Stanford: Stanford University Press, 1998.

McKay, Nellie Y. "The Narrative Self: Race, Politics, and Culture in Black American Women's Autobiography." *Women's Autobiography, Theory: A Reader*. Eds. Sidonie Smith and Julia Watson. Madison: University of Wisconsin Press, 1998. 96-107.

Ong, Aihwa. *Flexible Citizenship: The Cultural Logics of Transnationality*. Durham, NC: Duke University Press, 1999.

Santa Ana, Jeffrey J. "Affect-Identity: The Emotions of Assimilation, Multiracial-ity, and Asian American Subjectivity." *Asian North American Identities: Beyond the Hyphen*. Eds. Eleanor Ty and Donald G. Goellnicht. Blooming-ton: Indiana University Press, 2004. 15-42.

Singh, Amritjit and Peter Schmidt. "On the Borders Between U.S. Studies and Postcolonial Theory." *Postcolonial Theory and the United States: Race, Eth-nicity, and Literature*. Ed. Amritjit Singh and Peter Schmidt. Jackson: University Press of Mississippi, 2000. 3-69.

Smith, Sidonie. "Performativity, Autobiographical Practice, Resistance." *Women's Autobiography, Theory: A Reader*. Ed. Smith and Julia Watson. Madison: University of Wisconsin Press, 1998. 108-115.

Sollors, Werner. *Beyond Ethnicity: Consent and Descent in American Culture*. New York: Oxford University Press, 1986.

Tanner, James T.F. "Walt Whitman's Presence in Maxine Hong Kingston's *Trip-master Monkey: His Fake Book*." *MELUS* 20.4 (Winter 1995): 61-74.

Walker, Alice. *Meridian*. New York: Pocket Books, 1976.

—. *The Way Forward Is with a Broken Heart*. London: Women's Press, 2000.

Wardi, Anissa Janine. *Death and the Arc of Mourning in African American Litera-ture*. Gainesville, FL: University Press of Florida, 2003.

White, Evelyn C. *Alice Walker: A Life*. NY: W.W. Norton & Company, 2004.

Wong, Sau-ling Cynthia. "Autobiography as Guided Chinatown Tour? Maxine Hong Kingston and the Chinese-American Autobiographical Contro-versy." *Multicultural Autobiography: American Lives*. Ed. James Robert Payne. Knoxville: University of Tennessee Press, 1992. 248-275.

Pirjo Ahokas is Professor of Comparative Literature at the University of Turku, Finland. She is the author of *Forging a New Self* and co-editor of *Reclaiming Memory: American Representations of the Holocaust*.